NO
KIDDING
AROUND!

NO KIDDING AROUND!

AMERICA'S YOUNG ACTIVISTS
Are Changing Our World
And You Can Too

by

Wendy Schaetzel Lesko
Activism 2000 Project

Information USA, Inc.

Published in the United States by
INFORMATION USA, Inc.
P.O. Box E, Kensington, Maryland 20895
(301) 942-6303
First printing, 1992.

Publisher's Cataloging-in-Publication Data:

Lesko, Wendy Schaetzel, 1950-
        No kidding around!: America's young activists are
changing our world and you can too / Wendy Schaetzel Lesko.
p. cm.
Includes bibliographical references and index.

ISBN 1-878346-10-5
1. Politics, Practical—United States. 2. Political
activists—Vocational guidance. 1. Title. II. Title: America's
young activists are changing our world and you can too.
JK1711.L4 1992   320
                        QBI92-568

Summary: Oral histories of young citizen activists supplemented by a resource guide,
demonstrating how Americans of all ages can participate in our democracy and make it work for them.

Cover design by Sally Whitehead.
Illustrations by Nicholas E. Galifianakis.

We can't wait until we are adults to start doing something about the things we care deeply about. Pollution, endangered species, the homeless, drug abuse, whales, the ozone, or rain forests — if there is some problem you're concerned with — find out what you can do and DO IT!

— Kristin Johnson
Woodinville High School '92
Woodinville, Washington

Acknowledgements

I am but one of the authors of *No Kidding Around!* Dozens of young people took the time to share their own stories with me. So, first and foremost, my heartfelt thanks to each of my coauthors whose names do not appear on the front of the book.

Tracking down these citizen activists was not easy. I had a big assist from public interest advocates, teachers, principals, legislative aides, and people from all walks of life, including Dennis Bader, Ann Bland, John Blood, David Bragdon, Bill DeRosa, Gretchen Griffin, Kit Keller, John Schwartz, Linda Tracy, Connie Tucker, Peg van Patten, Andrea Vicent, Judith Webb, and John Williams. Organizations such as the Hunger Project, Maryland Student Service Alliance, National 4-H Council, National Safe Kids Campaign, Peace Development Fund, and the Washington Leadership Institute supplied me with many fruitful leads.

The focus of my research evolved gradually and Nancy Stefanik, more than anyone else, convinced me to concentrate on the efforts of young people. I have Mike Pertschuk and David Cohen to thank for all they taught me about oral history as a technique for chronicling citizen movements. The moral support from everyone at the Advocacy Institute and fellow activists like Geri Denterlein made writing this book a joy.

Sally Whitehead channeled so much creative energy into designing the book cover and succeeded at conveying the spirit of *No Kidding Around!*. I also am indebted to Nick Galifianakis for his inspired illustrations which enliven the text and his bandwagon series capturing the theme that more and more of us must rally round to rebuild our world.

Nancy Breslau Lewis, my editor, exceeded all expectations. Her own belief in political participation by young people made the editing process philosophical instead of merely mechanical. Researchers Maria Ott and Laura Retzler gathered essential information and both of them contributed much in the way of ideas. I must sound a final note of gratitude to a devoted production editor, Beth Meserve.

Table of Contents

Introduction

The emergence of democracies around the globe is a powerful reminder that ideas incubated over two hundred years ago in France are still potent enough to tear down walls, open gates, and rewrite political history. Citizens all over the world are demanding a say in the social and economic restructuring of their countries.

Here in the United States, the revolutionary fervor of 1776 cooled many generations ago. As our own brand of democracy enters its third century, visionary leaders seem few and far between. Who in American politics dares us to pursue truly innovative solutions to old social problems? Where are American Lech Walesas and Nelson Mandelas? Or twentieth century Thomas Paines?

It is among youth that we still see a compulsion to act sooner rather than later. It is young people who refuse to despair about the possibility of finding solutions. So often teenagers are cynically branded as being self-absorbed and irresponsible; yet an increasing number of them express a sense of duty to future generations. Although their involvement is most apparent in working to safeguard the environment, these activists are grappling with social issues as well; especially those which directly affect kids.

It is so rare these days for ordinary Americans to participate in our democracy that people actually pay attention when concerned citizens who are not yet of voting age take the initiative. Kids are pursuing remedies and reforms, by working with their school boards, city halls, statehouses and the federal government. These teenagers are not carrying out someone else's agenda; they are forging ahead with their own. Their impact is phenomenal. Experienced lobbyists express disbelief and confess: "If it weren't for the kids, that law would never have passed."

Kids have an uncanny ability to get a foot in the door of decision makers at a time in our history when campaign contributors seem to enjoy the easiest access to our lawmakers. The honesty of these young citizen activists is disarming. "Children everywhere can stop us short with their unnerving moments of innocent good sense," writes Robert Coles, child psychiatrist and author of *The Political Life of Children*.

The successful campaigns of these Americans are based on reasoned, pragmatic solutions. Their innovative ideas have resulted in the first bicycle safety helmet law in the nation, a new high school history course, and a model community center created and run by teens. They are willing to go out on a limb, too; ready to oppose board of education policies or to take on a state legislature when ecological assets are at risk.

The real legacy of their political involvement goes beyond the actual accomplishments achieved by these young people. Activism at an early age has the potential for becoming a lifetime habit. Nothing can match the exhilaration of having your ideas tested and accepted in the real world. Even those campaigners who are weary from the fight seem ready and willing to face the next round.

All levels of civic activism spell hope for our aging democracy. A legislator's thoughtful reply to a letter makes our representative government more familiar and less intimidating to a teenager. Even when elected officials are not responsive to a student's letter or campaign, the young constituent quickly learns that the government is not a closed and monolithic body. Strategy can often be refashioned to circumvent an opponent, since our government is composed of hundreds of decision makers and power centers. Instead of feeling detached from the democratic process, young activists feel plugged in. Once a teenager has canvassed the neighborhood collecting signatures for a petition, testified before a legislative committee, or spoken at a news conference with the cameras rolling, the foundation for future advocacy has been laid.

When teens encourage elementary school age children to get involved in a grassroots campaign, their self-esteem soars. These young adults rekindle in the next generation a belief that society is capable of perfecting itself, and that all citizens, regardless of their age, have a stake in that process.

This sense of idealism and social responsibility has no single stimulus. Some young activists, whose parents are still tethered to the protest politics of the 1960s, are quite naturally inclined to challenge the status quo. There are others, however, who come from families where political involvement is nonexistent. Many parents are uneasy, even suspicious, of their sons' and daughters' involvement with politicians, whom they distrust completely. Ironically, their children's activism sometimes reawakens a sense of civic responsibility in those same mothers and fathers. After all, thirty years ago most of these parents were young idealists themselves, who took to heart President John F. Kennedy's famous inaugural charge: "Ask not what your country can do for you; ask what you can do for your country."

A new effort to combat political cynicism and apathy is sweeping the country. Many educators, especially social studies and science teachers, are instilling the ethical imperative of participatory democracy in their students. Yesterday's teaching methods — field trips to the statehouse and mock legislative sessions — are no longer sufficient. "*Doing* is the most effective way to learn about citizenship," stresses Carol Kinsley of the Community Service Learning program in Massachusetts.

The remarkable growth in community service, now a requirement for graduation at an increasing number of high schools, is providing an opportunity for students to share the firsthand knowledge they gain from volunteering. Their service on the frontlines of a homeless shelter or a nursing home can spark a personal search for remedies to such daunting problems as caring for the disadvantaged and disenfranchised members of society. Imagine the potential for change if all this concern and compassion could be converted into action! Indeed, such prominent leaders as Ernest Boyer of the Carnegie Foundation for the Advancement of Teaching sees the need for our schools to be "a staging ground for action."

It is not uncommon for student governments and other youth organizations to take the lead on such controversial issues as school violence or censorship. Many community recycling programs and efforts to detect pollutants in streams have been initiated by school ecology clubs.

This book is filled with stories about young Americans who are throwing their ideas into the ring rather than throwing in the towel. These activists realize that democracy is not a spectator sport. They disprove the prevailing view that ordinary individuals are powerless. They show how anyone, at any age, can play the game of politics, and how participating in the process is crucial, rewarding, and even fun.

Ryan Tedeschi, a 'senior' citizen from a Massachusetts high school, urges everyone to step up to bat. I'll let him throw the opening pitch: "If you really believe in something, go for it! Life is too short to stand around and watch. Doing the hard work pays off, and you can look back and say, 'Yeah, I had fun and I worked for that fun and it was really satisfying!'"

Wendy Schaetzel Lesko
April 1992

PART I:

LAUNCH YOUR OWN CAMPAIGN
Mapping Out Your Game Plan

LAUNCH YOUR OWN CAMPAIGN
Activate!

A ship in the harbor is safe,
That's not what ships were built for.
— Sheed

Many navigators are needed as America tries to steer a new course into the next century. Young people in communities across the country are taking hold of the rudder and assuming personal responsibility for charting new directions in political activism.

"Young people must wake up to their power," says Maureen Gemma, who has been working to combat global hunger since the age of fourteen. Her message expresses urgency:

> *We have permission to be outrageous about*
> *the state of the planet. I see myself as*
> *accountable for the present state of the world*
> *and the future since it is our future. Don't wait*
> *until you are twenty-one to make a difference.*
> *Too much is happening.*

Once you view yourself as an agent of change, the next step is realizing how hard it is to achieve change. Ideas that challenge the status quo inevitably attract opposition. Apathy can suffocate even a non-controversial proposal. Peers may ridicule; parents may scoff.

The next barrier is not being taken seriously by decision makers. Jeff Curry, a high school senior who participated in a grueling two-year campaign with the state legislature, debunks the traditional attitude that children are to be seen, not heard:

> *Most kids think it is an 'adult world' and that*
> *they cannot touch it. They think it is just*
> *beyond them and they cannot do anything*
> *about it. They should realize that they can, if*
> *they work hard enough. Kids should be taken*
> *seriously because they share their true feelings*
> *about an issue and they are not paid to feel a*
> *certain way.*

Our society, which is so accustomed to public misrepresentation and falsehoods, tends to be stunned by, and then attentive to, a youth-led initiative free of suspicious motives. After all, who would dare to turn off the flow of ideas proposed by the next generation since today's young people will inherit the problems their parents cannot solve?

Young political activists are not guaranteed a smooth passage, however. Plenty of decision makers may initially display the welcome mat for them, but later resort to hardball politics and backroom maneuvering. Your odds of success will increase by playing by politicians' rules and letting them know you'll be back if you get shut out. Even if the chance of victory is nil, young citizen activists are willing to draw battle lines. Andrew Holleman, who stopped an $11 million condominium complex from being built in a wildlife habitat, remembers being warned, "Don't expect to win." His response was, "If you really believe in something, you have to stand up for it. If you don't, what are you worth?"

The next generation is proving that there is no minimum age for leadership. These kids are contributing their ideas and tackling complex problems. They have their own distinctive styles and are politically involved to varying degrees. Some are quiet collaborators, others are strident agitators.

These young activists are setting an example for everyone. Seventeen-year old Kristin Johnson says, "Let people in power know what you think. You live in a democracy and need to take advantage of it. The government is there for you." Great things happen when individuals concentrate their energies on a cause greater than themselves. Americans of all ages can sign aboard and help steer this country in a new direction.

"Launch Your Own Campaign" will help you choose your game plan every step of the way. There are numerous approaches and strategies, and no magic formulas. How could there be? That would take all the fun out of designing your own campaign!

STAGE 1: WARM UPS
Get Your Adrenaline Pumping

Today, because of communications technology, children know as much as the wisest nobles knew in the past . . . When people were illiterate, they had to elect the lawyer or the doctor or whoever had access to information and knowledge to represent them in government. But today the peasant has more information than the politicians, who lose their time in sterile partisan fighting. This kind of democracy is out of date.

— Jacques Cousteau

If you are in search of a mission, in our Information Age the sky's the limit. If you invest a little time to learn more facts about a problem, you can arm yourself with knowledge. This will make you more comfortable with the complexities of an issue and will whet your appetite to pursue solutions. Once you've focused on an idea and are ready to get started, it's time to begin gathering the information that is readily available.

WRITING FOR FREE INFORMATION

A few postage stamps can generate more information than you would imagine. This fact-gathering technique also works well for any research project, including term papers and other school assignments. Instead of relying on encyclopedias and magazines, exploring other information sources will give you a real advantage.

Andrew Holleman, the young environmentalist whose story is included in Part II, dug up volumes of information on both state and local laws regarding wetlands protection. He contacted the local health department, the housing commission, the regional office of the U.S. Environmental Protection Agency and many state and national environmental organizations during his ten-month campaign to save a wooded wildlife habitat. Andrew's father, a medical technologist familiar with the world of science, recalls: "All the environmental and scientific information that has come into the house through the mail and what I have learned from all this is astounding."

Several overlooked national resources which can help you get the big picture on a specific issue include:

★ U.S. Congress

> Nearly fifty House and Senate committees and several hundred subcommittees conduct an average of seventy-five hearings each week the Congress is in session. The records of these formal information-gathering sessions are printed months later. Dozens of experts from all walks of life testify. You can identify all the major national groups as well as community organizations that are supporting or opposing a particular legislative proposal. For example, the Senate Committee on Labor and Human Resources hearings entitled *The Issue of National Service*, or the House Energy and Commerce Subcommittee on Health hearings on *Tobacco Advertising*, acquaint you with different areas of controversy. You gain a historical perspective from these documents and also learn what has been tried in different states and cities around the country.

> Most published hearings are free. The only cost will be the frustration you experience in trying to track down the appropriate committees. All the congressional committees are listed in Part IV; once you think you've found the committee in charge of the issue you're interested in, write or call the committee documents clerk. Alternatively, send a request to your representative or one of your two senators asking them to find out what committees have conducted hearings on a specific issue. See if they can arrange to have the committees send the hearing documents directly to you. Simply write to either of your Senators, U.S. Congress, Washington, DC 20510 or your Representative, U.S. Congress, Washington, DC 20515.

★ U.S. General Accounting Office (GAO)

> The GAO serves as the fiscal watchdog for the entire federal government. A few examples of very current and readable reports produced by GAO include: *Greenhouse Effect* (RCED-90-74BR), *Metric Conversion* (RCED-90-131), *Noncriminal Juveniles* (T-GGD91-30), and *Supplemental Student*

Loans (HRD-90-33FS). You may want first to request the *Annual Index of Reports and Testimony*, and from that simply indicate your choice by using the appropriate order numbers and writing: GAO Distribution, PO Box 6015, Gaithersburg, MD 20877 (202) 275-6241 Fax: (301) 840-3638. There is no charge except for the stamp on your postcard or letter.

★ Congressional Research Service (CRS)

The CRS at the Library of Congress generates hundreds of fact-filled reports and Issue Briefs; for example, *Corporal Punishment in the Public Schools: A Fifty State Survey* (91-798A) and *Regulating Record Lyrics: A Constitutional Analysis* (IB87632A). Also available free of charge are CRS Info-Packs, which are more comprehensive; for example, *Drug Abuse in America* (IP030D) or *Native American Heritage* (IP454N).

The only way to obtain a CRS publication is from a member of Congress. One approach is to make a local telephone call to the district office of one of your senators or your representative and ask the staff to consult the *Guide to CRS Products* to identify the titles and report numbers of the specific subject areas you are investigating. It's possible that the local office will not have this catalog and it will be necessary to contact the legislator's Washington office. Let your member of Congress know you need this information for your campaign. Congressional offices often deny student requests if they think CRS reports will be used for a term paper. The Capitol Hill switchboard operator at (202) 224-3121 can connect you to any legislator's office or you can write to either of your senators at U.S. Congress, Washington, DC 20510 or your representative at U.S. Congress, Washington, DC 20515.

★ Federal Government Agencies and Departments

In addition to the legislative branch, most federal offices generate a tremendous amount of information. The U.S. Environmental Protection Agency has a special office geared to respond to public inquiries. Write to Public Information Center, PM-211B, EPA, 401 M Street SW, Washington, DC 20460 (202) 260-2080. Many of these government departments and offices are included in Part IV.

★ State and Local Government Agencies; Community Groups

You'll find more data than you can easily digest; for example, your state department of natural resources and the city department of sanitation will both have a boatload of information on landfill capacity and recycling initiatives. Your state commission on human rights will have figures on hate crimes, domestic violence, and sexual harassment. Community groups and state organizations are other promising sources of information. For

instance, California's Community Reclamation Project and the Neighborhood Youth Leadership Center in New York City are battling gangs and
can share their different approaches for dealing with urban violence.

★ National Organizations

You will discover that an association has been formed to represent the
interests of just about any group, ranging from the National Soft Drink
Association, the Society against Vivisection, and the Freedom of Expression
Foundation to the International Movement of Catholic Students. These
groups churn out volumes of information which they will often share with
you even if you are not a member. Organizations involved with issues
directly affecting kids are included in Part IV and the most exhaustive
reference source is the three-volume *Encyclopedia of Associations* found at
most public libraries.

★ Think Tanks

Comprehensive proposals considered by our elected representatives are
often first hatched by the experts and scholars. Some think tanks lean more
to the political right or left while others are non-partisan including the
Kettering Foundation's National Issues Forum, 100 Commons Road,
Dayton, OH 45459-2777 (800) 433-7834. The National Issues Forum
produces over a dozen issue books which present different perspectives on
major topics and examine the costs and consequences of various courses of
action. The purpose of these reports is to encourage public discussion
through informal study circles and locally organized forums. Examples
include "Growing Up at Risk," "The Drug Crisis: Public Strategies for
Breaking the Habit," and "Boundaries of Free Speech: How Free Is Too
Free?"

VIEWING VIDEOS

Scout around for films and videos on issues you're curious to know
more about. First, check with the librarian at your school media center to
find out what videos are in the school district's collection. Next, explore
your public library system. The audiovisual resources are usually centralized
and located at one branch. Here are some films and videotapes typically
available from public libraries:

Acid Rain: Requiem or Recovery
The AIDS Movie
The American Handgun War
The Klan: Legacy of Hate in America
If You Love This Planet [atomic bomb]
No First Use [nuclear war]
Books Under Fire [censorship]
Better Safe Than Sorry [child abuse]
Bluebirds: Bring Them Back
Drunk & Deadly [drunk driving]
The Solar Advantage
Becoming American [immigrant family's culture shock]
Bombs Will Make The Rainbow Break
Harvest of Shame [migrant farm workers]
Home Sweet Home [joint child custody]
Beyond Black & White
Energy: New Sources
Promises to Keep [homelessness]
A Love Canal Family [chemical dump near Niagara Falls, NY]
Replanting The Tree of Life [rain forests]

National organizations, ranging from Amnesty International to Greenpeace, produce videos with their own particular spin on an issue. Some nonprofit groups will loan you a videotape at no cost. For example, the Center for Marine Conservation offers a ten-minute video entitled "Trashing The Oceans." Leads to organizations offering videos are included in Part IV.

One other source is the National Audiovisual Center which serves as a clearinghouse for approximately 8,000 titles produced by the federal government. The *Media Resources Catalog* is available at most public libraries, or you can contact the National Archives and Records Administration, Customer Services Section P2, 8700 Edgeworth Drive, Capitol Heights, MD 20742 (301) 763-1896.

Also, if you live in a university town, it's worth checking out the collection on campus. It may take a little effort to arrange to borrow a film, but it's worth a try. Film distributors have very expensive rental fees and many universities have copies of these documentaries.

One talented young musician and songwriter recently used a film to drive home her message of compassion for the homeless. "Everyone knew me for my piano-playing during my sophomore year," says Anna Deeny who is now at Shepherd College in West Virginia, thanks to both a music scholarship and an ethnic minority leadership scholarship. Music has always been a part of Anna's home life; visiting grandparents and uncles from Puerto Rico would sing and strum on guitars in the living room.

Anna continually searches for compelling visual images to enhance the notes and words of her music. At her high school talent show, she presented a music video unlike anything you've ever seen. The theme had been brewing in her mind for well over a year. Anna recalls:

One night I was out with my friends during Christmas break. I had seen these homeless people downtown. I thought: This is terrible. I got home that night and wrote "Humanity Cried."

HUMANITY CRIED

*Each time I look into
his fragile eyes,
I see the pain
of a thousand men combined.*

*The city sees itself
in this man,
but no one wants
to look at him.*

*And each time I look
into his gentle face,
I see the face of God
crying out to me.*

*With haggard face
and time-torn clothes,
he's ugly outside
but his beauty's enclosed.*

*He holds his hands
up to the sun;
even when it rains
he prays that it will come.*

*And when he died
humanity cried,
but no one could
look straight into his eyes.*

Reprinted with permission by Anna Deeny.

Anna explains:

Have you ever noticed you cannot look a homeless person right in the eye? It's like you look at them for a second and then look away. I think it is because in that homeless person you see the weakest part of yourself. To look at them, we have to look at ourselves. To have these people on the streets is a sad reflection of our society.

As a senior I wanted to do something very special for the school talent show. When I play music I always imagine something visual. I thought maybe I'd just rent a movie about homeless people. I called the public library and they were extremely helpful. My disappointment is that more people don't use the library's services and don't realize all the knowledge that's available to them. The librarian mentioned that she had the movie "Promises to Keep." I was really happy about that because it was about homeless people in Washington, D.C. So I went in to watch the film. The whole beginning was just perfect — I decided to use the first six minutes of the film with the movie's sound turned off to accompany my words. I thought, "This has to work."

Before five hundred students and parents, Anna sat at a grand piano in a darkened auditorium. Her silhouette punctuated the message of the first song she sang:

IN THE DARK

*Imagine standing in the dark,
the more you look,
the more you start
to picture images
that you thought
were never there.*

*And as you start to walk along,
you once thought
that you were strong
enough to handle this.
Then you trip,
and then you fall,
and in the corner of your eye
you see images that now fly.*

Reprinted with permission by Anna Deeny.

The footage of homeless men, women and children then flooded the screen as Anna played and sang "Humanity Cried." Anna remains proud:

If I had to pay to be in the talent show, I would have done it. It was great. A lot of students were happy that I did that. They were screaming. There were a lot of people who cried. I think it made them think about the homeless . . . and about themselves.

After presenting this "multimedia performance art" at her college, Anna decided to continue performing at other events hosted by homeless advocacy groups.

INVITING A SPEAKER

While films and videos have an immediate visual impact, there is often no substitute for the emotional wallop packed by a public speaker. Your chances of easily reaching a speaker depend on where you live. Your options increase if you live in the state capital, since many national organizations will have state chapters located there. Although many large groups have their main offices in Washington, D.C. or New York City, plenty are based in Atlanta, Chicago, Dallas, Minneapolis, San Francisco, and other major cities. Federal and state government offices tend to be located in the larger metropolitan areas, often not in state capitals. In smaller cities and towns you'll find a local Sierra Club, Humane Society, and many other groups; so check out the public library or the telephone directory.

Here are a few examples of some local and national organizations that can usually put you in touch with a speaker:

American Civil Liberties Union (ACLU)
. . . on free speech and censorship
American Lung Association
. . . on clean indoor air and smoke-free zones
Board of Education
. . . on school rules and curricula
County Health Department
. . . on AIDS and teenage pregnancy prevention
Environmental Protection Agency (EPA) Regional Office
. . . on air pollution, water conservation, etc.

Federal Aviation Administration Regional Office
 . . . on noisy airplanes and flight patterns
Local Newspaper, Radio and Television Reporters
 . . . on their "beat," which means whatever subject area they cover
 (youth employment, education, environment, crime, etc.)

Refer to Part IV for many other organizations which may be able to arrange a speaker for your group.

Rennie Salomon recognized the value of contacting public speakers back in elementary school. She remembers first learning that Florida panthers were an endangered species in the fourth grade. That's when she realized "The world was in trouble and I was just surprised that not everyone was doing something, because this world belongs to everyone."

Even though Rennie moved hundreds of miles away from the Everglades, her knowledge of this vast swampland and wildlife refuge fueled her continuing concern about the environment, especially the rain forests. Rennie was working on a book report when she stumbled on the idea of getting a resource person to speak to her sixth grade class:

For Hannukah, I got "Going Green: A Kid's Handbook to Saving the Planet." It's a how-to book and it tells you a little bit about the problems, what you can do, and some people you can call.

For my book report I zeroed in on the rain forests. In one section of the book, under the letter "I" it said "Invite a speaker." That's when I started looking for organizations. I came up with Friends of the Earth. I was trying to think of a group that would know about everything, not just the rain forests.

It was a Sunday and I wanted to call somebody. Someone was at the organization's office, but I was told to call back and talk to Beth Stein. When I reached her, she said she'd love to come in. We had a lot of phone calls — about ten to fifteen —including a long-distance call. She wasn't in a lot. Over spring break, while we were in California, I got in touch with her and gave her my teacher's phone number and she called him and they set a date for the speech.

She sent a big package of things: "How to Plant a Tree" and a lot of different environmental materials. I copied them for my class and handed them out. My teacher really liked that. I introduced her: "Now here is Beth Stein from Friends of the Earth, who graciously donated her time." She talked about all the things you could do when you wake up in the morning until you go to bed at night; like don't waste the water when you brush your teeth, and when you go to school take a bus or car pool. She brought a big garbage bag and let everyone feel how much trash one person throws away in a day . . . She was really open to people and everyone liked her presentation.

Rennie's interest in the environment continues to grow and she has helped form an activist group at her synagogue called Seven People Trying to Make a Difference.

HINTS

▸ Decide with your teacher or group on several possible dates and times to propose to the speaker.

▸ If you leave a message and your phone number, suggest they call after 4:30 p.m. or whenever you're sure you will be home.

▸ Expect "telephone tag" and don't become frustrated. It's often difficult initially to reach someone.

▸ See if your teacher or counselor can take an incoming call during school hours.

▸ You might ask if the speaker wants to pass out any material to the class or group. Check to see if the speaker needs any equipment to show a video, film, or slide show.

▸ Consider asking the speaker about his or her background, which will make it easier for you to introduce the speaker. If you don't want to make the introduction, get someone else who is comfortable with public speaking to make a short intro.

▸ Once the date is set, be sure to write or telephone the speaker about the time and place.

▸ Send the guest speaker a thank-you note and also ask for more information about any unanswered questions.

TELEPHONING EXPERTS AND ON-LINE CONNECTIONS

Pick up the phone and you'll be surprised how much current information you can accumulate within a week or two. One call will often lead you to contact other organizations and information centers. If you are concerned about the use of Styrofoam packaging in the lunchroom, for example, find out about your school board's policy by calling them. Then you may want to browse through Part IV and contact government agencies and organizations. These groups may have comparative analyses on paper packaging as well as on new Styrofoam products which supposedly don't release chlorofluorocarbons (CFCs) that harm the ozone.

To avoid long-distance calling, refer to Part IV for toll-free hotlines and clearinghouses. For example, the U.S. Department of Justice operates a toll-free number (800) 638-8736, in Maryland (301) 251-5500, and can send you free, three-page crime file study guides. There are thirty-two in the series, including "Neighborhood Safety," "Gun Control," "Juvenile Offenders," "Death Penalty," "Drug Testing," and "Victims." Local law enforcement agencies, community organizations, and elected officials can provide data, speakers, and other resources.

Computer on-line networks linking young people are the wave of the future. There are more electronic bulletin boards in the United States than newspapers. Electronic pen pals, now popular at many schools, pave the way for more information exchanges. The Coalition for Children of the Earth is pioneering an international telecommunications network to involve kids in the 1995 U.N. World Summit for Children.

Nancy Stefanik, one of the designers of this youth-oriented network, sees computer conferencing as the critical linchpin linking the world community. She explains how one international network for tobacco control advocates enables individuals to pursue their own local goals while keeping an eye on the global perspective.

Let's say you're a lone activist lobbying to remove vending
machines from places kids can easily access. You know that

most smokers start before the age of seventeen and a high percentage before the age of fourteen, and that it's likely they will never smoke if they make it to age eighteen. You've made vending machine restrictions your mission but then you learn about what the tobacco companies are doing in the Third World; how they are making up for declining sales here in the U.S. by aggressively promoting their products to women and children in developing countries . . . You're not going to stop your own efforts, but perhaps make part of your mission informing Americans about how we are increasingly being considered promoters of death because of the actions of the U.S. Trade Representative in support of our tobacco companies. You learn that this ethical issue involves the whole planet.

The opportunity to fish in a vast ocean of ideas and use whatever information or strategies fit your own priorities is made easier by having access to a computer and a modem. Contact national organizations to find out whether the network is open to non-members and whether the users group in your area can introduce you to the many local electronic bulletin boards operating close to home.

ATTENDING A CONFERENCE

The conference business has become a booming industry and many conferences are geared for kids. Organizations like the National 4-H Council and the Kettering Foundation's National Issues Forum sponsor conferences around the country with the goal of encouraging the next generation to focus on the challenges that lie ahead.

These annual meetings often are work sessions where bold initiatives are debated. A lot of networking also occurs. Having the chance to meet other people who are deeply involved with the issue you care about can really spur you on.

Kristin Johnson, who lives near Seattle, decided when she was in ninth grade that somehow, someday, she would travel to the Amazon to study the rain forest. Reading Andrew Mitchell's book, *The Enchanted Canopy*, only heightened her enthusiasm. With her dad's help, she put together a slide presentation on the rain forest for her science class. For the past four years Kristin has been giving this lecture to area schools. She believes she made a quantum leap in the level of her commitment because of all the people she met at a conference. Kristin was fifteen at the time:

My dad and I went to my first conference on the rain forests. I was lost most of the time because I didn't know what these scientists were talking about. It was like a two-day flood of information that would have been better to get over a period of a few months. I had only done the slide presentation four or five times. But while I was there, I met the director of the Rainforest Action Network, Randall Hayes, and a native woman from the Amazonian rain forest, plus I met a woman from the Woodland Park Zoo who told me about volunteering there.

Since then, Kristin's involvement has taken off. Not only did she get "tons of slides from scientists and my friends at the zoo," but Kristin created the Rainforest Awareness Information Network, which consists of a dozen or so students who present her slide show to area schools. Her contacts from this conference and others that she has attended enabled her to get prominent tropical biologists like Donald Perry to come to Seattle to speak.

Like Kristin, hunger activist Maureen Gemma remembers how the first conference she attended solidified her own commitment:

I realized that it is important to raise money [for food relief organizations], but I also wanted to do different projects in which I actually had the opportunity to educate people. So, I went to a Youth Ending Hunger (YEH) conference in Rochester. YEH had gotten my name somehow from my participation at my high school and they invited me.

Participating in these YEH conferences has enabled Maureen to move into an international league. In 1991, she addressed the Global Youth Conference on Hunger in Kyoto, Japan, and spoke in front of 375 people from 60 countries. She knows her father's encouragement and willingness to pay for airline tickets allowed her commitment to blossom, however. Maureen says that this sort of parental support is unusual:

This summer when I was calling people to go to this conference in New York, I noticed parents wouldn't pay for their child's plane fare and the kids had to raise the money themselves. I think that parents supporting their kids in whatever humanitarian project they dream up is important. Youth are passionate about helping people. Parents, I think, sometimes suppress their feelings or do not allow their kids to fully swing out and participate.

Developing Hidden Strengths

Once you've picked your mission and have started fact-finding, take a few minutes to jot down your ideas. Often your initial solution for solving a community problem is beautifully simple, yet effective. Be aware that your original idea will most likely undergo a metamorphosis as you absorb the ideas of supporters as well as opponents. After all, debate and reaching consensus are what our democracy is all about.

BRAINSTORMING

Float your idea by talking about it with friends, parents, classmates, teachers, advisors, relatives, or neighbors. Ignore those well-meaning individuals who are enthusiastic but warn you against trying. Usually they want to protect you from failure, which is certainly a very real possibility. Be prepared that most people will not share your zeal and determination.

Pay attention to those who like your idea but offer specific suggestions. Also, listen closely to those who voice objections. Understanding different points of view is essential and will make you both smarter and more effective in convincing others to become active allies.

Every conversation you have, every argument you hear, every article you read, and every fact you dig up will make you better informed and that much more persuasive. In other words — do your homework!

William Sangster, a Massachusetts teacher who has guided many students through several campaigns with the state legislature, explains the evolution that takes place.

The hardest part when you get involved politically is to withstand all the negativism. The secret to launching a campaign is there has to be a period of dissatisfaction. Something has to be bothering people, or forget it. There has to be a grassroots annoyance. When that begins to happen, then someone champions the cause. Now you begin to get people on the bandwagon — people who agree with you. You have to sell it to your own. So the first thing anyone has to do when they start thinking about proposing a law is get the people in your immediate environment to think it is a good idea and say, "Yes, you've brought up a good point that bothers me."

John Fudala, an avid skateboarder, remembers listening to an avalanche of complaints voiced about backyard skateboard ramps at a zoning board meeting. He was sixteen at the time and had the biggest ramp in town. The city of Virginia Beach had outlawed skateboarding on streets and sidewalks as well as on private ramps. The debate centered on how to accommodate the "wild maniacs" in a way that wouldn't disturb the peace and quiet of this resort community.

There weren't that many of us there at the zoning meeting, maybe thirty or thirty-five. Some were skaters who had their ramps prohibited or taken away. I remember there were some kids we didn't even know who were doing some petitioning. My dad and other parents spoke for us. There were a lot from the other side so we heard both sides. It came down to what the city was going to do for us.

The skateboarders and the zoning board reached an understanding. Once the City Council decided to build a public skateboard facility, it was the parks and recreation department experts who *listened* to John's ideas and used his designs for a vertical ramp ten feet high and almost thirty two feet wide. Located on the only hill (actually a landfill called Mt. Trashmore) in Virginia Beach, this ramp has become a smashing success and tourist attraction. The "grassroots annoyance" voiced by some teenagers and their parents was heard by the powers-that-be, and both sides found common ground on which to build a compromise.

EVALUATING SOLUTIONS

"People need to be clear on what is wrong. The more you understand problems, the more you'll understand solutions." That sound advice comes from John Williams, editor of *Bicycle Forum*, who has seen many bike paths that are poorly designed or downright dangerous for cyclists. He can take credit for devising innovative trails that are recognized as national models. Good solutions don't evolve out of thin air but from solid research and careful thought.

We might do well to draw on the Seventh Law of the Iroquois. Before making a decision, these Native Americans consider the impact of an action seven generations into the future. Our search, too, should be for long-term solutions rather than quick fixes.

This process of thinking creatively and critically about complex issues is being emphasized more than ever in the classroom. You may want to try to take advantage of one such curriculum that has been developed for all grade levels by the Future Problem Solving Program, 115 West Main Street, Aberdeen, NC 28315 (919) 944-4707. This step-by-step program encourages young people first to weigh all the information they have learned about such problems as terrorism, the arms race, poverty and inequalities in the American legal system. They then explore possible solutions, decide on a course of action and, finally, try to carry out their proposed solutions.

> **HINTS**
>
> When evaluating long-term solutions:
> ► Be open-minded and curious.
> ► Gather information from many different sources.
> ► Seek out contradictory facts and statistics.
> ► Be tolerant of other perspectives.
> ► Weigh other points of view.
> ► Consider alternative solutions.
> ► Make sure your proposed solution serves the larger public good.

Whatever the issue, the first step is to find out what has been tried in the past and what ideas have already been considered and discarded. Some detective work is also necessary to figure out who has the power to decide your issue; whether it is the school board or the state legislature. It is also worth learning what other cities and states have done in trying to solve similar problems.

DETERMINING WHO HAS THE POWER TO DECIDE

You want to make sure to bark up the right tree and usually there are several trees in the forest from which to choose. Getting funds for a teen center probably means going to your city council. If you are concerned about global warming, human rights, or some other international issue, it will mean bypassing your local and state governments and perhaps joining a national effort that is trying to gain support in the U.S. Congress or at the United Nations.

If your proposal pertains to education you will no doubt be working with the local school board. Board members are usually elected, except in a few districts where they are appointed by the mayor. Youth representatives on the board of education, even though they are not usually voting members, can often become your allies. The elected members of your city council or county council have the final say on some school decisions.

School policy also can be determined at the state level. For example, the requirement that every high school graduate perform a certain number of hours of community service was voted on by the Maryland State Board of Education. In New Jersey, however, mandatory community service is being debated not by the state board of education but in the state legislature.

If you have a choice between trying to get action by your local government or the state legislature, consider these three questions:

★ Is the statehouse reasonably close to where you live so you can make several trips to meet and talk with lawmakers?

★ Will the state legislature be in session for several more months?

★ Do you know your state representative or state senator, or do you know someone who will arrange for you to meet either one or both of them?

If the answer is "yes" to all three questions, you should probably consider taking your campaign to the state level.

As a general rule of thumb, follow the principle: "Think Globally, Act Locally." Stay close to home and see if you can get some action through your city council. If you succeed, this kind of victory often serves as a stepping-stone to winning at the county or even state government level.

In Maryland, for example, one town council outlawed cigarette vending machines and that precedent helped prod the county government to adopt a similar ban. In Minnesota, however, after twenty municipalities voted to get rid of cigarette vending machines, the tobacco industry went to the state capitol to lobby for a bill that would preempt or overturn the local ordinances. When students in Oakdale, a community located about fifteen minutes away from St. Paul, heard about this controversy they got fired up.

Under the guidance of Curt Jackson, their social studies teacher, they drafted a petition in favor of banning vending machine sales of cigarettes and collected nearly six hundred signatures in one day. Without any affiliation or communication with the American Cancer Society or other health organizations which were trying to defeat the tobacco industry bill, the students met with their state senator and representative and then testified at the committee hearings. At this juncture, the legislation had already passed the House and the prospect of defeating it in the Senate looked unlikely.

Five of the fifth graders then proceeded to speak before the Senate Commerce Committee hearings. Watching the videotape of their testimony, it's dramatic to note how the legislators actually sat up, listened intently and then voted to table the bill. As one seasoned lobbyist said, "It was the most remarkable thing I've ever seen. The kids made all the difference." And Mr. Jackson called it "one of the most exciting times in twenty-nine years of teaching."

Very often it will be obvious who has the power to decide. The next logical step is to try to learn what has already happened on this particular issue and whether there is any future action in the works.

FINDING OUT WHAT'S ALREADY IN THE PIPELINE

Often it is easier to move your ideas forward on a train that's already rolling down the tracks. One environmental group has a tradition of finding out the train schedule in advance. Every fall, members of the Severn School Environment Club, located in Annapolis, the state capital of Maryland, invite either their county councilmember, their state representative, or an environmental lobbyist to speak with them about pending legislation. The club then determines its priorities. These high school students joined in a successful campaign to lobby the county council to spend $3 million to complete a bike route. The club also pushed for state legislation, now enacted into law, which requires local developers to reforest a percentage of land as a part of any new construction.

Listening to the news and reading the local newspapers may provide enough clues about ongoing efforts. Usually one legislator or councilmember will be out in front trying to steer the debate on just about every major problem in your community. The primary government agency responsible for carrying out any new laws will be aware of the variety of proposals that are under consideration.

For example, in Washington, D.C., where drive-by shootings and stray bullets pose a horrifying risk, about two dozen streetwise teenagers linked up with the Police Chief's Youth Task Force to Prevent Violence. These young activists, many of whom have experienced violence firsthand, got the mayor to proclaim October as Violence Prevention Month. They created a calendar of events which included conflict-resolution workshops at many city high schools, ecumenical church vigils, "Turn In A Gun" Amnesty Week, and go-go rap concerts promoting "Peace in D.C." Weekly meetings of the task force continue.

Make a few calls to your city government or the school board and you stand a good chance of finding out if proposals related to your particular concern are moving through the pipeline. Many state legislatures have toll-free numbers so you can call to learn whether there has been any action on a proposed law. The telephone numbers for all state legislatures are listed in Part IV.

DISCOVERING WHAT'S HAPPENING AROUND THE COUNTRY

Getting a glimpse of the big picture is important. Let's say your city council is considering a curfew for teens. It's possible to find out how many other cities have imposed a curfew and ask for their crime statistics before and after the local law went into effect. This information should provide clues on the effectiveness of such a policy.

There are many shortcuts to sending letters to a dozen big city mayors or all fifty governors. You can get an overview of legislative proposals and innovative laws by contacting some national clearinghouses which track what is going on across the country. For instance, the issue specialists at the National Conference of State Legislatures are aware of what is happening in all fifty states on over two hundred topics including adoption, AIDS, animals, automobile insurance, home video regulations, and state holidays. This staff is very helpful; however, some of the other organizations listed below do not routinely respond to the public.

If you indicate that your request is not for a classroom assignment but is, instead, a serious initiative that you are pursuing with your elected officials, you will probably glean some first-rate information from these clearinghouses. Here are a few starting points:

Council of State Governments States Information Center PO Box 11910 Iron Works Pike Lexington, KY 40578 (606) 252-2291	National Governors Association 444 North Capitol Street Washington, DC 20001 (202) 624-5300
International City Management Association 777 North Capitol Street NE, #500 Washington, DC 20002-4201 (202) 289-4262	National League of Cities 1301 Pennsylvania Avenue NW Washington, DC 20004 (202) 626-3000
National Association of Counties 440 First Street NW Washington, DC 20001 (202) 393-6226	National School Boards Association Resource Center/Library 1680 Duke Street Alexandria, VA 22314 (703) 838-6722
National Conference of State Legislatures Office of State Services 1050 17th Street Room 2100 Denver, CO 80265 (303) 830-2200	U.S. Conference of Mayors 1620 Eye Street NW Washington, DC 20006 (202) 293-7330 U.S. Congress Legislative Information & Status Office Washington, DC 20515 (202) 225-1772

National organizations also monitor what is happening across the country and in the U.S. Congress. For instance, the National Commission on Drunk Driving publishes a chart comparing the laws in every state. The Student Press Law Center is aware of censorship cases involving school newspapers and yearbooks all across the nation.

To get the names of a few organizations that may have an overview, first refer to Part IV. If you don't find what you are looking for, consult Gale's *Encyclopedia of Associations* at your public library. Simply use the keyword index in this encyclopedia and you will be able to identify several organizations you can write or call to find out what has been tried elsewhere in the country.

GATHERING EVIDENCE AND STATS

Once you compile data on initiatives developed by other cities, school districts, or states, your next move is to get the facts on the situation in your local community in order to build your case.

On practically every issue, you will run into disagreement on the scope of the problem. Different organizations and interest groups will naturally highlight the data which buttress their own position. If you are not gathering conflicting statistics, then you had better keep digging. The numbers are out there and familiarity with divergent viewpoints is essential if you expect to mount a successful campaign.

Here are a few methods young citizen activists have followed to gather information, collect hard evidence, and conduct surveys and statistical research.

THE MASTER PLAN

After years of reading books about nature, twelve-year old Andrew Holleman knew a great deal about hydrology and the groundwater purification process. Andrew's knowledge, along with information he dug up from his town's master plan, provided the evidence needed to stop a developer from building a huge condominium complex. The master plan, which he discovered quite by chance at his public library, detailed exactly how many acres at the proposed building site had to be preserved as wetlands. (Refer to "Young Environmentalist Saves Wetlands" in Part II.)

Many cities and counties adopt a master plan that serves as a comprehensive blueprint for the future over the next ten to twenty years. Although the master plan can be modified, it is valuable research tool and can be a rich source of local zoning information.

NATIONAL STATISTICS & LOCAL DATA

In Virginia, there was an uproar when the **Fairfax County Board of Supervisors** proposed charging students a $100 fee to park their cars at school. High school students protested that driving to school was necessary for such things as extracurricular activities, sports, and after-school jobs. Scott Worden, who is the school newspaper editor at W.T. Woodson High School, investigated what the cost would be if an additional five hundred students depended on school buses for transportation.

> After checking with an official at the Fairfax County School transportation office, I found that each additional bus run would cost an average of $28.82 per day. With a maximum capacity of about fifty kids, ten additional bus runs and drivers would be required at an annual cost of more than $50,000. I doubt that many economists would endorse that plan as an effective method for reducing a deficit [a $30 million shortfall in the county school budget].

Although this editorial and other objections raised by students did not convince the board to rescind the parking fee, Scott Worden's argument undoubtedly carried more weight because he used facts to substantiate his opinion.

You can drum up statistics on just about anything. The more you can use local figures, the better. Instead of talking about the total number of kids nationally affected by drug addiction, point out statistics that show the extent of the problem in your school, city, or borough. This will be sure to catch the attention of your neighbors, the media, city officials, and elected representatives. Refer to Part IV for a listing of the many government agencies that collect data as well as the organizations that analyze these findings.

HARD PROOF

Two brothers staged a sting operation proving that signs on cigarette vending machines which read "You Must Be 18 Years" are meaningless. Barely four feet tall, nine-year old Morgan Lesko and his younger brother, Max, appeared before their county council describing how no one stopped or even questioned them when they were buying Marlboros and Camels from vending machines at bowling alleys, restaurants, and grocery stores. They explained, "Each time we bought cigarettes, our parents were out of sight. After we bought them, they would come and take our picture."

Simple photographs along with the tell-tale cigarette packs mounted on poster board added a human dimension to the familiar statistics recited by health experts, who also testified in support of a ban on cigarette vending machines. Councilmember Bruce Adams remarked: "These two guys slam-dunked all those high-powered lobbyists and interest groups that were fighting that legislation."

After their victory at the county level, the two brothers moved onto the Maryland legislature to argue for a statewide ban. Shortly before Max and Morgan testified before a Senate committee, they bought cigarettes at a well-known hotel less than a block away from the state capitol. When they served up this bit of evidence, even their staunch opponents on the committee winced. Although the chairman had the votes he needed to defeat the vending machine ban, a tobacco industry bill that contained a provision to overturn laws passed by local governments (which would have included the county's ban on cigarette machines) got trounced by the same committee.

Morgan and Max have every intention of returning to the Statehouse when this issue surfaces again. Their exposure to power wielded by the tobacco industry lobbyists seems to have only strengthened the Lesko brothers' resolve on the vending machine legislation and heightened their awareness for the need to curb the flow of money from lobbyists to lawmakers.

INFORMAL POLLING & SURVEYS

Christopher Maio and his high school ecology club in Massachusetts galvanized the student body and faculty into action. These concerned environmentalists conducted an informal survey asking teachers and seniors five questions related to school policy. Out of two hundred surveys distributed, one hundred and seventy-six came back. Only five people said they would not be willing to pay an additional five cents for using biodegradable paper cups in the cafeteria. Christopher presented the survey results to the faculty and student government and, as a result, Styrofoam cups and trays are no longer used at school. All it took to convince school administrators to change their policy was the evidence of an informal poll.

An example of students conducting a statewide poll occurred a number of years ago in Utah. Ridgecrest Elementary fifth graders learned that a statue of Brigham Young stands in Statuary Hall in the U.S. Capitol, and they wanted to get a second statue of a Utah native placed there. (Each state is authorized by Congress to erect statues of two natives.)

Under the guidance of their social studies teacher, Bruce Barnson, students compiled a list of twenty-one important figures in the history of the state. Then they asked nearly thirty other elementary schools to list their favorites. A smaller list was sent to five hundred households, and students also conducted an informal survey at a downtown mall. The clear favorite of both students and residents was Philo T. Farnsworth, whose claim to fame was being an early pioneer in the development of television.

The poll helped spur the Utah House of Representatives to second the choice of Farnsworth, but supporters of J. Willard Marriott of the Marriott hotel chain managed to persuade the Utah Senate to defeat the students' choice. During the next session of the state legislature, the kids were able to overcome the opposition. So, the next time you happen to visit the U.S. Capitol in Washington, D.C., look for one of the inventors of television when you tour Statuary Hall!

AN OBSERVATIONAL OR SCIENTIFIC STUDY

In Fairbanks, Alaska, precise scientific surveying proved to be a fruitful method of investigation. Erosion was causing an irreversible gully at a local playground. Jane Behike, a teacher at Weller Elementary School, describes how her class succeeded at getting the borough to solve the underlying erosion problem:

> *We used surveying skills, counted the number of erosion channels which were formed from week to week, estimated the water equivalence of the snow cover, interviewed experts in re-vegetation and in soil mechanics, and investigated the legal aspects of disturbing the existing flow patterns of water. We also documented the damage that took place during the seasons we studied the project.*

> *The students decided that it would be necessary to form a drainage channel around the playground, sloped toward a drainage basin, with an underground drain which would carry the water into the nearest storm sewer. The class recognized that it was not possible to simply drain the water down the hill because existing homes would be affected.*

> *We made a short video tape, but an oral presentation could have been as effective. The route our class took was to make an initial presentation to the principal, then to the Central Office personnel at the school district, and finally to the borough mayor. This was the solution that was ultimately chosen by the borough, and was implemented the summer after the study was completed.*

In addition to solid research, the teacher and her students were brilliant in their strategy. They informed the school authorities of their findings first and then moved up the ladder to the city officials who had the power to decide.

STAGE 2: TRAINING & CONDITIONING
Teammates

Once you feel you have a good grasp of the issue and the information you need, it's time to develop a strategy and line up the members of your organizational team.

BUILDING
A CORE GROUP

Involve enthusiasts early on. Ask for the ideas and help of a close friend, someone in your family, a teacher, or anyone who seems to support what you are trying to accomplish. The sooner a few allies are brought into mapping out a game plan, the better. Sharing in the development of a campaign will make this core group more committed. Not only will these soul mates share their brainpower and energy, but they will bolster each other's morale during the inevitable low ebbs.

"My mom was a coach. She gave me pointers on my testimony and a lot of moral support," says Brian Meshkin, who played a key role in the passage of the first bicycle safety helmet law in the country. Jenn Pistone and her classmates, who spent two years lobbying the Massachusetts state legislature, credits their faculty advisor with sustaining their determination in the face of opposition from other teachers and students: "Mr. Sangster was so proud of us and had so much confidence in us, and that really helped us to deal with obstacles."

Maureen Gemma remembers getting flack when she was working on a project to raise money for international food relief organizations:

*I walked into class late and my teacher said, "I don't care if
you are saving the dolphins or the world . . . I just want you
in class on time!" I knew I needed to be responsible for my
time and I should have been in class, but sometimes it feels
like you get stopped before you even get started on a project.
For me to keep going it takes awesome adult partnerships,
especially when I get stopped or stuck. So I worked with my
principal. It is always good to have an adult on your side.*

Like Maureen, the Oakwood Students Against Drunk Driving in
California frequently called on parents for help. When they decided to
make a TV public service announcement, "We got a lot of things donated
by people and a lot of it had to do with personal connections," says Lisa
Goldsmith, co-president of this high school group. Adults can sometimes
open doors that remain firmly closed or off-limits to kids.

One close friend, her mother, and her aunt made up the core group
in fifteen-year old Detra Warfield's successful campaign to convince the
Louisville school board to offer a year-long black history course. After
hearing through the grapevine about Detra's speech before the Board of
Education, her principal expressed regret at not being included in her
efforts to change the school district's curriculum. Detra was reluctant to
share her idea with the principal, or with any of her teachers, because she
thought they might try to stop her. In the end, though, Detra got all the
encouragement she needed from the people she trusted the most, namely
her family and her close friend.

Katy Yanda of Santa Fe, who helped organize a huge student
conference on the environment, describes the reaction of adults and offers
these words of wisdom:

*I think the main thing is to be genuinely interested yourself, to
really care about what you are doing. Then present this interest
to others. If you are excited about what you are doing, people,
especially children, will be excited also. With adults, it is best
to know what you are talking about and present it well. So
many adults were surprised that students were doing
something. I often ran into adults who were so happy because
we were showing initiative. Take advantage of being a student.
Believe it or not, people do listen. Find others who also care*

and work with them.

Having a few steadfast allies outside your core group will make all the hard work more tolerable and help keep your spirits up, too.

PROS AND CONS OF JOINING AN EXISTING CAMPAIGN

Linking up with a group or coalition that is pursuing more or less the same goal as your project poses a dilemma. Unquestionably there are advantages, such as sharing organizational resources and gaining clout through a unified campaign, especially for major events designed to raise public awareness. A perfect example of such a joint effort is the cross-country bicycle tour coordinated by Youth Ending Hunger (YEH). Maureen Gemma, now at Mills College in California, reminisces about one of her proudest memories:

The Tour de YEH started from the steps of the Capitol in Washington, D.C. It took forty-seven days, biking three thousand miles across the United States and over the Rockies. When we got to that last hill before the finish line in Seattle... Wow! What a feeling of accomplishment. On the Tour there were seventy-five people from twelve countries. The average age was about fifteen; two riders were thirteen years old.

We had presentations set up in each community we rode through. That summer we announced the World Summit for Children that was going to happen in September of 1990 at the United Nations. We invited people to participate in the candlelight vigils that happened all across the world. We asked them, pleaded with them, to write letters to President Bush asking him to attend the World Summit on Children.

In local towns, we met with political leaders and elected officials. I don't care how tough and corrupt they are. They will never be the same after having met with seventy-five young people from all over the world. They cannot forget the impact we made. We reached millions through the media. We were in "USA Today" four times. We were on the "Today" show. We were in every small-town newspaper in every community; some with only five hundred people.

The tour achieved its objective. The President joined seventy other heads-of-state and signed a declaration which spells out a comprehensive set of international legal guidelines for the protection and well-being of children all over the world.

Youth Ending Hunger happens to be a national organization that leaves the strategy planning to its members — youth. However, if you join a big group that is an adult-driven campaign you may become a team player wearing their uniform and playing by their rules. You stand a good chance of learning a great deal from this kind of training, though. In addition, you may become acquainted with some prominent leaders and experts.

Also, national groups usually will set guidelines for local chapters. Lisa Goldsmith explains why Oakwood Students Against Drunk Driving decided to remain independent of the well-established organization, Students Against Drunk Driving (SADD).

We never joined SADD because you have to pay dues and there was so much red tape. I was told that their policies are a bit different now. To use SADD's name you have to check everything through them and you can't do anything spontaneously. Everything is very exact which is fine for some people but I think at our school people were so motivated and committed that it wasn't for us.

Actually, SADD does grant some leeway to its chapters but because of the organization's tax-exempt status and its overall emphasis on education rather than legislation, it does not engage in political action.

The most important reason not to hook up with a campaign operated by adults is that the involvement of young activists may then be viewed with distrust. You could be seen as a puppet. The tearful testimony before a congressional committee by a fifteen-year old Kuwaiti girl, who described premature babies being taken from their incubators by Saddam Hussein's army, seemed to push the right buttons as Congress debated whether to declare war against Iraq. One year later it was revealed that this witness was the daughter of the Kuwaiti Ambassador to the United States. This bombshell only heightened suspicions about the manipulation of American public opinion by the government of Kuwait.

Motives aren't questioned when young citizen activists are not under the influence of adults and do not serve as emissaries for an adult-led organization. Jessica Early, who convinced four friends to testify with her on state legislation that would outlaw animal traps, confirms the importance of independence:

> *I really believe in everything groups like People*
> *for the Ethical Treatment of Animals stand*
> *for, but I think if we had been part of a group*
> *we would not have been as effective, and also*

*the legislators would have thought that we
were brainwashed.*

Credibility soars when young activists remain independent. One veteran lobbyist, speaking about the passage of legislation restricting over-the-counter sales of chewing tobacco and cigarettes, confirms this point: "Had it been the usual coalition of public health advocates, the bill never would have moved through the Statehouse."

Even if you want to remain independent, it is worth checking into the priorities of some of the larger, more established public interest and industry groups. Usually a phone call or letter to a couple of national organizations will clue you into any major campaigns that are underway.

Plan of Action

Before embarking on a plan of action, Aaron Hobart, a senior at Sandwich High School in Massachusetts, emphasizes the importance of commitment:

> *You've got to make sure you have the motivation. It takes work: you've got to do the letter-writing, the speech-writing; you've got to make a fool of yourself in front of your friends. If you're not ready to do that, then you aren't going to get anything at all.*

Doing the hard work is a theme expressed over and over again by activists like Aaron. They are not preoccupied with weighing their chances of winning. What is unacceptable to them, however, is losing the commitment to pursue their cause. Flexibility is the key to this "Never say die!" attitude. If one plan doesn't succeed, these teens try something else. Aaron Hobart sees the need to develop a sort of hybrid temperament that is passionate, pragmatic, patient, and persistent.

> *You cannot go into something and not expect to get it finished. I mean you cannot stop. We got totally shut down and we came back. You've got to have the willpower and backbone to get back up. You've got to do everything that you can, just to reap the benefits.*

Over a dozen imaginative strategies are introduced here which you can draw on to create your own game plan. If you are hesitant to go public with your ideas, reading about how others have moved from being dreamers to doers will convince you to take that most difficult first step. Once the initial paralysis is overcome, the major dilemma will be finding the time and resources to launch your own mission. We begin with modest, yet effective, action plans as well as ambitious long-range initiatives. The oral histories in Part II and Part III reinforce many of these tactics and introduce new strategies as well.

MAKING WAVES WITH A HARD-HITTING LETTER

One concise but detailed letter, written and signed by more than a dozen high school students, drew a city councilmember's attention in Springfield, Massachusetts. The interest of that elected official was all it took to get the city to clean up a huge trash heap next to the students' school. The teenagers' long-range goal of getting a playground built in the vacant lot, however, required considerably more action. (Their story, "Bump The Dump," is included in Part II.)

A social studies assignment prompted fourteen-year old Ruth Ellen Smalley of Kansas City, Missouri, to attack commercial dog-breeding operations, commonly referred to as "puppy mills." Her letter to members of Congress called for tougher regulations and enforcement, and was selected as one of fifty winners in the national "Speak Up for Yourself" contest sponsored by RespecTeen. Ruth Ellen traveled to Washington, D.C., with the winners from the other forty-nine states and met with several legislators, including her own U.S. representative. She was then invited to testify at a hearing on puppy mills at the Missouri state legislature.

In Connecticut, letters from elementary school students flooded the offices of state legislators about lighter-than-air balloons which float to the surface of the earth after the helium dissipates, often winding up in rivers and oceans. The students described how this airborne litter becomes a deadly meal for birds, turtles, and other marine mammals. They proposed ending the popular practice of releasing balloon bouquets into the atmosphere.

Most legislators thought this idea was a joke. State Representative Lenny Winkler, who had tried to get action on her own balloon bill since 1988, credits the torrent of mail from students with prompting the House Environmental Committee to hold hearings. In October 1990, a new state law went into effect banning the mass release of helium or any other lighter-than-air gas balloons.

HINTS

▶ Go beyond giving your opinion. Indicate in your letter what you want the legislator or government official to do; for example, investigate your complaint, conduct a hearing, or introduce legislation. Ask them to tell you what action they have taken on a particular issue in the past. A specific request is more likely to solicit a meaningful response, instead of just a polite letter thanking you for your views.

▶ "Put your age down on those letters," urges seventeen-year old Kristin Johnson. "Let people in power know what you think...we younger generations are going to be the caretakers of the future, and it is important for today's leaders to know what we care about."

▶ To find out the names of your elected representatives and their addresses, call the League of Women Voters or your public library. To write to any U.S. senator, all you need on the envelope besides the senator's name is Washington, D.C. 20510. For any U.S. representative, just change the zip to 20515. In other words, you don't need the street address or room number; just a name, city, and zip code are sufficient. The same holds true for writing to city councilmembers or state legislators.

▶ A legible hand-written letter may actually get more attention than a typewritten one. It looks a lot more authentic and heartfelt than computer-generated letters.

A group of sixth graders in Virginia discovered that hand-delivering letters had advantages that went beyond merely saving postage. By presenting letters in person to state legislators, the students' mail didn't go unnoticed. This classroom research project on toy safety turned into a sophisticated lobbying campaign where *every* House and Senate committee member received letters calling for legislation modeled after an Oregon law that requires doctors and hospitals to report any injuries or deaths caused by a toy. The state department of health would then issue a warning to consumers if a toy is linked to several injuries. The legislation passed the General Assembly and was signed by the governor in 1992.

PUTTING YOUR WISH LIST OR DEMANDS ON PAPER

In the summer of 1991 in the Nation's Capital, angry youths torched buses and police cars, and threw bottles and rocks after a Hispanic man was shot and seriously wounded by a police officer. In the aftermath of the riots, some Hispanic and African-American teens formed a group calling itself Young Minds That Care and developed a sweeping list of recommendations to deal with racial tensions.

Young Minds That Care outlined a thirteen-point wish list which included more money in the city budget for youth employment, better programs in schools to serve Hispanics who do not speak English, and additional recreational facilities for youth. The teenagers' proposal also recommended more Spanish-speaking police officers as well as sensitivity training programs for the entire police force. Their agenda, which resulted in a full-length newspaper story in *The Washington Post*, complemented other demands being formulated by the D.C. Latino Civil Rights Task Force. Community leader Pedro Aviles praised the contribution of this group, saying, "The young people were able to accomplish what adults had not been able to for years."

Teachers and students from two high schools in Staten Island, New York used a mission statement to publicize their project to eliminate graffiti:

> The primary objective behind our campaign is to educate all of Staten Island to the fact that graffiti vandalism is not some cutesy art form or harmless prank, but a deliberate criminal act. When you deface and destroy public and private property, you're committing a crime. The SICA Graffiti campaign hopes to promote awareness of the problem through an educational program that prompts students and teachers to take action to find a solution. The founders of SICA Graffiti firmly believe that each individual can make a difference and when enough people voice their disgust with graffiti vandalism, the problem will decline significantly.

This one-page document, which looks quite official, helped enlist the support of other schools, community leaders, and local businesses. Many merchants and organizations collaborated with the students' "Adopt a Wall" program and the campaign can boast that over five hundred locations are graffiti-free. Widespread community support, plus twenty-five hundred signatures on petitions calling for increased enforcement and stiffer penalties for graffiti vandals, have influenced the borough president to view graffiti-removal as an integral part of the Staten Island Beautification Program.

DRAFTING A PETITION

Even though the right to petition is indelibly etched in our minds from U.S. government classes, it's surprising how many Americans of all ages are hesitant to exercise this First Amendment prerogative.

Ingrid Brodegaard of New York describes how she got up the courage to spend hours on a street corner getting strangers to sign her petition.

> *I read in the newspaper that the Central Park Zoo might be closing. What didn't make sense to me was the city had just spent all this money to fix it up and then when they finished, all of a sudden, they decided to close it.*
>
> *I went to the zoo and they had signs up that said "Zoo Closing" and "Help Save The Zoo." I signed a petition there. I went home that day and I wanted to do something to help keep the zoo open, and I wasn't quite sure what I should do. My mother said, "Well, you could do what the zoo is doing." I said, "Oh, you mean start some petitions?" I wasn't sure whether I was allowed to and she said, "Don't worry, there is nothing wrong with petitioning." So, I thought I could start a petition and stand outside on the corner, near our apartment building. The petition read, "Help Save Our Zoo." I made a poster that said: "It's Not the End of the World But It May Be The End of the Zoo." I also got some pamphlets*

when I was at the zoo and put them on the poster.

HINTS

A petition can serve many purposes:

▸ A petition is an effective tool for expressing the collective will or views of many. After all, numbers count. Elected officials pay more attention to hundreds of names than just a few individuals.

▸ The process of explaining the issue reaps results beyond obtaining signatures. A petition is an indirect way of asking for help and a few like-minded people may want to do more than simply sign their name.

▸ Petitions can help publicize your campaign. A huge stack of petitions or a thick computer printout with signatures is a good visual prop that may provide a TV camera crew or newspaper photographer with just the shot they are looking for.

▸ Petitions provide you with the names and addresses of supporters. High school sophomore Detra Warfield of Louisville circulated a petition to her classmates to gauge what they felt about her idea of starting a year-long black history class. After she testified before the board of education and won their support for her proposed curriculum, the school system sent out a mailing to all those who had signed Detra's petitions. These students were then invited to a special black history program offered to both kids and their parents on Saturday mornings. (Detra's story is in Part II.)

For about four hours that day I had people sign my petition. At the beginning it took me a couple minutes to get started. I felt really bad when people just walked by and made mean faces. It felt really good when people came up to me to sign my petition; then I knew how to say everything. This police officer came by, signed my petition, and started yelling to people on the street: "Help this girl! Help her save the zoo." Then I really knew it was okay to do petitioning.

A lot of people complimented me for taking a Sunday to do this. The next day I spent three hours petitioning and it was really tiring. I sent about five hundred signatures to Ms. Powers, who works at the Central Park Zoo, and then I got four hundred more signatures. After school on Monday, I got some more.

I never thought I would do something like that. I'm really surprised at myself and it feels great that the zoo is still open. A newspaper article was even written about what I did. If they try to close the zoo again, I'll try my hardest to save it.

I think other kids should be aware of what's happening in the world. If you see something on the news or if there is something you would really like to do, don't say, "Oh well, someone else will take care of it." There is something you can do.

If eleven-year old Ingrid could get this kind of response in "The Big Apple," where New Yorkers have a reputation for ignoring sidewalk hustle and bustle, think how much easier it would be to approach your own friends and neighbors. Andrew Holleman did just that, spending hours going door-to-door in his small New England town with an incredible, information-packed petition he had drafted. (Andrew's petition is reproduced in Part II.)

TESTIFYING AS A WITNESS

"Never underestimate the power of your voice," says Lynn Terrill, one of the student leaders of a tobacco-free schools initiative. "We took twenty to twenty-five kids to testify at the State Capitol and we all had different opinions, a different way of speaking, and each way was effective. The fact that you have numbers behind you and that you believe so much in something will make a difference."

Speaking as a witness at an official public hearing can have a real impact. Even though hearings are as common an occurrence as hourly weather reports, concerned young people who share their points of view stand out from the typical parade of adult witnesses, who include experts, professionals and representatives of various organizations and interest groups. In contrast to the lobbyists and "hired guns" whose job it is to testify, young people have no ulterior motive except for the few who relish being in the spotlight.

It is next to impossible for even an arrogant, corrupt politician with a closed mind to turn a deaf ear to the ideas offered by the next generation. Legislators may vote against the proposals young people advocate, but they are likely to listen — really listen. "Kids don't bring to the political arena the ability to lie without being caught. The purity is there, unlike adults who have learned through years and years of practicing facial things, and how to lie," explains William Sangster, the Massachusetts faculty advisor who encouraged Lynn Terrill and other students in their successful anti-smoking campaign.

Since the experts and professionals who testify tend to overwhelm with data and statistics, one alternative strategy is storytelling. It is important to include facts and hard-hitting information that you've dug up, but sharing your firsthand knowledge on the subject really catches legislators by surprise. After all, they spend hours every week trying to appear attentive while listening to the less colorful testimony of dozens upon dozens of professional witnesses.

Seventeen-year old runaway Janna Koschene of Aurora, Colorado, presented a vivid account of sleeping in cars and overnight shelters in Arizona and California at hearings conducted by the U.S. Senate Judiciary Subcommittee on Juvenile Justice. She also included in her testimony detailed recommendations based on her own positive experiences with Urban Peak Youth Center, a daytime drop-in center for homeless and runaway teens in Denver:

> *I believe that if we give street kids time and alternatives they will turn their lives around. Urban Peak offers specific alternatives that I personally believe are the most valuable...a transitional living program for kids so they can learn to live on their own, and a medical clinic where girls can receive prenatal care, counseling on pregnancy choices and have access to birth control. It is also important that youth have a phone number and address and receive other help getting identification [cards] so they can work.*

After the formal hearing, Janna had lengthy conversations with several senators and the subcommittee staff. At a time of budget cuts, Congress voted a modest increase for federal funds earmarked for crisis shelters and other community-based alternatives to youth detention homes and jail. The more lasting legacy, perhaps, is the imprint Janna had on this newly created Senate subcommittee. "Janna opened their eyes to the problem and made an important first impression," says a lobbyist representing the National Network on the Homeless.

In this and other situations, it is important to be well-prepared and primed to answer unfriendly questions. See "Stage 3: The Main Event" for more on stage fright and other tactics involved in testifying.

MEETING WITH DECISION MAKERS

Plenty of alternatives exist for making your views known to lawmakers, besides testifying at hearings. Try to get ten minutes to talk with the head of the city council or one of your members of Congress. A prominent politician can help get the ball rolling or serve as your emissary when legislation is apt to undergo a metamorphosis at the stage when amendments are being considered. Don't be offended if your appointment with an elected representative turns out to be a meeting with the legislator's staff aide.

Here's one example of how such a face-to-face meeting produced results. Seventeen students from Jackson Elementary School in Salt Lake City started the Leaf It to Us Children's Crusade for Trees. They signed a handwritten letter to their U.S. Senator which read:

> Dear Senator Hatch,
>   We are asking you for as much money as you can get for kids to plant trees across the nation. Kids could match 10% to 20% of the money you get for them. The money could be put in a fund just for kids. Money could be kept in a fund in Washington, kids could apply for grants. They could plant the trees in their own states on public property.

> The reason we want to plant trees is because one tree in its 50 year lifetime cleans up $62,000 worth of air pollution. Trees will also prevent soil erosion, recycle water, give off oxygen. Trees help cut down the greenhouse effect.
>
> Thank you. Can we do something more to help?"

These students are real pros. Under the guidance of Barbara Lewis, their talented teacher and also the author of *The Kid's Guide to Social Action*, they had earlier made history by lobbying successfully for the Utah Superfund Law to clean up hazardous waste dumps.

One of the Jackson Elementary students, Audrey Chase, who is featured in the documentary film "Take Me to Your Leaders," traveled to Washington, D.C., to meet with several members of Congress. While she had no opportunity to testify before the Senate or House committees because hearings had long since been held, the opportunity for input still existed. Audrey spelled out the idea of funds for reforestation. Senator Hatch's legislative assistant still remembers being amazed by her poise and determination. Several congressional staffers drafted an amendment and managed to attach it to a bill that had cleared all but the final hurdles of the legislative process.

The Utah students scored a home run. Two words, "youth groups," are included in the federal law called the America the Beautiful Act of 1990, in large measure thanks to Audrey's lobbying efforts:

> ...to award matching grants to nonprofit organizations including youth groups for the planting and cultivation of trees to ensure that our descendants may share the pride of their ancestors when referring to their land as "America the Beautiful."

The traditional approach for scheduling a meeting with an important official involves calling again and again in the hope of eventually getting an appointment. But remember — kids have an advantage over lobbyists who are paid to persuade and cajole lawmakers. Heidi Hattenbach, who joined twenty-four others in a cross-country cycling tour a year after Maureen Gemma's nationwide bicycle marathon, describes how she and other teens had remarkable luck meeting with members of Congress about world hunger without any prearranged meetings.

On the cycling tour we carried a petition and got thousands of signatures across the country urging President Bush to sign the

U.N. Convention on the Rights of the Child. We had decided that we wanted to bring our 'Ending Hunger' message directly to some of our elected officials in Washington, D.C., and to talk to them about specific legislation.

We would walk into senators' offices with no warning and say, "Hello, my name is Heidi Hattenbach and I just bicycled thirty-five hundred miles to meet senator so and so . . . When can I see him?" We saw seven senators that day in person. Then we had meetings with the chief-of-staff or with other staff people who were responsible for hunger and domestic issues for thirteen other senators. We saw twenty percent of the U.S. Senate in one day.

When lobbying groups heard about what we were doing, they said they couldn't do that in a month. I think it is because they don't walk in with the fresh, new energy we had. Our attitude was just . . . "Hello, of course I should see my senator! After all, he is <u>*my*</u> *senator!"*

HINTS

See if your mayor, county executive, or governor have instituted regular five-minute sessions with ordinary citizens. San Diego Mayor Maureen O'Connor, for example, offers "a meet the mayor" program which she believes "just might save our cities from bankruptcy, terminal boredom or a premature death inflicted by the modern drone of pollsters, consultants, and experts." Mayor O'Connor explains:

Admirals visit as well as police officers, Boy and Girl Scout troops, taxi drivers, square dancers, anti-litter fans, bowlers, the F.B.I. and streams of worried parents, abused wives, inventors of anti-graffiti materials and all those stuck in the traffic jams of a modern bureaucracy . . . These people have had their small say, have received help and made a big difference in my sense of governing. They have given me a street-sized perspective on a high-rise job.

If no open-door program exists in your city, you might want to propose such an idea to your mayor.

Meeting face-to-face can make a lasting impression. The chief difficulty is getting your foot in the door. The rest is easy.

PURSUING A PROCLAMATION

Getting legislation passed is a major feat and usually lawmakers will not act until they see evidence of a groundswell of support. Landmark legislation such as the Americans with Disabilities Act of 1990 was the result of over ten years of lobbying and negotiating by a broad-based coalition of citizen activists. Keeping an issue alive that long can be a struggle.

A proclamation issued by the mayor or the governor, though largely symbolic, can be an enormous boost to a campaign. Incremental victories are essential for maintaining momentum. Also, an event that lasts only one day or one week is a perfect match for the media's short attention span.

Issuing a proclamation is one of the easiest gestures for a political leader to make. The Oakwood Students Against Drunk Driving, the high school group in Los Angeles, invited the mayor to speak at their press conference. Although he declined, his office declared April 30th "Sober Driving Day" in L.A. The next year the governor proclaimed the last day in April as "Sober Driving Day" throughout California. On the heels of this statewide support, the Oakwood School's campaign to lower the legal blood-alcohol limit stretched to distant cities. The mayor's office in both Chicago and New York agreed to hold rallies on April 30th.

This strategy can be conducted nationally by getting the U.S. Congress to designate a day, a week, or a month for your cause. It's not as long a shot as you might expect. Nearly one-third of all the laws enacted by Congress are commemoratives such as World Food Day on October 16, National School Breakfast Week in mid-March, or National Red Ribbon Month in November. Some say that the issuance of proclamations is a substitute for the real legislating they should be doing on Capitol Hill!

PROTESTS AND RALLIES

Unlike testifying before a legislative committee or the school board, there are more spontaneous ways to speak out. A rally has the added advantage of getting news coverage, because television producers are a lot more likely to send out a camera crew to film a crowd rather than talking heads.

The disadvantage of rallies is that they occur so often that lawmakers and the media sometimes ignore them. But numbers count. A demonstration that is part of an ongoing campaign can have a real impact.

In Chicago in the fall of 1990, an unusual protest occurred at a public hearing conducted by the commissioner of health on shutting down a community health clinic that provided services for poor pregnant women and infants. Nearly fifty children attended the hearing and sang in both English and Spanish:

> *I have a message for you,*
> *We have a right to be healthy,*
> *We have a right to the future because we are the future,*
> *Please don't close our clinic.*

Those four lines overwhelmed the opposing testimony of city budget planners and health professionals and the clinic remains open today. Magda Elias, a doctor originally from Guatemala who risked losing her job because of her involvement mobilizing opposition to the city's plan, says, "The parents were so afraid, but these little children inspired the grownups to take a stand." After the kids sang, the crowd of adults erupted in applause. Dr. Elias says with pride: "Children taught the adults something. Now there's more respect for their kids. And those children will never forget that experience."

The student government at Eleanor Roosevelt High in Maryland organized a sit-in inside the school lobby protesting budget cuts approved by their board of education. The principal tried to discourage the protest but then gave permission to students to spend the night. Some two hundred students stayed overnight, doing homework and writing letters to the governor, state legislators, and county councilmembers, arguing that short-term budget problems shouldn't jeopardize long-term investment in education. This sit-in, together with many other demonstrations as well as a massive letter-writing campaign, contributed to a political atmosphere in which the county council voted to increase the energy tax rather than make severe cuts in the public school system.

In Alabama, student sit-ins took place at both Selma High and the city hall over school policy. African-American students and their parents argued that blacks typically were "tracked" in classes that not only reduced their chance of going on to college, but encouraged them to drop out of school. The rift between the protesters and the school board and mayor widened following the sit-in. ("Track Me To Freedom" in Part II reveals the impact of the students' non-violent campaign that was met with police brutality.)

BYPASSING NORMAL ROUTES

When your chances of achieving success through conventional channels are next to nil, there are almost always effective alternative routes. In 1990, forty-three states and the District of Columbia used the referendum.

Young people helped collect thousands of signatures for a ballot initiative in San Francisco to amend the city charter to guarantee funds for children. The proposition, which passed by a healthy margin in 1991, ensures that a small percentage of existing property tax revenues be dedicated for recreation, tutoring, delinquency prevention, child care, and other programs for kids. Coleman Advocates for Children and Youth, a local organization, pursued this strategy of bypassing lawmakers and taking the initiative directly to the voters after the board of supervisors ignored previous proposals.

Youth Ending Hunger is one organization that uses the United Nations as a way to pressure the U.S. government to give more attention to both domestic and global hunger. A massive national petition drive and candlelight vigils coordinated by numerous religious and hunger organizations certainly contributed to President Bush's decision to attend the World Summit for Children in 1990.

Also organizing at the international level, oceanographer Jacques Cousteau mobilized young people around the world to write letters to the heads-of-state of Britain, France, the United States and other countries, urging them to sign a treaty restricting mining and economic development on Antarctica. A new international agreement safeguarding the continent's resources is now in place, thanks to the combined efforts of those young activists, numerous environmental groups, and the governments of many nations.

WINNING A SEAT ON THE BOARD

It is no longer a rare phenomenon when policy makers seek input and feedback from youth representatives. The Governor of Washington state's Youth Initiative is designed to include kids in discussions about truancy, gangs, and state programs for children and teens. Many philanthropic organizations such as the United Way and the National Crime Prevention Council have given some of the decision-making power to young people to determine the best way charitable funds are to be distributed for worthy causes.

Youth representatives on school boards, most of whom are non-voting delegates, serve as an important channel for students to send their views to the board of education. Similarly, student governments play a critical role in negotiating school policies on such controversial issues as censorship or distribution of condoms.

Another means of insuring that the next generation can make its voice heard is by having a youth representative in city hall. High school junior Cassie Fuller of South Carolina, a community leader who persuaded the county council to pay the salary of a youth development director at a student-run teen center, convinced the councilmembers to institute the practice of letting a student speak at every monthly meeting. Now there are two youth representatives who offer their perspectives on the needs of children and teens at each council meeting.

CONDUCTING A STUDENT SUMMIT

It doesn't take an established organization to convene a group of concerned people to examine problems and explore solutions. Certainly, legislation alone can't provide all the remedies to social and political ills.

Laws don't automatically change attitudes and behavior. Lasting solutions often are those built over time through education and public awareness.

Katy Yanda of Santa Fe, New Mexico is someone who believes that "We will have to change the way we look at things if anything is going to get better." Katy is one of the leading characters in *Rads, Ergs, and Cheeseburgers*, an engaging story written by her father. The story contrasts the behavior of the inhabitants on several planets who squander the natural resources to the kids on one healthy planet where they don't make the same mistakes and became prudent energy consumers. During her junior year of high school, Katy, who shares her father's concern for the environment, helped stage a major student summit to consider new perspectives on environmental issues.

> *I was part of a youth organization called YouthVoice, a group that makes it possible for students to publish articles in local papers. About five or six of us put together an environmental conference called Symposium for the Protection of the Environment and Action by Kids (S.P.E.A.K.) with the help of a fantastic guy named Ken Richards.*
>
> *Our purpose was to educate students on current issues concerning the environment, and then have the students come up with solutions for the problems. On the first day participants chose the workshop they wanted to be a part of: Endangered Species, Deforestation, Trash, Animal Testing, or the Disappearing Ozone. They heard experts in those fields talk about their subjects, and then discussed them on their own. S.P.E.A.K. was able to get Peter Bayhouth, the director of Greenpeace, for our keynote address because he was interested in a student-run conference. Take advantage of being a student! Believe it or not, people do listen.*
>
> *Over four hundred students from five different states attended S.P.E.A.K. It was wonderful to see how many people cared about the environment and that they were willing to do something about it. Each student group came up with a solution and those solutions were presented at a press conference on the last day of the symposium. All of those students delivered the same message — the only way anything*

is going to be changed is through education. If children know from the very beginning how important the environment is, then they will grow into adults who respect it.

Changing the mind-set of an entire country or the whole world is quite a large task to undertake, but it can be done if we teach the children. There are more and more people who are starting to realize what problems there are. Just let people know you are interested. Then do something about it! Whether it is a recycling program at school or a symposium like ours, anything helps. And that will start others thinking about what they can do.

CREATING A SPEAKERS' BUREAU

Over and over again teenage activists speak of their responsibility to future generations. So often kids are criticized for being self-absorbed; yet these young people express a greater sense of urgency to repair the world than many adults. Teenagers have a special gift for awakening the concern and interest of younger people.

Katy Yanda visits elementary schools and helps with science club projects. She says, "It is good when a not-quite-adult speaks and works with them because they see that it isn't just a faraway problem. I really suggest that high school and college students who are interested get involved with children. The benefits you receive in smiles and understanding faces are wonderful."

Kristin Johnson, the high school senior in Woodinville, Washington, has created an educational campaign on the disappearing rain forests that can serve as a real model to others. Her mission began in the ninth grade when she decided to give a slide show and lecture to her science class for extra credit. The next week she gave the same talk on the rain forests at a nearby elementary school. Kristin has continued giving this one-hour presentation to individual classes and school assemblies once or twice a week all through high school, and has trained thirteen other students for a speakers' bureau.

The script Kristin has written is as colorful as her slides. She explains that her speakers travel as far as two hours away to visit both inner-city public schools and private schools. Her history teacher calls the group "granola-eating environmentalists." Kristin says:

> *They are a great group of young adults who have a lot of fun and are all kind of in the mainstream of high school life. We've been training about a year now, and they are beginning to go out and do the actual talks. At least three of them are experts now. Two of the girls are in ninth grade, and the rest of us, including four guys, are in high school.*
>
> *During our slide show, we take the kids on a tour of the rain forests — mainly the Amazon because I like it the best — from the very bottom to the rivers and to the top emergent layer where the birds are. For instance, when we show a slide of an anaconda and caiman, we say:*

> "Here we have a seven-foot caiman who is having a very bad day. That's an eighteen-foot long anaconda wrapped around him. Even though that caiman has a very tough armor over his back, and very nasty teeth, he does not have a very good chance of escaping from the coils of the anaconda. The anacondas are a type of constrictor. That means they squeeze the victim just hard enough to cut off the blood circulation of the victim, and make it so he can't breathe.

> If we were walking in the Amazon forest, and came upon a thirty-eight-foot anaconda, we wouldn't have to worry too much about it attacking us for two reasons. One, the anaconda is extremely slow, and also, they are not very bright. Their eye is only an inch or two off the ground, and when they look up they probably think we are giants."

> *Then we talk about what the plants give to us — a lot about medicinal values and foods — and then we go on to the*

native people of the forest and try to explain what they have been put through, and the special knowledge they have of their forests.

Talking about what is happening to the rain forests is hard. For one thing, by that part of the slide show we are running out of time, and another thing — it is hard for us to explain reasons for something we ourselves do not entirely understand. But we try to get the basics across concerning the destruction and the consequences.

We have a couple of slides on the forests of the Pacific Northwest. It is more difficult living in Washington and doing something that's very controversial like a presentation about our own national forests — but it is perhaps more important. We want to make the talk as unbiased as possible, but both sides [loggers and conservationists] make that extremely hard to do with the conflicting information they send us. We want to include everything, between the radical environmental groups that spike trees and loggers that shoot spotted owls. The media usually highlight the extremes like 'Jobs versus Spotted Owls.' But there must be common ground somewhere. In the last three or four years both sides have done a little more talking together rather than at each other. It is looking very positive if we can stop some of these bills that the timber industry is pushing through Congress.

We give kids ideas on what they can do to help the forests. We used to have them write letters to the President. I sent President Bush about two hundred letters from kids and received a form letter back that did not even make a reference to rain forests. We are going to start sending the letters closer to home now, such as to our Washington state senators and our governor where perhaps they will do a little more good.

From what I have seen in the past couple of years of doing this, I think our being high school kids and not adults doing these presentations does make some difference. Students really look up to us; sometimes they want to take us on a tour of the playground, or ask all sorts of questions related to being

*a big kid like "Do you have a boyfriend?" They have even
asked for our autographs before, and Katie was asked out on
a date by a fourth grader, which she politely declined!*

*We want to get across to our young audience that if
there is anything in their hearts that they care about, no matter
what it is, there is something they can do. I think we illustrate
this very well because we are not just worrying about what is
happening to the forests — we are doing something about it.*

Recently Kristin was working with her father on a Northwest Forest
slide show, putting the finishing touches on a packet called "Empowering
Children through Conservation." She is also creating another presentation
designed to interest corporations in donating money for a facility in Costa
Rica where tourists could see the top of the rain forest canopy, not just the
bottom. No wonder Kristin was selected as a "Giraffe," a prestigious award
presented by the Giraffe Project to people of all ages in all walks of life
who "stick their necks out."

Kristin cannot share her copyrighted slide collection but is eager to
send a copy of the R.A.I.N. script to any students who want to use it as a
model for creating their own presentation on whatever issue concerns
them. (Send a self-addressed, stamped envelope to Kristin Johnson,
R.A.I.N., 18802 185th Avenue NE, Woodinville, WA 98072.)

Getting the Word Out

The more people hear about your mission, the better. Also, the sooner the opposition makes its arguments, the more time you will have to consider those views, outline a rebuttal, negotiate and possibly compromise.

Stirring up a hornets' nest when necessary will do more to keep the issue alive than almost anything else. Controversy equals honey in the minds of reporters, and media coverage will help focus the public's attention on the issue. When an issue gets air time on radio or television or captures a headline in the newspaper, legislators are more likely to pay attention. Another side effect of a news story is that like-minded individuals will seek you out, offer to help, and even donate money to cover expenses such as phone bills, printing, and postage.

FINDING AN INSIDE ALLY

Thank goodness not everyone believes politicians only pay attention to their big campaign contributors. Although money unfortunately buys first-class access to our lawmakers, it doesn't mean that everyone else is shut out. Our representatives routinely do favors for their constituents to win reelection. Even if you are not yet of voting age, the inclination of most politicians is to respond favorably to your request because they know you will soon be casting your vote. And you may even find legislators who share your concern for a particular issue and will no doubt be delighted to have you on their side.

It is a cinch for a councilmember, state legislator, or member of Congress to introduce a bill. It's a way for them to make their constituents happy. However, it is unusual for a lawmaker really to put a lot of effort into nursing a proposal through the legislative process. Most bills are stillborn.

If your goal is to get a law passed, it is crucial to have an inside ally who will not simply sponsor the bill but push it through the legislative labyrinth. It's wise not to prejudge your potential supporters by their political affiliation. In the case of the precedent-setting bike helmet law, student leader Brian Meshkin describes how his faculty advisor at Glenwood Middle School in Maryland succeeded at getting this issue moving by contacting Councilmember Feaga, who happened to be the only Republican in the county government at the time. Brian, who leans in the direction of the GOP, believes there was an advantage to having Mr. Feaga take the lead, since "Republicans have been labeled as the political party that doesn't care about the people." Not only did Republicans rally around the helmet legislation, but enough Democrats were brought on board and bipartisan support made the difference when it came time for the final vote.

If you read Brian's story in Part III it becomes evident why getting a bill introduced is a big step, but only a first step. In order to get action on a proposal, it is essential to make your elected representative and other key lawmakers, such as the committee chair, aware that many people care about this issue. William Sangster, the teacher who now is on a first-name basis with the Speaker of the Massachusetts House of Representatives as a result of several lobbying campaigns by his students, explains how to turn up the heat:

> *There are a lot of things going on in the statehouse that you and I don't know anything about. So you begin writing to elected officials who have fifty thousand other things to do. Then I had to get the people of the town to say the legislation was a good idea. That's when we started championing the idea that kids go knocking on doors around the neighborhood to get everybody around involved, not only a core group.*

The staying power of these students in their two-year effort with the statehouse was extraordinary, as you will discover reading their account in Part III; but it isn't only their persistence that brought results. Two unpredictable elements are also critical for success: a favorable political atmosphere and good timing. In other words, if the committee responsible for your proposal already has a full agenda, you are out of luck. But remember, "In politics, a day is a long time." The political climate can change overnight.

A few years ago, seniors at Robinson High School in Fairfax, Virginia, became outraged over how the federal government continues to operate trillions of dollars in the red and spend hundreds of billions of dollars just servicing the interest on that debt. As one student put it: "My generation is going to be paying for this mammoth deficit and that's irresponsible." At the time, U.S. Representative Dan Rostenkowski (D-Illinois), the powerful chair of the tax-writing committee in the House of Representatives, was pushing hard for legislation that would eliminate the deficit by tax increases, spending cuts, and freezes on social security benefits. The students' teacher called the congressman's office, attempting to schedule a meeting, and was told, "Rosty doesn't do kids."

The chairman changed his tune as his political base of support waned. In the process of looking for some way to recapture the momentum for his deficit-reduction package, Rostenkowski's staff pursued a "photo-op" with the Robinson high school students. On March 21, 1990, with television cameras rolling, four yellow bus-loads of teenagers embarked on a field trip to the U.S. Capitol. Although the students were very aware that they were really doing a favor for the congressman, they also knew that their concern over the deficit was receiving valuable publicity.

Remember — your councilmember or state senator may be doing you a "favor," but chances are that elected official stands to gain some good publicity by supporting a youth-sponsored initiative.

PUBLICIZE!

Leadership by ordinary citizens, especially those not yet of voting age, is a human interest angle the media adores. Just the fact that a teenager or young person is taking the initiative to solve a problem will attract a reporter. William Sangster explains:

Local media are dying for stories. Human interest stories are almost as high up on their list as tragedy. It's not going to sell papers but there is a reporter out there with a heart of gold looking for someone who has a good idea. If you can find that person, they will push you.

How do you find that journalist? You write and call the reporter, and do it over and over again if necessary. Someone will pick up your story. Even though you will want to contact both the print and broadcast media, a newspaper article or editorial carries a credibility which will often prompt a television station to do a story.

The more your issue is in the news, the brighter the spotlight will shine on a lawmaker's action or inaction. In nearly every campaign recounted in Part II and Part III, publicity through the news media proved to be a critical success factor. And, of course, it's fun to see your picture in the paper or on the TV screen!

COMPILING A PRESS LIST

The first step is to develop a list of news outlets. The best source, which can be found at your public library, is *Gale Directory of Publications and Broadcast Media*. This three-volume reference can supply you with all the pertinent information you need about every magazine, newspaper, radio and television station in the city or state where you live. The next step is to telephone the local newspapers and magazines to find out the name of the reporter who covers the issue you are working on. Your letter or news announcement is less likely to disappear in the newsroom if it is sent, for example, to "Metro Editor" or to an individual journalist.

Your press list should include all newspapers as well as the major dailies and any community, suburban or weekly papers. Don't overlook the most likely outlet for publishing an article: your school newspaper. Another possibility might be church bulletins. Several news-gathering services run by or for young people are always looking for stories about activists. Consider spreading the word about your campaign nationwide by sending a press release or other information to these news organizations that enjoy a readership of over a million high school and middle school students:

Youth News Service	Children's Express	Current Events
Attn: Managing Editor	Attn: Cliff Hahn	Attn: Charles Piddock
1320 18th Street NW #200	30 Cooper Square	245 Long Hill
Washington, DC 20036	New York, NY 10003	Middletown, CT 06455
Tel: (202) 429-5292	Tel: (212) 505-7777	Tel: (203) 638-2400
Fax: (202) 429-9423	Fax: (212) 505-7885	Fax: (203) 638-2788

Similarly, try to get the names of radio and TV reporters by calling each station. You may also want to get their fax numbers, since faxing winds up being a faster and cheaper delivery system than the mail. Besides your favorite radio stations, make sure to check in with all-news stations and the public radio station. You can also take advantage of programs aimed at children; for example, "Kid's Corner" on WXPN-FM in Philadelphia, "Radio Aahs" on WWTC-AM in Minneapolis, and "The Round Table" on KAOS in Olympia.

In addition to the major television stations, don't forget cable; especially your public access channel, which often is called community television. It's possible you might be able to interest a volunteer film crew in producing a program on the issue. Not only would the program be broadcast on the cable station, but it could be shown on many occasions to schools and to community groups. Many public access stations allow teenagers to attend training classes and join intern programs.

DEVELOPING A PRESS RELEASE

There are many other ways to get the word out. You can produce a short news bulletin describing your campaign or a press release announcing an upcoming event.

The more the news release looks like your own creation, the better. A handwritten release will stand out from the dozens of professionally generated news releases that newspapers and radio and television stations receive every day.

Be sure to include your name and telephone number so interested reporters can call for more information. You may want to keep the news release to one page in length, and consider using an eye-catching headline.

Remember the "four W's" when writing a release:

WHO — Mention the school or youth group involved and the students' age.

WHAT — Describe how unique, important and newsworthy this event is.

WHERE — Consider a location that would offer good visuals for cameras.

WHEN — Often Mondays and Fridays are slower news days and reporters actually hunt for stories to cover.

HINTS

► Sometimes a catchy name or motto for your campaign can attract attention. It can be used on letters, petitions, or press releases. Stick to a creative, clever concept and avoid being precious. One of my favorites is "Leaf It To Us," the student group that was instrumental in lobbying for passage of a federal law providing matching funds to youth groups for planting trees.

► When choosing a name, you might want to emphasize the positive rather than the negative. The Oakwood Students Against Drunk Driving instituted a major name change and now call their organization the National Campaign for Sober Driving.

► A constructive slogan can reinforce a campaign's message. Youth Ending Hunger adopted the powerful expression suggested by sixth grader Tammy Rheault of Anchorage, Alaska: "Don't let hunger end youth. Let youth end hunger."

If the purpose of the news release is to lure the media to attend a news conference or event, try to send out the release at least two weeks ahead of time. A week later, you may want to call each newspaper, radio and TV station to make sure they received the announcement. Usually your news release will get buried with the rest of the mail, so plan to offer to fax or mail them another one. On the morning of the event, call each newspaper and station to remind them of the time and place. (See page 81 for more last minute suggestions.)

WRITING LETTERS TO THE EDITOR

High school sophomore Brian Meshkin has an insatiable appetite for politics. Brian's attempts to get his opinions published in local newspapers provided him with valuable training for his role as a citizen activist. He has developed a real flair for commenting on controversial issues, including the education budget and the sale of assault weapons. Brian's letters to the editor in two different newspapers helped influence the passage of a bicycle safety helmet law in two counties.

Like Brian Meshkin, members of the Environment Club at Severn School in Maryland are quite skilled at publicizing their views on pending legislation. This group of high school students takes a position on any proposal that could undermine forest conservation and especially housing and highway construction bills. They voiced strong opposition to the Governor's proposal to increase the state sales tax on gasoline by drafting a letter to the editor arguing that without the gas tax increase, the road-building budget would decline by 18.6%. Their letter, sent to thirty newspapers statewide, won space in several newspapers. The wide distribution of the students' letter prompted their local paper to write a feature story on the club's campaign.

A letter to the editor or an editorial that appears in the city paper validates the importance of an issue. This type of exposure in the media builds public awareness and adds momentum to a campaign. Massachusetts teacher William Sangster remembers the boost a newspaper editorial gave the Students Against Smoking campaign:

> *What really got us going were the letters to the editor. In the library we looked at a directory, and Bingo! We found all the addresses of local and statewide newspapers. We sent a letter to the editor of every*

HINTS

▸ Keep your letter to the editor brief. Usually the maximum is around five hundred words. Be sure to include your name, address, daytime telephone number, and age. (An editor may need to contact you about your letter.)

▸ Mention that your letter is in response to a specific article that appeared in their newspaper or a proposal being considered by the legislature, school board, zoning commission, city council, etc.

▸ Send your letter to suburban and community newspapers, weeklies, and the major dailies.

▸ Newspapers are inundated with letters to the editor. Don't be disappointed if yours doesn't get published.

▸ Sending a flood of thoughtful letters to the editor is one way to push the newspaper to publish more articles about the issue. The newspaper's editors and reporters often debate the issue among themselves. Letters from readers may help them reach a consensus and write an editorial officially stating the newspaper's position.

▸ If your letter to the editor is published, send copies of it to local radio and television stations. This may prompt them to do a story on the issue.

single newspaper.

The editor of The Cape Cod Times showed me that politically we were on target. I remember my heart was pounding as I started to read the editorial saying, "Great idea, this is something we need in schools." That support helped me talk to all the people I hadn't talked to, knowing they read that column. They started calling our school and the school committee started to tell the superintendent, "Bill Sangster has something really good going. Why don't you have him come and see us and we'll help him out."

I was bringing some really positive publicity to a town, and now all of a sudden they wanted their children involved because they were starting to see, "Hey, this is going to work!"

Your published letter to the editor may have a domino effect in catching the attention of reporters at other newspapers as well as at TV and radio stations. By winning the early support of "opinion leaders," such as a newspaper editorial board, you wind up creating a more favorable political climate. If you write your elected officials, send copies of your printed letters, noting which newspapers the clips come from. Policymakers pay close attention to letters to the editor. They believe that every letter to the editor represents the views of as many as several thousand people who did not write. Those invisible people are potential voters.

SPREADING THE WORD OVER THE AIRWAVES

Television camera crews are likely to cover an event like a rally or demonstration. Exciting visual images are what producers crave, in contrast to newspaper or radio reporters who can run a story without pictures.

Oakwood Students Against Drunk Driving are pros at drawing the media to cover their news conferences. These young activists from North Hollywood, California know just how to use their hometown advantage. In this community outside of Los Angeles, where headlines about the entertainment industry often overshadow world events, screen actors have leading roles in the student-led campaign to get drunks off the roads. Lisa Goldsmith, who shares the highlights of the Oakwood students' triumphant campaign in Part III, puts it bluntly: "You've got to have a celebrity or some very prominent political figure to get at the top of the news." The high-profile involvement of a big shot is often what it takes to snag the attention of jaded reporters.

HINTS

▸ Usually the postal service or a courier delivers press packets to stations, but hand-carrying your news release or announcement is such an unusual occurrence that you increase the odds of getting air time.

▸ Rock-and-roll stations will be more likely to mention student-initiated campaigns, so be sure to call them.

▸ Definitely contact the all-news radio stations and those with listener call-in shows. Telephone the station and ask to speak to the producer in charge of a particular program. Briefly describe your campaign and let them know you could participate in a live radio show as a studio guest. In the event you get a cool response, ask the producer to suggest a few reporters at the station who might be interested in your story.

▸ Chances are, more stations exist than you know about. In Los Angeles there are seventy-nine talk shows. Washington, D.C. is the ninth largest market with fifty-eight talk shows.

MAKING A COMMERCIAL OR A PUBLIC SERVICE ANNOUNCEMENT

The powerful broadcast media reach millions of people instantly. Luck and timing have a lot to do with what stories get aired. It's not unusual for television and radio reporters to ignore your story even if you badger them constantly and suggest all kinds of different angles.

A radio commercial is one way you can make sure your message plays. No doubt you're thinking that ads are prohibitively expensive and require all kinds of sophisticated recording equipment to produce. The provocative documentary, "Guerilla Media: A Citizen's Guide to Using

Electronic Media for Social Change" (a 120-minute video produced by Varied Directions in Camden, Maine), debunks that myth. Media guru Tony Schwartz says anyone can create a thirty-second ad using a simple tape recorder and a decent microphone. About $100 is what is might cost to have the ad run during rush hour on one of the major radio stations. Odds are that the decision makers — who are the targeted audience — won't hear the ad, but plenty of people close to them will. "Guerilla Media" offers an example of such a radio ad, narrated by a young girl:

> *Governor Carey, you prevented me from going to camp this summer and I'm mad at you. You opened a prison for teenage murderers, robbers and rapists within a mile of my Girl Scout camp. Shame on you, Governor Carey. I don't want to be mad at you. Male voice concludes with the standard line: Paid for the Committee of Concerned Parents and Residents of Duchess County, New York.*

The ad played in the state capital, and according to Schwartz, the station manager said he had never had such a response to a commercial. For ideas on how to raise money for ads or other campaign promotions, refer to the next section on donations.

A more ambitious strategy for getting a message out is a public service announcement (PSA). Here again, the Oakwood Students Against Drunk Driving managed to get a Hollywood production company to donate its services and the result was a very professional thirty-second PSA that has aired on the NBC network, as well as on local television stations. (The story of the filming and distribution of this PSA is included in Part III.)

High school senior Erik Oleson of Fairfax, Virginia, single-handedly created such a powerful thirty-second PSA that the National Highway Traffic Safety Administration of the U.S. Department of Transportation distributed it to television stations across the country during Child Passenger Safety Week. The inspiration for Erik's script came from an image he had tucked away in his mind while driving on an interstate. There, he saw a toddler sitting in the front seat of a car, without the protection of a car seat.

Later that year, on "senior skip day," an old friend of Erik's was seriously hurt while riding in a Jeep that ran up an embankment and flipped over. Nathan Rasmussen was the only rider not wearing a seat belt at the time and the only person injured. When he heard that Nathan was in a coma, Erik immediately recalled the frightening image of the unbuckled toddler and he decided that "We must reach people when they are very young."

Over the summer of 1991, Erik solicited and received approximately $15,000 worth of donated services, including a film truck and crew. He made arrangements with the local police, rescue squad, and fire fighters to play visible roles in the shoot. Lacking about $500 for incidentals, he followed up on a suggestion made by several people that he apply for a grant from the National Highway Traffic Safety Administration and quickly received the money he needed.

PSA Clearinghouse

The Community Action Network (CAN) serves as a national clearinghouse to recognize and recycle public service announcements and news stories about effective solutions to social problems. The CAN Databank shares over one thousand ideas reported in the media on such local community concerns as AIDS, alcohol abuse, education, environment, homelessness, runaways, and teenage suicide. The Oakwood students' public service announcement on drunk driving won third place in the 1991 CAN Annual Media Awards. For more information about the Network's databank or its competition, write: CAN, 211 East 43rd Street, Room 1203, New York, NY 10017 (212) 818-1360.

Erik's PSA begins in full color with the screen filled with stuffed animals in a baby's nursery. The song "Pop Goes the Weasel!" plays softly. Then black and white shots show a boy coming over the back seat toward the windshield as his mother tries to get him to settle down and at the same time keep her eye on the road. A panoramic sweep of the nursery in color follows. Black and white footage reveals the aftermath of the crash with a medic walking away shaking his head. Back in the nursery, a tear falls from the eye of a stuffed animal as you hear word "Pop!" Then the words "Buckle Up or We'll Do It for You" appear as two hands buckle a seat belt around a body bag and lift the stretcher into the ambulance. As one traffic safety education administrator comments, "It's one of the most powerful PSAs I've ever seen."

Now at New York University, Erik has produced a public service announcement on homeless children and Nathan is making a remarkable recovery.

Donation$

Producing a public service announcement may require serious money and donated services, but even modest campaigns on limited budgets incur expenses such as postage and printing that add up. Often a newspaper article about a campaign will result in small contributions and in-kind donations that trickle in from strangers. Direct requests for money often yield results.

Letters of support containing checks for as little as $5 surprised Andrew Holleman, the boy who successfully stopped a housing development from being built on a wooded wetland. As his preservation efforts intensified, a neighborhood association formed and asked for financial help in its bulletin to cover such costs as hiring a lawyer and an environmental consultant. "We raised about $16,000 . . . members of the association, people from the neighborhood, across the state, and abroad donated too," Andrew reports.

SMALL CONTRIBUTIONS

A white elephant sale, recycling cans, selling T-shirts, and benefit concerts are popular methods for raising money. Persuading corporations based in the community to underwrite specific projects worked with the California student group that got Budget-Rent-A-Car to print and distribute a brochure they had written on drunk driving.

Another approach which increases public awareness about an issue and simultaneously brings in some money for a campaign is described by William Sangster, the faculty advisor to Students Against Smoking:

> *We went from the Lung Association to the Lion's Club, from*
> *the School Committee to the PTA. We told everyone in town*

what we are doing. Retirees love a group of kids coming in. The Rotary Club would say, "What can we do for you?" "Can you give us some money for stamps?" "Okay, we'll write you a check for $100." "Please make it out to Sandwich High School." I had my own account. Each kid got their parents to donate $10. You've got sixty kids — that's $600. That paid for stamps and for buses so our campaign war chest didn't come out of the school budget, not that we couldn't have gotten any money from them.

GRANT MONEY

A more ambitious strategy that requires considerably more energy and time is competing for grant money which is awarded by private institutions and government agencies. In Fort Yukon, Alaska, where there are more caribou than cars, teenage Native Americans and their parents got a sizeable federal grant approaching $10,000 to repair a dangerous section of road. An elderly woman had been killed by a police truck and another pedestrian fatally injured by a snowmobile on this same incline. With the grant money, the steep hill was leveled, street lights were installed, and the teenagers worked as the construction crew to build a sidewalk.

In the lower forty-eight, Cassie Fuller and her friends at the 4-H New Horizons club persuaded the city of Sumter, South Carolina, to donate a building for a teen center. Then she wrote several grants that paid for "a tile dance floor, paint, a drug abuse prevention flyer, the Mini-Teen Institute, and the Teen Sexuality education program." This high school junior landed $3,000 from the Rotary Club and several government organizations, including the U.S. Bureau of Justice Assistance Office for Drug Prevention. No doubt part of her success was due to her searing firsthand experience at the age of fourteen, when "suicide, drugs and alcohol were becoming a normal part of my life." Now in its second year of operation, the New Horizons Teen Center draws some two hundred kids on Saturday evenings and hosts alcohol-free graduation parties and numerous other events. (Cassie's story is included in Part II.)

Even though budgets are tight, Uncle Sam is still providing funds to states and communities at record levels. For example, the 1991 Federal Highway Act dedicates significant grants for mass transit and bicycle paths. There are several reference guides to locate sources for grant money readily available at your public library. The U.S. government publishes the *Catalog of Federal Domestic Assistance* twice a year. However, if this publication is not part of your library's collection, consult the more user-friendly reference book *Lesko's Info-Power*, which describes both federal and state agencies and their grant programs.

The Foundation Directory describes money given out by philanthropic organizations and private foundations and the *Annual Register of Grant Support* lists both private and public grant programs. Most grantors have strict guidelines and do not award money to individuals. However, a school, youth group, community group or an official organization you create may well be eligible. The Babcock Foundation, Ben & Jerry's Foundation, Charles Stewart Mott Foundation, McKenzie River Gathering Foundation, Sierra Pacific Foundation, and the Surdna Foundation are just a few of the foundations committed to social change. They can send you their annual report and general information about applying for grants which is admittedly a very competitive process.

STAGE 3: THE MAIN EVENT
Win, Lose or Draw

Practice and persistence make perfect. The fun will come after the work. There is always a reward for everything you do. It may take longer than you hope or expect but one day you will sit back and say, I did that!
— High School Senior Cindy DeNaples

Let's suppose you are at the point of making last minute preparations before the launch of your campaign. Your adrenaline is surging now. The culmination of all your work may be a pivotal event such as testifying at a public hearing, speaking at a news conference, meeting face-to-face with the governor and other elected officials, or perhaps staging a sit-in inside city hall.

It's not easy to predict what the outcome of these public happenings will be. Usually a lot more of your energy will still be required to keep attention focused on the issue. Competing proposals or staunch opposition often crop up. When the going gets rough and the result is uncertain, diehard campaigners often find themselves fighting battles on their own. But in the event of victory, expect all those supporters who previously dropped out of sight and even some naysayers to jump on the bandwagon.

FINAL PRACTICE

Dividing up tasks among your teammates in advance will reduce the inevitable frenzy when last minute snafus occur. If you're running into problems securing a city permit for a rally, call on the mayor's office or your councilmember for help. Now is the time when you may have to seek out generous souls who will lend you the use of their copier machines or public address systems.

Since the news media often provide the oxygen that keeps a campaign alive, devote as much time as you can to persuading reporters to cover the main event. When reviewing your posters, press announcements, and speeches, see if you can come up with a ten-second "sound bite," which amounts to the auditory equivalent of a bumper sticker slogan. That snappy message is just what radio and television reporters look for to liven up their report and explain the issue.

Rarely will a reporter or producer promise to come to a hearing, rally, or press conference. Not only will they be noncommittal, they'll often be disinterested or downright rude. That's how the media treat nearly everyone, except the publicists who work for big-time politicians or celebrities. So don't take offense. When a television station says they never received your news release about an upcoming event, offer to fax them another or hand-carry one over. When they say, "We don't cover that sort of thing," be ready to convince them why this event is newsworthy. Make sure to emphasize that *young* activists — a rare breed indeed — are the driving force behind the campaign. This fact is often considered more newsworthy than the issue itself!

The California teens concerned about drunk drivers discovered a great trick for getting the word out over the radio on the day an event was scheduled. Student leader Lisa Goldsmith explains:

We paired up in twos and went to a radio station in the morning and gave them a package of information about our rally, with a balloon. We also brought them doughnuts. I remember somebody said that they'll let you in if you bring them food. So we just went to the radio station and said, "Hi, we've got some doughnuts for the staff and the DJ," and they let us go in. I went on the air and talked about the rally and told people to come.

This publicity attracted additional media coverage and helped maintain the momentum of this student initiative which was then in its third year.

A dress rehearsal is a worthwhile exercise prior to testifying. You can get more mileage out of your speech by investing a little time beforehand. Here are a few suggestions:

HINTS

▶ Time the length of your testimony. If there is a two-minute limit, shorten your speech if necessary to make sure you don't go too long because the committee chair may cut you off.

▶ Type out your statement even if you don't plan to read it. Make enough copies to hand out to all council or committee members and to the news media attending the hearing.

▶ Practice your testimony, perhaps

using a video or tape recorder, and ask a friend, parent, or teacher to give you some coaching.

▶ The day of the hearing, call to confirm the time and location. The committee clerk may be able to tell you the total number of witnesses and where you stand in the witness line-up.

▶ Consider faxing a copy of your statement prior to the hearing to any reporters who expressed an interest in your campaign.

Besides attending to these nitty gritty details, try to anticipate what questions you might be asked. Do some role-playing and think through how you might answer zingers. One way to predict the areas of controversy is to contact one of your inside allies before the hearing is held. For example, the five teens who planned to testify in favor of legislation banning steel animal traps learned from their state representative that a weakening amendment was going to be offered. The girls managed to include in their statement a compromise proposal to this "killer" amendment that won approval over the objections of the trappers. (Their story is included in Part III.)

What happens in the public arena under the glare of the spotlights is very different from the deals concocted privately behind the scenes. Politicians may make promises and commitments but a smile and handshake usually are not much of a guarantee. Remain vigilant by staying in contact with key staff members who can keep you informed of action or inaction.

There's a lot of truth in the joke heard on Capitol Hill: "How long does it take Congress to cook minute rice?" The slow, deliberative process of lawmaking at any level of government partly explains why the advantage rests with those who want to defeat a proposal. As a rule, it's easier to block legislation than to propel it through the pipeline. Depending on your position, one strategy is to turn up the heat which might mean presenting a stack of petitions or holding a demonstration. The teens in South Carolina who created the youth community center mobilized immediately after learning that the county council planned to renege on its commitment to pay the salary for the center's full-time director. Overnight, a telephone tree took root and kids got hundreds of their friends to call councilmembers. Many teens voiced their support publicly for the first time and the Sumter County government responded by voting to fund this new, paid position for the teen center director. In Alabama, round-the-clock demonstrations by black students and parents at city hall pressured the mayor of Selma to appoint more African Americans to the school board.

Toppling the opposition has its place in the political arena, but so does collaboration. The search for middle ground requires more patience and energy. Negotiating with the other side is commendable under most circumstances because it signals tolerance and respect for other points of view. A carefully crafted compromise can build broad-based unity in a community.

THE ART
OF COMPROMISE

Two stories recounted in Part III reveal how the willingness of young activists to consider alternatives kept proposed laws on track when opponents nearly derailed legislation. Student leader Brian Meshkin recalls how county councilmembers philosophically opposed to a mandatory bike safety helmet ordinance proposed an amendment to require bicyclists of *all* ages to wear the protective gear. While arguments about potential economic hardship on poor families and parents' prerogatives were raised against the student proposal which only covered bikers under the age of sixteen, the "strengthening" amendment provoked vehement public outcry. After listening to the arguments of his adversaries at the second round of hearings, Brian recognized the political game being played out and testified in support of a bill covering all bicyclists. In the end, the revised measure offered by those opposed to any helmet law backfired. The original bill for bikers fifteen and under became the first law of its kind in the nation.

Similarly, the successful two-year student campaign to persuade the Massachusetts legislature to prohibit smoking on school property came under heavy fire from the chairman of the House Health and Education Committee. After their bill remained bottled up in committee, the students explored ways to meet the chairman's objections and negotiate. As William Sangster told them, "You learn that compromise doesn't mean you lose."

The second time around, the new bill included teachers and won the chairman's approval. However, the Senate, under intense lobbying by teachers, dropped school faculty from the bill. Hardball politics ensued but students prevailed by getting the House, in a highly unusual procedural move, to overrule its own committee chairman and pass the Senate version of the legislation.

The young people involved with the bike helmet bill and the smoke-free schools measure listened to their opponents and accepted a fundamental change to keep their legislation alive. The irony is that both of these laws now on the books mirror the original bills first proposed by the students.

Ordinary citizens, especially young activists, have a distinct disadvantage during the negotiating process. As Harry Boyte of Project Public Life emphasizes, "Political skills and arts are learned, like basketball or music." Experienced lobbyists also are aware of the horse-trading conducted between lawmakers and can anticipate parliamentary ploys. Moreover, these 'hired guns' usually enjoy first-class access to the movers and shakers, thanks to their campaign contributions. Yet the dogged determination of novice lobbyists often proves to be a surprisingly powerful weapon.

The unwavering commitment shown by student activists seemed to pierce even the thickest-skinned legislators in the Massachusetts Statehouse. Jeff Curry, one of the core group members, remembers the response they received when they returned to the capitol after their proposal was defeated the first time: "I think what really got their attention was our persistence. We wouldn't take 'no' for an answer." Jeff's classmate, Lynn Terrill, says "We were as adamant as ever to make it work. I think essentially the defeat was a learning process. It showed that we were really sincere. It also showed that we would fight until the end."

BEYOND THE FINAL SCORE

Action over apathy. Courage over cynicism. Whatever the tangible outcome of your campaign turns out to be, you'll know you have fought the good fight. Here is where you write the ending. Perhaps it reads along the lines of Ryan Tedeschi's essay which he submitted with his college applications:

> Many people go through life hoping to make a mark for themselves or on society. I can proudly say I have already accomplished one of these goals. Even if I go through the rest of my life not making a big name for myself, or being in the public eye, I will always be able to say that perhaps I helped save a young person from developing the life-threatening habit of cigarette smoking.

The pride of discovering a forum for your views and being heard is another reward with lasting significance. In the story, "Bump The Dump" recounted in Part II, the students at an alternative high school express amazement at how their ideas were taken seriously by an adult world which had often looked upon them as lawbreakers. These 'at risk' teens had a taste of empowerment and now speak of their readiness to help solve other problems in their community.

There are other, subtle rewards in immersing yourself in a grassroots campaign. Maureen Gemma describes how her long-term advocacy work has transformed her lifestyle:

> *I think any activist project really doesn't fit into your schedule. It's something you have to invent and create into your day. It has become*

*a habit now for me to wake up excited and
inspired about my life.*

A modest victory or even defeat, represents a win in terms of making that first connection with our democracy. Once you've plugged into one outlet, it becomes apparent that many other outlets exist for every issue and cause. All the power centers where policies are debated and decided for our schools and streets, cities and states, and even the global community, are no longer are viewed as off-limits. They represent public arenas that actually accept the high-voltage ideas of concerned and informed people.

High school graduate Katy Yanda of Santa Fe believes it is crucial for activists to inspire others:

> *If you are genuinely interested and excited, others will be too. People who care need to teach others to care. I would also tell students to follow through as much as possible. The amount of difference one person can make is amazing; the amount a group can make is even more.*

Katy's message holds true for everyone — not just those who picture themselves as leaders. Activists come in all sizes, colors, and ages. They are living proof that ordinary citizens are not powerless. Reform-minded citizens should be encouraged to question conventional wisdom and challenge the status quo. What a different decade the 1990s could be if activism became viewed as the essence of patriotism!

Sharing your story nationwide is one important way of inducing other Americans to get involved. The Activism 2000 Project is eager to hear from you and possibly include your campaign — whether it proved victorious or not — in a future edition of *No Kidding Around!* Also consider sending information about your campaign to national publications such as the consumer magazine *Zillions*, the Humane Society's *Student Network News*, or the environmental magazine written by kids titled *Ozone*. It's a long shot, but it is conceivable that major publications like *Newsweek*, *People* or *Seventeen* might pick up your story.

It may seem egotistical, but also consider putting your name in the running for particular awards or nominate one of your key allies. View this as another way to convince Americans of all ages they, too, can make their voices heard and shape public policy.

Recognition and Awards

A growing number of government agencies and private organizations showcase the contributions of America's dreamers and doers. Here are just a few examples:

★ The prestigious President's Environmental Youth Awards Program sponsors an annual regional certificate program and a national awards competition. Contact the U.S. Environmental Protection Agency, Communications & Public Affairs, Washington, DC 20460 (202) 260-2080 or your regional EPA office.

★ The Giraffe Project chooses individuals of all ages across America who "stick their necks out." Contact: PO Box 759, Langley, WA 98260 (800) 344-TALL (206) 221-7989 in Washington state.

★ Six Colorado counties participate in the Metropolitan Mayors and Commissioners Youth Award to recognize "unsung" local youth heroes. Contact the Denver Commission on Youth, 303 West Colfax Avenue, Room 1600, Denver, CO 80203 (303) 575-2621.

Local chapters of national advocacy groups such as Common Cause and Audubon Society often recognize ordinary people responsible for extraordinary accomplishments.

PART II:

IN THEIR OWN WORDS
Righting Wrongs, Filling Needs

IN THEIR OWN WORDS
Righting Wrongs, Filling Needs

It is individuals who change societies, give birth to ideas; who, standing out against tides of opinion, change them . . . It is my belief that an intelligent and forward-looking society would do everything possible to produce such individuals instead of, as happens very often, suppressing them.
— Doris Lessing

The following oral histories offer living proof that indeed individuals — not government institutions or the establishment — are changing our world. These young Americans are proposing new directions for our schools and cities, and some even dare to try to reorder global priorities. None of them were invited to join ongoing debates before their county council or zoning commission. These ordinary kids who felt compelled to get involved and change things simply invited themselves. Many of them still express surprise over their participation in the democratic process. Never before had they presented their ideas in a public forum.

Each one of these concerned citizens has an individual style that rarely conforms with a standard definition of leadership. They don't view themselves as modern day Pied Pipers. Most claim to be average students whose parents feel disconnected from government. Others are labeled "at risk" and have even had brushes with the law.

Common to all is the ability to break down problems into manageable pieces and successfully design cost-effective solutions. Their prescriptions for fixing our educational system, tackling teen pregnancy, drug abuse, hunger at home and abroad, or environmental destruction represent either significant stopgap measures or innovative initiatives. These teenagers manage to get action on issues that have been consistently neglected or routinely dismissed.

The following oral histories — which are the product of taped interviews — capture the young activists' pioneering spirit. What makes them tick? Where do they get the courage to challenge the status quo? What makes them overcome the apathy or cynicism that greets their energy and vision? What makes them even more determined when they experience setbacks or defeat? Which strategies work and which don't? Their genuine, impassioned voices help us realize that these narratives aren't mere stories but actual history in the making.

YOUNG ENVIRONMENTALIST
SAVES WETLANDS
Developer Builds on Old
Drive-In Theater Lot Instead

Some people just don't let problems get them down. Take Andrew Holleman of Chelmsford, Massachusetts, for example. Because Andrew suffers from terrible allergies, he cannot have pets like cats and dogs. Instead, this animal lover temporarily adopts such animals as a wounded raven he named Edgar Allen Crow. Andrew let the bird perch on his shoulder and hand-fed it water and popcorn. On more than one occasion, neighbors have called asking for Andrew's help with injured skunks that have been hit by cars or caught in animal traps.

Andrew's bookcase reveals his passion for the natural world. The shelves are filled with such classics as Gerald Durrell's *A Zoo In My Luggage* and an extensive rock collection. Over the years, Andrew has acquired expert knowledge about the importance of wetlands as a home for many species of wildlife, as a flood plain which absorbs water and releases it slowly over time, and as an area where the plants and soil purify the underground water that feeds local wells.

When this twelve-year old learned that a housing development was being planned nearby, he instinctively fought to protect his favorite woods and the animals that made their home there.

IN HIS OWN WORDS . . .

One day my mother signed for a registered letter and I asked if I could see it. It was from a developer saying he wanted to build a 180-unit condominium and the letter stated that a meeting would be held at the town hall. I read it and knew something had to be done. I told my mother we had to go to the library and she took me a couple of days later. She suggested looking in the law books and went off to do a little bit of shopping. I went to the section where they have the Annotated Laws of Massachusetts. I found pretty much everything about the Hatch Act [Massachusetts law protecting wetlands].

I asked the librarian if there was anything that would help. She said, "Not really," but then she added, "This might help." It was the town master plan. I had no idea there was a town master plan. It's big but not difficult to go through. So I started looking through it and found the ammunition I needed — only 2.2 acres of the 16.3 acre site were considered sound enough to be developed.

A neighbor told me, "Don't expect to win," since the developer was a "townie" who always gets his way. I try never to get my hopes up about anything and I just do what I can. You'll never get anything done if you don't try.

I drafted the petition against the condo development within the week. I figured that's how you get things done. I must have seen it done on TV or something. I knew if you get a lot of people to speak out you have a better chance than just one person.

> During the past month many people have been concerned about the low income condominiums that may be built between Farms One and Concord Rd. in Chelmsford, MA. My name is Andrew Holleman. I am twelve years old, and I am very opposed to the proposed site for the buildings, and not because they are for low-income families. What I am against is the pollution of our drinking water, the pollution of the wetland and woodland areas, and the killing off of the wildlife. These areas are right where the condos will be built. Everyone talks about the protection of our environment for the present and future generations. Is this how they protect our environment?
>
> The following facts will prove why I am very much against the construction of these 180 units.
>
> 1. The area for the buildings according to the Town of Chelmsford Massachusetts Master Plan, dated Feb. 11, 1986, is on 16.3 acres of land: 8.5 acres of which is wetland, 5.6 acres is poor soil, and only 2.2 acres is developable. This area is surrounded by conservation land. Inevitably, it will be polluted.

2. The Wetlands Protection Act (1972) says that a permit has to be obtained from the Chelmsford Conservation Commission for any project which is located within 100 feet of any wetlands. These units will be on wetland.

3. According to this survey in the Chelmsford Master Plan there are only 2871 vacant acres of land in the town, of which 2188 acres are wetlands, leaving only 5% of developable land. Land development has increased since this study, and wetlands have probably been destroyed.

4. The residents living in Farms One will be getting sewerage in the future because of the poor drainage in this area. Only 40% of Chelmsford is getting sewerage proving the desperate need not to pollute our environment.

5. The Massachusetts Wetlands Protection Act (Hatch Act), I believe, will be violated because of where the buildings may be constructed; on wetland and with conservation land on both sides of it.

6. Please see the map showing proposed building area and the stream running through it.

7. Please sign the paper provided if you agree with me.

After three hours of walking I'd come back with five signatures and my mom would say, "What happened?" Well, when somebody invites you in for a Coke and starts discussing it with you, it takes a while. A lot of people didn't seem to realize what was going on even though they also got a registered letter. After going around to a few houses in the general radius of our house, I got to people I didn't know. Only two refused to sign. As I went around I had a copy of that letter and I'd tell them when the meeting was and they could come just to show their support. Apparently they listened because a whole bunch of people came to the developer's meeting.

I collected about one hundred and fifty signatures. Elizabeth [Andrew's younger sister], as well as my parents, helped get petitions signed, too. The petition really helped in gaining publicity and built awareness.

HINTS

Andrew's petition is remarkable. Unlike most brief petitions, this one truly informs. Many people, after reading such a detailed document, talking with Andrew, and signing the petition, became involved in the issue. For example, Andrew impressed one neighbor, a member of the Housing Review Commission, who invited him to come speak at one of their meetings. She also took the initiative to call the newspaper and the result was the first of many articles about Andrew's campaign. His petition proved to be perhaps the most effective tool in mobilizing the community.

There's a grapevine in this town about two hundred miles long. Many students signed the student petition and offered support, but I was learning myself as I went along and really had no time to teach others how to help.

[Here's a typical letter.]

Dear Andrew Holleman:

My name is Chad Feeney and I'm in the 8th grade at the McCarthy School. I am in favor of what you are doing and would like to help support your project. I am also surprised that these people would ever propose a condo development on a wetlands area when the Massachusetts state law, the Hatch Act, protects these areas. I'm interested in wildlife and would like to know the type of heron and wood turtles if you do know. I would like to sign your petition and would be honored if I could. I'm not sure there are many people in the world who would try to stop this. It seems to me it is always kids our age who take the first step. If I could sign your petition, I am in Homeroom 108. I would also like to be your friend. Not because you're in the newspaper, but because of who you are. You are the type of person that keeps our nation together and alive. I thank you for your time.

Sincerely yours,
Chad Feeney

My parents would bring me to the library so I could copy the petitions and then I would deliver them to the town hall and place copies in the mailboxes of each selectmen's office and the zoning commission office and board of health office.

THE FIRST OF MANY PERSUASIVE SPEECHES

Dressed in sneakers, jeans, and a sweatshirt and holding the shell of an old turtle, Andrew was an awful difficult image to overcome.
— Joseph Shanahan, Developer & Attorney
Russell Mill Pond Realty Trust Inc.

The meeting at the town hall started out in a small room adequate to hold approximately twenty people — those that received the registered letters — but then was moved to the gymnasium because there were about two hundred and fifty people. I invited the rest. After the developer discussed his project, he was going to take some questions but he let me speak first. I was really nervous.

It was the first time I had done anything really except maybe book reports in front of my class. We must have practiced my speech forty times. Elizabeth knew it by heart. We had it on tape and Mom would play it back and she would say, "You want to fix that."

I knew anything that is too emotional you'd get called a loony and be thrown out. I never really get that emotional about anything. I know you have got to keep your cool or you'll just fall flat on your face.

[Holding 3x5 index note cards, Andrew walked to the front of the gymnasium. The audience clapped for twenty seconds. A polite applause lasts about five seconds.] I began my speech by saying: "My name is Andrew Holleman and I am twelve years old." [Andrew spoke about how sewage from this 180-unit condominium would eventually pollute the town wells because of the poor soil.]

[Holding the shell of a wood turtle he'd found in the woods, Andrew described how this development would destroy such endangered species as the blue spotted salamander, the wood turtle, the red fox, the blue heron and various kinds of hawks. Andrew suggested that a better place for building condos might be the abandoned drive-in movie lot in town. As he concluded his three-minute speech talking about protecting the wetlands for "future generations," Andrew received yet another thunderous round of applause.]

The developer, Mr. Shanahan, then tried to discredit the information I used rather than attack me. Mr. Shanahan said, "Andy's done a lot of research at the junior high school library," and I broke in and said "No, it was done at the main public library."

Yes, all the applause was a comfort. I had lots of people there who said, "All right, Andy, let's go!"

After that night, I wrote letters to many state representatives and also to a local TV anchorwoman. I included my petition in the letters. Someone suggested I call up the "Helpline" of the Massachusetts Audubon Society. When I called I got Dr. Dorothy Arvidson; she thought I was an adult. She's a biologist and now a good friend. She took a real interest and told me to keep my fight local and that I should approach town representatives because national and state organizations wouldn't be much help.

When I told her I was only twelve years old, she said, "Well, that's no excuse."

Meetings were held almost every week. A lot of them were either the conservation commission, zoning board of appeals, or town selectmen meetings where the developer's proposal got reviewed. The conservation commission passes it if they think it is all right. The selectmen have the power to override the conservation commission if they think it is better for the town and the zoning board of appeals has the ability above everybody. Those were the three main places where I went to speak.

It wasn't exactly fun. I enjoyed doing it and I would do it again any day. But it's not fun when you've got at least three hours of homework a night, go to a four-hour meeting and go to Boy Scouts. I had to learn how to organize my time. Lots of school kids do it — those who have jobs, belong to a club or two at school, plus homework. That's 26 hours a day!

I got calls in school. During the middle of Spanish class, Mr. Tymowicz, my Spanish teacher back then, got this call for me to come down to the office and he said — in an attempt to be funny — "If you want to get closer to the environment, I will plant you in the ground."

We'd go to one meeting and then they would say that we're going to have another meeting. And we'd swing by the town hall and look at the big calendar with all the meeting notices on it just in case we missed something. I also went to a couple meetings of the health board and the housing review commission. People were getting used to me being around.

Shanahan was an adversary. At a Board of Health meeting, he said, "I'm not going to discuss hydro-geological information with a twelve-year old." Then we got to know each other and we'd say "Hi" every once and awhile. He said he'd pull out of this development if we'd support him for another development at the drive-in. We said we wouldn't support him but we wouldn't fight him either because that was a good place to put it. He was already getting fought by people who lived in that area. It was just NIMBY — Not In My Backyard. By ripping up a couple of acres of tarmac [at the drive-in lot] and putting in some real plants, the condo development could actually help the environment.

ANDREW'S FIGHT GROWS INTO NEIGHBORHOOD FORCE

I was bucking heads with Andrew and his group for eleven months. For a youngster he did a heck of a job organizing the community.
— Joseph Shanahan

For the first month or so, I was alone, although my family gave me a lot of support. Then after that, the Concord Road Neighborhood Association was formed and we all worked together. Dad almost didn't let me become a member but I insisted. I think he figured that I was too young and I didn't belong there. Mom wasn't part of the organization but she should have been! She did enough — typing, encouragement, driving me to meetings, suggesting ideas, etc.

Each of us had our own specialized area. One person had access to printing so we printed all the bulletins. We had a chairman who did speaking for the group. My dad and I worked a lot with the conservation commission but anybody else was free to work with them, too.

We asked for donations in our little bulletins. Members of the association donated, people from the neighborhood and abroad donated, too. We raised $16,000. We hired a lawyer and an environmental scientist.

Shanahan continued to dispute the town master plan and the town zoning maps. His surveys indicated less wetland and little-to-no groundwater run-off. We made videotapes showing wetlands that were not marked off and large areas of excessive groundwater.

After nine months, the state Department of Environmental Quality Engineering came to the proposed site to do "deep hole" soil and groundwater tests. This checks the soil's drainage by seeing if a deeply dug hole will fill with water [which means the land couldn't absorb the condominium sewage treatment system]. I was fairly confident that the site would fail because I had known that land a long time. But I can tell you that when the test confirmed my beliefs, I was excited and relieved.

The town denied a comprehensive permit to the developer to build his 180 condominiums so nothing of that magnitude can ever be built there. Shanahan and his group are now building in the drive-in area.

The battle isn't over yet because some developer could try to get a couple of single family houses built back in the woods. I'm trying to acquire some money from different sources so that the town can purchase the land and make it conservation land. Besides being a dream of mine to see this land protected, I know it will be one more step in the preservation of our environment and the saving of our world.

PREDICTIONS

Andrew Holleman became the youngest winner of the U.S. Environmental Protection Agency's Regional Merit Award, and in 1989 was chosen by the United Nations Environment Program for its Global 500 Award for Achievement. Chances are, he will study environmental law. Andrew has been named a "Giraffe" for sticking his neck out and thanks to the Giraffe Project, he recently traveled to Russia. Dr. Dorothy Rodwell Arvidson of the Massachusetts Audubon Society, Andrew's mentor and friend, observes that "He is a role model for his peers, and I hope there are many thousands more like him somewhere in the world."

Andrew's entire family sings his praises. In a third grade creative writing composition entitled "A Special Occasion," brother Nicholas captured the whole story in a few sentences.

> My special occasion is when my brother saved our environment. He saved it by stopping Shanahan from building condos behind Cappel's Pond. My family passed out notices and we got 180 people to sign petitions. My brother won so Shanahan won't build back in the forest.

Elizabeth, an ardent environmentalist who routinely convinces local shoppers to use paper rather than plastic grocery bags, gives her brother all the credit: "Even though Andrew is only sixteen months older, he has taught me so much about the environment. Now I can answer other kids' questions."

"He opened my eyes," confesses Mrs. Holleman. "I grew up being told, 'Don't make waves' and thinking it's better not to do anything to avoid being disappointed. But now there are a few issues I want to get out there and fight about!"

Andrew's father beams with pride: "It was a once-in-a-lifetime opportunity, particularly working with somebody as young as Andrew was at the time. It is something every parent would love to be able to say. Boy, what a wonderful experience it was!"

INFORMATION STARTERS

First, contact your state department of natural resources for an overview of the laws governing wetlands. The following national organizations and federal agencies can provide you with a wealth of information.

★ **Environmental Law Institute**
National Wetlands Newsletter
1616 P Street NW, Second Floor
Washington, DC 20036
(202) 328-5150
Serves as a clearinghouse and offers free information.

★ **National Audubon Society**
950 Third Avenue
New York, NY 10022
(212) 546-9100
State chapters can be of help but Andrew was especially lucky when he dialed the Massachusetts Audubon Society's statewide toll-free number (800) 541-3443 and spoke with Dr. Arvidson.

★ **National Home Builders Association**
Environmental Regulation
15th and M Streets NW
Washington, DC 20005
(202) 822-0484
Plays an active role in this public policy debate.

★ **National Wetlands Coalition**
1050 Thomas Jefferson Street NW, Sixth Floor
Washington, DC 20007
(202) 298-1822
Represents industry alliance which includes gas and oil companies.

★ **National Wildlife Federation**
  1400 16th Street NW
  Washington, DC 20036-2266
  (202) 797-6800
Focuses on wildlife habitat protection.

★ **Nature Conservancy**
  1815 North Lynn Street
  Arlington, VA 22209
  (703) 841-5300
Purchases nature sanctuaries, including wetlands, to safeguard them from development.

★ **U.S. Army Corps of Engineers**
  Regulatory Branch
  20 Massachusetts Avenue NW
  Washington, DC 20314-1000
  (202) 272-1785
Responsible for federal wetland areas as they relate to flood control.

★ **U.S. Environmental Protection Agency (EPA)**
  401 M Street SW
  Washington, DC 20460
  (800) 832-7828 Wetlands Hotline
  (202) 260-2080 General Information
Provides free information on the Federal Wetlands Protection Act, the Clean Water Act, and other environmental issues.

★ **U.S. Fish and Wildlife Service**
  U.S. Department of Interior
  4401 North Fairfax Drive
  Arlington, VA 22203
  (703) 343-5333
Oversees federal wetlands areas along with the U. S. Army Corps of Engineers and the U.S. Environmental Protection Agency.

OFF THE STREETS
Community Center
Created by Teens, for Teens

Right now, teens in America are fighting a war, and we are scared to death because our friends are dying. Our friends are trying to kill each other and killing themselves . . . I don't think it works for adults to push messages about drugs and alcohol and AIDS on teenagers. Teenagers need to hear those messages from other teens.
— Cassie Fuller

The rats no longer occupy an old warehouse that is as wide as a four-lane interstate. The building, especially on Friday and Saturday nights, is filled with young people who flock to the New Horizons Teen Center. It was an uphill battle to convince the southern community of Sumter, South Carolina, that kids desperately needed a place to hang out and have fun.

Cassie Fuller and several other high school students active in 4-H were determined to create a recreation center in Sumter. They believed that the best way to win the "war" was for teens to help teens. At fourteen, Cassie says "My world was constant chaos and death. Suicide, drugs and alcohol were becoming a normal part of my life." Although a casualty of the "war" on sobriety and sanity, she survived and remains determined to help other kids whose pain she understands only too well.

In the following account, this Texas-born "loudmouth," as Cassie describes herself, retraces her steps which involved winning the support of the county council and the governor, as well as obtaining nearly $3,000 worth of grants. The New Horizons Teen Center has become a national model, and is a testament to Cassie Fuller's drive to change her corner of the world.

IN HER OWN WORDS . . .

I went from good girl to bad girl. I went through a very long wild streak, but I benefitted from it. One thing that my father, who comes from an old Southern family, taught me is whatever is given to you and doesn't kill you, will make you stronger and you have to help others because there are those who won't be able to survive what you did.

I was part of a gang once. I did drugs to some extent. I drank. I attempted suicide twice. I'm not proud of these things but if I had not done those things, I could not have helped others. I see kids who were younger than me in the same pain that I knew and I would feel and know their pain. No child should go through things like this. There are kids out there who are really adults at twelve and I felt that wasn't right.

We are looking to adults around us for comfort, for safety and for support. We teenagers are lost and we are looking for help from others. What we are getting are programs that tell us, "You are a good person," and "Just Say No to Drugs." We feel pain inside that we have never felt before and we're hurting like we've never hurt before. Saying "no" to something that is going to make us forget the pain and hurt and feel good for a while is really hard to do.

There really is a big generation gap and it's not a joking matter anymore. Kids can no longer look up to adults to take care of them and to make it all better. We've got to start to hold each other's hand. I think if you can work inward from the teenage community and out that is one way to work through these massive problems.

Most kids in the beginning do not have major life-threatening problems but what happens is they have no one to talk to and nowhere to turn so they turn to drugs, alcohol, sex, or whatever. Kids need a place to go and talk to other kids who aren't going to down them and judge them. And those who have already turned to drugs — I personally believe anyone can change themselves. I didn't go to a rehab center. I didn't go to a psychologist or therapist. I did it on my own with the help of friends. That was my basic philosophy behind the teen center.

I had just turned fifteen when I moved to South Carolina. I did not want to be here. There's nothing in Sumter but to cruise up and down. A friend introduced me to a 4-H group called New Horizons. They had gotten a old warehouse donated by the city and had applications to open a teen center, but the structural problems of the building and actual community programs had not been worked out yet. When they told me about their idea, I had a lot of ideas on how to make this work.

We only had five members — four boys who were juniors and seniors in high school and I was the only girl, a sophomore. My worry was to get this place looking good enough so we could open the doors once a week. If we could get kids into the center and let them dance and hear a deejay, then we could hit them with the punch and get them to claim the place as their own. Then they would want to make it the very best it could be.

It took four years of long, hard work to get it where it is now. The community rallied around us with a very cautious attitude. We were baited, given scraps like you would to a dog, and then told this is all we can give you. I felt if the teenagers alone could get money and build the structure and if we could do everything that we had to do on our own, then I could go to community members and organizations and say, "We've done all this, now give us money so we can do more."

There is still denial. Sumter is a very prosperous community but the drug problem prospers, too. It's a perfect geographical place for drugs to be shipped in. We are very close to Myrtle Beach, Charlotte, and Columbia. Sumter is a small town, low profile, and a lot of people did not want to see the growing problem.

We started finding different grants that we could apply for. I found out about them through the 4-H and the South Carolina Drug and Alcohol Commission. They'd get the applications for me or tell me whom to call and I wrote the grant. The first grant we got came from the Bureau of Justice Assistance Office of Drug Prevention in Washington. That money was for tile we needed for the dance floor.

One of the things I put in the grant is that the teen center is positioned on the southern side of the county which is the roughest end of town, where the poor people and the gangs are. The center's location might have been accidental but part of it, I think, was a gift from God because those are the kids we need to hit first. High-income and middle class kids need to be targeted as hard as you target low-income children but first of all I wanted to get the low-income kids working with us for two reasons. First, to get them in and off the streets and second, because I needed them to provide protection for the Teen Center. If I had kids and gang members from that area working with us I knew we wouldn't be attacked. That plan has worked for the last four years.

It started out with fifteen to twenty youths. Now the center hosts around two hundred kids at various events and activities, including recreation and youth development programs. Our attendance has gone way up. It started out as one high school crowd but since then we've branched out to five high schools and that was one of our goals. Teens are just like adults — when you succeed, everyone jumps on the bandwagon.

We initially opened on Friday nights and it was a white upper middle class group of kids. On Saturday night it was primarily black. Now there is more of a mixture. We tried to do a program on race but it was shot down. There is just as much racism against whites as there is against blacks. Everyone is becoming racist and ignorant of everyone else. But the one thing about the Teen Center is we are there to dance. No one is different there.

The Teen Center is run by a core group and that group is constantly revolving — new leaders, teen DJs, and high school bands. Teens do the accounting, some do grants, some others search people at the door for knives and stuff because of the gangs.

MORE THAN A PLACE TO HANG OUT

We started a Sex Ed program which is essentially peer counseling done within the Teen Center. Our group discussions are about how to respect yourself and have responsibility for what you do. We also have doctors and nurses come to the center and these professionals talk to the teens in their own territory. People were afraid I was going to distribute condoms and they didn't want their children hearing about sex from strangers. By this time I was seventeen, and my answer was: "Well, they aren't hearing about it from you and I'm tired of seeing these fourteen-year olds pregnant." We have flyers in the bathrooms about condoms, where to go to get birth control pills, and what is the safest protection against AIDS and gonorrhea.

We started a Government in Action program. Two students now attend every meeting of the county council and speak about teen problems. Before this program began, I felt teens were being ignored. I told the council that it's only going to take you ten minutes — five minutes for each child to speak — and you might learn something. Since then the council has sponsored summer programs, all sorts of government programs for teenagers, and kids who are interested in politics can spend a day with a county councilmember.

We also help with resumes, and find volunteer work for kids at the center. We're involved with recycling and environmental projects. The Teen Center gives you a place to let your guard down and lets you find out who you really are. It's especially for all the wonderful kids who aren't the star pupils and don't make straight A's and are basically considered outcasts. They don't fit in a clique or their parents don't have enough money and teachers and principals overlook them and they don't get picked to go do the special things. If a kid comes in the Center and has an idea and has worked it through, we'll show him where to get the money and the support. If he fails, we'll help him figure out how and why.

STREET SMARTS

I hate to be patted on the head and told "Good girl . . . Go home." That's what a lot of politicians did to me. When they did it, that got me more fired up. I believe in the old kind of democracy when every individual really did have a say. We need to band together now. I've done it with the Sumter teen community.

I told Governor Campbell once if all teens could band together and go against the government you would have no government. Kids are tired of it. Everyone is saying you've got to do something. It's overwhelming even to me at times. The bureaucratic process is so slow and so complicated.

Everyone has views and ideas of how it can work. Americans are too scared or too fed up to try. If I didn't have 4-H and the state Drug and Alcohol Commission, I really wouldn't have known where to go for help. They showed me which people you need to go to for what. The average American doesn't know where to begin.

Sometimes I would call Governor Campbell instead of my mayor, primarily on the pregnancy issue and AIDS. I didn't have the information I needed. I think Sumter is second in the state for teenage pregnancy. That's devastating to the community. I'd go and say, "Look, what are you going to do about this?" I used my age to get my foot in the door. To speak with Governor Campbell, I would get an appointment with one of his aides and tell him what I needed: "This is going to help the state's image and it is going to help South Carolina economically," I'd say. By promising the politicians that I could make them look good and make their state look progressive, they were saying, "This little girl is still in high school and is promising us national recognition in an area that we are so behind in."

You have to play their game. That's what really worked for me. I was under eighteen and I knew so much. I could speak their language in very big words. I could play ball with them even though I was so young. And I think that shocked people and while they were shocked, I went in for the kill. They would take what I was saying about kids on the street, where they are getting drugs, sex and diseases and they would set it alongside their data and my information would be right on. They had spent billions of dollars of research to learn what I've learned in sixteen years.

I got involved with the Kettering Foundation; it's a giant think tank. They offer materials on different topics for community groups to sit and discuss. They believe in democracy and town meetings. We filled out an application for a grant from the foundation and mainly because of the Teen Center I got a scholarship to go to Washington, D.C. I got to speak with Presidential advisors on education and drug policy and the President's Deputy Assistant for Domestic Policy and Economics. I was invited back and I brought back five people to tell the government what it could do. After that we started a national newsletter for anyone who wants to start a teen community activity group. Things really skyrocketed.

We had done all this work on our own and I received a promise and a handshake that the Sumter County Council would give us the money for a Teen Center Youth Development Director. I was out of town at a convention of the Drug and Alcohol Commission for teenagers from all over South Carolina.

One of the guys who had started out with me in New Horizons was home on vacation from college and heard that the council had decided not to fund the youth director position. Over four hundred teens called the councilmembers at ten, eleven, and twelve at night. They had their parents call. Kids from all walks of life telephoned, even those who wouldn't outwardly support the Teen Center. Three hundred kids showed up at the council meeting to make sure that vote went through and it did. We have our youth director and the Teen Center has blossomed because of him. I'm particularly proud that I helped create a job for an adult.

The Teen Center is going to carry on. Teens created it and adults just made sure it was legal. It could be adapted to a smaller town, or even a big city like Atlanta. Come steal the ideas from the center and make it fit your community. To me, that's the greatest compliment!

I'm now an adult. I vote, I pay taxes and I want to be heard. There's my sister's generation — she's sixteen — and the generation under her. All those kids deserve the chance to speak their minds. I know more kids who know more about what's going on with drugs, alcohol and sexual problems than adults whose job it is to know.

PREDICTIONS

Cassie Fuller aspires to be "the first teacher in the Senate — not a lawyer — but someone close to the people." Another dream of hers later on in life is to live in a small city like Sumter with a community center available for her own children. For now, Cassie is at Old Dominion University in Virginia, pursuing a double major in education and political science. As the recipient of the 1991 National 4-H Council's Citizenship Award, she remains in the public eye, still staring down politicians for not having the guts to act and urging teens to fight the "war" in their communities.

Amy Howell, Cassie's successor as president of New Horizons Teen Center, has proved to be another remarkable young leader and serves on several policy-making committees in Sumter. Community support for the center has grown, and recently the county council voted 34-1 to keep it open after a police officer was stabbed trying to break up a fight between two gangs outside New Horizons. After this incident, the teen center, which always has had tight security and used metal detectors, has come to symbolize a safe haven for teens in today's urban war zone.

INFORMATION STARTERS

For more information on sources for grant money, refer to pages 77-78.

★ **ACTION**
 Drug Alliance Program
 806 Connecticut Avenue NW
 Washington, DC 20525
 (202) 634-9759
Supports drug-free environment youth initiatives.

★ **Kettering Foundation**
 100 Commons Road
 Dayton, OH 45459-2777
 (800) 221-3657 (800) 433-4819 in OH
Offers scholarships to teens to attend its Youth Policy Institute in Washington, D.C.

★ **National Clearinghouse for Alcohol and Drug Abuse Information**
 5600 Fishers Lane
 Rockville, MD 20857
 (800) 729-6686 (301) 468-2600 in MD
Refers to organizations and provides a free resource catalog.

★ **National Crime Prevention Council**
 1700 K Street NW
 Second Floor
 Washington, DC 20006
 (202) 466-NCPC

Works closely with the U.S. Department of Justice. The Council provides grant money to groups like the New Horizons Teen Center as part of its "Teens As Resources Against Drugs" program.

★ **National 4-H Council**
7100 Connecticut Avenue
Chevy Chase, MD 20815
(301) 961-2800

Sponsors many youth forums and conferences. Cassie Fuller's local 4-H club served as the community group that helped launch and sponsor the center.

★ **New Horizons Teen Center**
PO Box 2377
Sumter, SC 29151
(803) 773-5561

Welcomes your inquiries about New Horizons and its community programs. Tom Cloer is the center's director.

★ **Office of Juvenile Justice & Delinquency**
U.S. Department of Justice
633 Indiana Avenue NW
Washington, DC 20531
(202) 307-5911

Works closely with numerous youth organizations.

BEYOND BLACK HISTORY MONTH
Student's Proposal
Wakes Up the School Board

One day at Moore High School in Louisville, Kentucky, a light bulb flashed in Detra Warfield's mind and she did something many of us never do. Instead of merely thinking about her idea, this fifteen-year old embarked on a plan to tackle an issue affecting all the schools in her county.

After reading Detra's story you might expect her to hold some elective position in student government or perhaps serve as a youth representative on the school board. However, she describes herself as a normal student who gets lots of B's, but some C's and D's too. Detra proves that many of us have untapped leadership qualities that just need a little encouragement to emerge. The support she received from her family, especially her mother and her aunt, made all the difference in her decision to make a difference.

IN HER OWN WORDS . . .

It was February and Black History Month. My English teacher asked us to do a report on a famous black American who contributed something to America. So, I picked Booker T. Washington and I wrote about him. That was all we did for that month. In all my other classes, I didn't have another assignment about Black History Month.

It made me begin thinking about why we were limited to studying black history during the shortest month of the year. I called my aunt and asked her what I should do. She writes for newspapers and she encourages me to do anything. My aunt said "Just get a petition up first and see how many people agree with you." She told me after passing out the petitions to write a speech and go to the Board of Education.

The next week I got a petition up; I'd never done that before. I just asked people in my school — both blacks and whites — would they like to have a class to learn more about black history? Some of the students wouldn't sign because they thought they would get in trouble. Some asked what it was for, and I told them it was for a good cause. I collected over one hundred names from my school.

Then I asked my friend, Ian Cooley, who is two years younger than me, to get some names from her middle school. We started collecting the signatures in March and by the third week we had collected over three hundred names.

Then I just looked up the Board of Education in the telephone book and called. I asked if I could present a speech about a black history class in the Jefferson County schools and was given a date to come in.

There were about ten school board members. Lots of people from other schools were there for other issues. I was nervous; my leg was shaking. I had practiced at home but I was still nervous. I wrote my speech all on my own but my aunt helped me. She told me to put three questions in my speech and to get a group of black and white students to answer them.

The first question was "Who was the man who raced against a steam-driven machine and won?" The second question was "Who was the woman who freed over two hundred slaves in the underground railroad?" And the third question was "Who was the man who chopped down the cherry tree?" Probably half the students could answer just question three. The other two questions are about African Americans and half the students probably didn't know the answers to those because they are about black history. [Answers: John Henry; Harriet Tubman; George Washington.]

I just presented my ideas that black people have made a lot of contributions in America and some people just don't know about it. I said that a class would teach everybody who wants to know about black history and let them appreciate the African Americans who have done so much.

I was giving my speech and my time ran out. One of the board members — he was the only black member — said "Let her go ahead," and I finished my speech. The Superintendent of Jefferson County Schools said,

"We'll look into this." After the meeting, I had people come up to me saying that it was a great speech.

About two weeks after the speech, a newspaper reporter interviewed me and Ian. The headline was: "Discovering a Heritage: Black History Month Leaves Two Students Wanting, Asking for More."

The one black board member got Montest Eaves, the Assistant Superintendent of Jefferson County Schools, to help me out. I met with Mr. Eaves about a month later. He was interested. It was the first time anybody showed an interest since they had a black history class back in the 1970s. Then Mr. Eaves asked me and my mother to join a committee.

The committee included the Assistant Superintendent and his secretary, teachers, my mom, and this other student and his teacher. This guy, a junior from Manuel High, came to the meetings because he wanted the same thing I did. In the end he asked me and my friend, Ian, to come over to his school to talk about it.

The committee met about every two weeks throughout the summer. My mom and I went to every one of those meetings. We talked about what we wanted for a black history class and what we needed, like books and how teachers would be chosen to teach this year-long class.

That summer the committee and I used the petitions to get students' names and addresses to start up a Saturday Academy. It was a class held every Saturday from 11 a.m. to 2 p.m. for all ages and taught people about African Americans.

By September we got an African-American History class started in four or five schools. I was amazed at how quick it took to get a class in the schools. The class for the 1991-92 school year at Moore is completely full. It's only for juniors and seniors. So far this year we've learned about the geography of Africa, and right now we are reading *Native Son*. We have a white teacher. As long as she can teach history, it's okay with me. The other students in the class said it was all right, too.

I have a dream just like Martin Luther King and I am hoping to keep it alive. I hope that my idea will grow and that eventually the class that includes the contributions of blacks and other people of color won't have to be called Black History. It will be called American History.

PREDICTIONS

When Detra first thought of doing something about Black History Month she had no experience organizing anything and had never held a leadership post. But by diving in head-first, she accomplished her goal and is now the winner of the Young and Teen Peacemakers' First Annual Award. Detra wants "all students — black, white, Asian, Hispanic, all of them — to learn something they don't know about other races so there will be more understanding and there won't be any fighting among people different from each other."

She wonders, "When I grow up, will the class still be there? Will it be bigger and better? Will it be mandatory rather than elective?" The answer is probably 'yes,' judging from the growth of multicultural programs in high schools and colleges across the country. In the meantime, the Jefferson County School administrators are sticking with their commitment to Detra to infuse African-American studies throughout the curriculum for all grades.

Chances are when Detra Warfield is older she'll be at the front of a class. She wants to major in history and become a teacher or a professor. Between now and then, Detra intends to rely on the guidance of her aunt and offers this encouragement: "*Never* give up what you really want to get."

INFORMATION STARTERS

★ **Educational Research Information Clearinghouse on Social Studies**
Indiana University
2805 East Tenth Street
Bloomington, IN 47408-2698
(812) 855-3838
Serves as a central information exchange for social studies teachers.

★ **Jefferson County Public Schools**
   PO Box 34020
   Louisville, KY 40232-4020
   (502) 473-3011
Provides information on its African-American history course.

★ **National Association of State Boards of Education**
   1012 Cameron Street
   Alexandria, VA 22314
   (703) 684-4000
Provides information about policy decisions which local school districts must implement.

★ **National Council for Black Studies**
   Ohio State University
   115-A Independence Hall
   Columbus, OH 43210
   (614) 292-1035
Provides information on African-American black studies.

★ **National Council of Social Studies**
   3501 Newark Street NW
   Washington, DC 20016
   (202) 966-7840
Plays a key role in analyzing and revising curricula.

★ **National School Boards Association**
   Resource Center/Library
   1680 Duke Street
   Alexandria, VA 22314
   (703) 838-6722
Provides information about school board decisions and other education policy across the country.

★ **Young and Teen Peacemakers**
   37 Lebanon Street
   Hamilton, NY 13346
   (315) 824-4332
Concentrates on conflict resolution. Currently there are thirteen chapters across the country. Their national magazine, *Peace On Our Minds*, is published four times a year.

BUMP THE DUMP
How Teens Moved a Mountain

Adults often blame kids for causing many neighborhood problems. In one New England city, however, adults made a mess and it was the kids who got the city to clean it up.

It all started when Catherine Harraghy, who teaches American Government at Bridge Academy, rebelled against using textbooks that were published in 1976 and were nearly as old as her high school students. Using outdated texts was especially frustrating for Ms. Harraghy since motivating her class is a very real challenge. Many of the students need to be encouraged every day to stick it out and get their high school diplomas.

"For most of their lives these kids have been told that they are losers," explains Ms. Harraghy. "Bridge Academy is for students who probably won't make it," says seventeen-year old Lisa Mojica. This public school in Springfield, Massachusetts is an alternative route for youth at risk of dropping out, including pregnant girls and teenage parents as well as minors who've become runaways or had problems with the law and are on probation. Often their only encouragement comes from teachers like Ms. Harraghy.

Back in 1991, a mountain of rubble grew in plain view of Ms. Harraghy's classroom window. To save money, the city of Springfield had stopped its bulk trash pick-ups and a trash heap mounted next to Bridge Academy. The school principal had called city hall and the department of public works about the illegal dumping but her complaint fell on deaf ears. Ms. Harraghy figured this might be a job for her American Government class to take on.

Robbin Kraulter, Lisa Mojica, Adalis Santiago, Miguel Torres, and Zulma Torres (who isn't related to Miguel) are some of the Bridge Academy students who spearheaded this project they called "Bump The Dump."

IN THEIR OWN WORDS . . .

MIGUEL: The dump was a real big pile. It would almost fill up a basketball court. There was no fence; kids could get hurt. There were stoves, cribs and those kinds of things. I think it was more embarrassing to adults. They expect young people to make the mess out here, but the dump was an adult thing.

LISA: The dump was embarrassing. Who wants to go to a school next to a dump? It makes us feel like we're dirty. Central High School is so beautifully clean and the grass is cut.

ZULMA: You'd pass by and the smell would get you sick. There were a lot of cats and dogs. And the number one thing was a lot of kids could get hurt so we decided to do something about it.

LISA: Everyone in the class wrote a letter, then Ms. Harraghy took the best from each letter. My best sentence is the second sentence of the class letter. Then Zulma's was the third, then Robbin's, then Miguel's; everyone was included. It was all bonded together.

[All members of City Council received this letter.]

Dear Councilor:

We are the students of the Bridge Academy government class. The neighbors adjacent to our school are growing a dump instead of flowers. This dump is located on Eastern Avenue. The dump is very dangerous to children in this neighborhood because the yard is not fenced in to keep them out. So if they were playing in the dump, they could get seriously hurt.

Health hazards are also involved with this pile of trash. We are also concerned about rabid animals. Children can also get cut on the sharp objects which can cause an infection. We also enclose in this letter a list of things in the dump.

1. Stove and Washing Machine
2. Bureaus
3. Bed Mattresses
4. Large Wood pieces with nails
5. Chairs
6. Baby Carriage
7. Bike parts
8. Aluminum sidings
9. Car tires
10. Trash

Sincerely,
BRIDGE ACADEMY
Government Class

ROBBIN: At first it was like a class assignment but then we started seeing things happening. People started coming into our school and talking with us about it. I think with all the kids in the class writing letters, they responded to us because of all the letters.

ADALIS: It was more than just writing letters to get a grade. We hoped the letters would do something. At first we didn't think they would even bother to read our letters, but they wrote us back. Then some people came to see the dump, and not even two weeks went by before they had some men working on getting all the trash out.

LISA: There was no one leader. It was all a team effort. Half the class would like draw posters or write letters. Tara has two kids and she graduated last year and she volunteered to do a lot of the typing and doing the letters real right, copying and sending them out. I did some posters and put them up at the school. Everyone had something to do. That's why the project made us feel good.

MIGUEL: Some of the students called city councilmembers. I guess Mr. Foley, our councilman, took an interest because he didn't like what was going on. After we wrote the letters, he came to our school. And then they cleaned up the lot. We wrote him a letter back thanking him. Then he wrote us back saying that the job wasn't done and that they were going to come back to finish hauling away the rest of the trash.

MIGUEL: One of the kids at school called the newspaper. A reporter came and the story she wrote about the mess embarrassed people in the neighborhood.

LISA: The article helped a lot because it went all over Springfield. Some of my friends from other schools called me. Because this is an alternative school, kids at other high schools could say like, "Oh, wow! Bridge did something!"

ZULMA: We had a lot of proof. We had pictures and we described everything that was in there that we saw that could have hurt smaller kids. And the dump could attract lots of druggies and problems could have happened. I live about three blocks away and it's a clean neighborhood.

> **HINTS**
>
> In the case of "Bump The Dump," thank you letters from the class spurred further action. Even a handwritten note thanking your allies will often encourage them to support you further. A few words of appreciation will cause the person to whom you are writing to think, "That's so nice. They don't take me for granted. I should do more to help them!"

LISA: When I saw them working to clean up the dump I felt very proud. [The city sent a crew of six to eight men and it took them an entire week to remove eight separate truckloads of rubbish.]

ROBBIN: I think they paid more attention to us because we were trying to do something for the community. And the people who came to our school to speak with us really listened. It is not usually kids who try to do something like that.

LISA: Mr. Foley came to our class to speak. We all had good ideas on what to do with the dump. Some kids said we should put in a basketball court. Some kids said a playground. I suggested a parking lot for whoever lives there. When we spoke, they listened. Yes, I'm very surprised. It's very nice that someone out there at least listens to us because hardly no one does. I think they listen maybe because they realize that what we're saying is true. And another thing: This is our school and if we make the effort to become proud and to become comfortable going to Bridge, then they should listen and react to what we say and the way we feel.

ZULMA: The group wanted to see how far I would go since I wasn't into school and I especially hated the government class. So they figured maybe if we give her the chance, she might prove herself and go represent the school at a Community Service Roundtable Meeting. So I did! It was the first speech I had ever given. I was very nervous. I went with Ms. Harraghy to the top floor of the Bay Banks Tower and spoke in front of over fifty people. We had city councilors there, the mayor, the superintendent of schools, and there were a lot of business people. I had five minutes. I introduced myself. My speech was on how dangerous the dump was and what we expected to be done. We especially wanted a playground since the school doesn't have a gym. The neighborhood also could have used a playground because there aren't many around. The part I enjoyed most from the project was to see the class united and how we became friends with each other and how it gave us a chance to learn from each other.

MIGUEL: There is no dump next to the school now. Anyone caught putting more trash there would be fined. But it's just wasted property. It would cost too much to put a basketball court in and stuff like that. The budget in Springfield is all messed up and now we have to live with it. The parks and the swimming pools — that's what we mostly do out here in the summertime — are closed.

ADALIS: We'll still try to get a playground or something there. This dump project gave me the opportunity and motivation for speaking up for what I want and not holding back on what I think is best. I believe when you want something in life, you must work hard in order to get it. As a student I feel proud of what we accomplished, and as a teenager, it is good to know that older people will understand and hear your words. It's a great feeling to succeed.

ZULMA: I always say, if you have a lot of pride in yourself and a high self-esteem you can accomplish anything in life that you set your heart on. Some people have bad influences on others and intend to keep them down, but I have learned "Don't give up until you succeed." I'm half Indian and half Hispanic and I also have learned that it doesn't matter what race you come from, you can accomplish what others can.

PREDICTIONS

No playground has been built yet because of the city's budget crisis but these Bridge Academy students seem poised to try and lobby for it when the time is right. Miguel says, "If I want to do something again, I'll write a letter or call them . . . before I didn't even know who to call." Miguel's soft voice, full of confidence, reflects his involvement as one of the youth representatives on a task force to reform the city's public high schools.

Zulma started going to class regularly and justifiably boasts that "I almost had second Honors. I missed it by one mark." Lisa reflects: "When I was doing this project I was very shy. I wouldn't speak to anyone. The experience helped me out with my writing and drawing. I'm not embarrassed anymore to go to Bridge. It was the best thing I ever did."

Even after Adalis, Robbin, and the others graduate, there will be more students who will probably follow in their footsteps to try and get the city to transform this public land in a way that will benefit both Bridge Academy and its neighborhood.

Zulma, who will graduate from Commerce High School in '93, promises, "I'd always go back and help them at Bridge Academy, because I feel like we started this project and that we, as a group, should finish it!"

INFORMATION STARTERS

★ Your local government — the county health department, the department of public works, and the housing commission — can often provide information about who owns a property and what the regulations are regarding upkeep by the property owner, as well as the fines for dumping. In "Bump The Dump," getting the attention of elected officials was vital in getting the city to clean up a mountain of trash. This approach is increasingly necessary because local agencies don't have the money to take care of such "minor" problems as litter.

★ Your local parks and recreation department is a good place to check out what short-term and long-range plans are available for building new playgrounds and other recreational facilities.

★ Your state tourism agency may take an interest in helping you clean up abandoned trash heaps and dump sites when you point out the potential negative impact on tourism posed by these eyesores.

★ The U.S. Environmental Protection Agency regional office should be called in to investigate if you believe a particular dump may be hazardous or toxic (refer to Part IV).

★ America the Beautiful Act, a new federal law, provides matching funds to any youth group for planting trees. Many states have similar incentives. Consider investigating what grant money may be available to you once an area is cleaned up.

YOUNG PEACEMAKERS HEARD IN MOSCOW
International Letter-Writing Campaign Touches World Leader

Heidi Hattenbach of Santa Barbara, California has been putting her idealism to work for well over half her life. She admits matter-of-factly, "I am not waiting to be an adult for anything to happen. I am doing it now."

When she was eleven, her first letter to the editor appeared in the newspaper. Heidi explains, "It was on how people in stores treat kids like we are going to shoplift. So I wrote a letter to the editor telling storekeepers to be nicer to kids."

All through secondary school, environmental issues and political campaigns drew Heidi's attention. After she spent a month in Russia as part of a student summer exchange program, her interest in international affairs grew. Her advocacy work on world hunger began in earnest during her first year at Portland's Reed College, when she learned about the student-led international group called Youth Ending Hunger (YEH).

Her story about the impact of young peacemakers brings to mind an old German legend called "The Naumburg Children's Festival." In the fifteenth century, as the tale goes, General Procop of Bohemia led his armies from one town to the next, killing innocent men, women and children. When Procop surrounded the walled city of Naumburg, surrender seemed unavoidable. However, the townspeople instead plotted to soften the heart of the ruthless general. Singing children paraded to the enemy camp and innocently asked Procop to play with them. The General stared in disbelief, and then smiled. After a day of games and laughter, Procop's army surrendered, realizing that the brave youngsters of Naumburg should not suffer.

In this contemporary version of an old story, the young peacemakers of Youth Ending Hunger did not confront Ethiopian military dictator Mengistu Haile Mariam but challenged his primary weapons-supplier — the Soviet Union — to exercise its influence to end the civil war in Ethiopia.

IN HER OWN WORDS . . .

The Peace in Ethiopia Campaign actually was the brainchild of Eli Cohen, a seven-year old boy in London, England. He had heard about the civil war in Ethiopia and how millions of children were starving to death there. Even if food shipments did get through, the people were kept in a state of chronic hunger because their money, land, and energy went into the war rather than into economic growth. This just didn't make sense to Eli.

Eli wrote a letter to Mikhail Gorbachev, who was then at the height of his power as the leader of the Soviet Union. Eli had decided that since Mr. Gorbachev could bring down the Berlin Wall, he could do anything. He asked Mr. Gorbachev to try to halt the civil war in Ethiopia so the famine could be ended.

Eli's mother suggested he tell his class at school about his letter. Soon, all of his schoolmates wrote letters and somehow the Youth Ending Hunger organization in London heard about it. YEH decided that this letter-writing campaign would be a really great global project for the organization.

I had been introduced to YEH and the issue of hunger when I went away to college. There was a guy named Andrew in my dormitory who wore this shoddy bracelet that said "End Hunger." I didn't understand why this guy, who always dressed so nice and was such a neat person, wore this string bracelet. It turned out he was one of the people who started YEH in the United States. He and other YEH leaders said they weren't going to take their bracelets off until hunger ended.

I had never heard that forty thousand children die every day from hunger. Maybe I had heard it in the news, but I never realized that was *forty thousand children*. The number can seem so unreal that it is really easy to stay out of touch with it. It hit me so deeply. I had nightmares, I cried, I was scared. It just didn't make sense, so I decided to do something about it. I got involved in YEH and we started activities at our college. We now have a large group organized on campus.

GLOBAL LETTER-WRITING CAMPAIGN

Youth Ending Hunger in the U.S. directed the letter-writing campaign more towards President Bush than Mr. Gorbachev. In only a few weeks we collected about six thousand letters and sent them to Bush.

Andrew and I did assemblies in high schools and junior highs around Oregon, talking to hundreds and hundreds of kids about hunger and poverty, and letting them know that they could do something about it. I was surprised that setting up the assemblies was so easy.

During our presentations, we'd show a video about the distinction between chronic hunger and famine. We talked about global and local hunger, including the war and famine that was going on in Ethiopia. We told the schools about the United States' and Russia's involvement in the war as far as sending ammunition, money and other things.

We'd also talk with students about hunger in the United States, and invite people to start a Youth Ending Hunger club in their school, and then see if they wanted to do the letter campaign as their first project. Sometimes we'd have everyone write a letter to President Bush. Some teachers thought that was a really good homework assignment. I think it is a wonderful thing just for people to know they can write a letter to the President and make a difference with it.

Youth Ending Hunger collected about sixty-five thousand letters from all over Europe, from a couple of countries in Africa, the United States, and Canada. Eli Cohen and the other people who worked on the campaign decided that once we had all these letters, there was no way we were just going to mail them to the Soviet Union. We decided to deliver them in person to Mr. Gorbachev, and the campaign formed quickly behind that. Through some contacts that we had in Switzerland, we got a private

airplane donated to fly us from London to Moscow and we also got a meeting with Raisa Gorbachev. Actually we did try to meet with Mr. Gorbachev, but he was out of the country.

One of the neat things about the Ethiopia Campaign was that a lot of the letters were from kids who were just learning to write. They would draw pictures like a gun with an 'X' through it and draw food and say things like "Dear Mr. Gorbachev . . . Please end the war so the kids won't die." The spelling was horrible but it really came from their hearts. I think that type of letter makes so much more of a difference than corporate stationery and pre-printed postcards.

One person was invited from each of the countries that gathered letters and several countries like the United Kingdom and Germany had extra people come. We had a delegation of twenty people representing twelve countries. I was selected to represent the United States because of the work I had done on the campaign, gathering letters to President Bush. I had written a pretty good letter to Bush that a lot of people had read and liked. It was a letter telling him that it wasn't okay with me that forty thousand children were dying from hunger every day and it wasn't okay with me that around five million children stood to die within the next couple of months. I knew he had the power to do something about it. I called on him to take responsibility for the children of the world who need to be taken care of.

When I told my professors at school that I was meeting Raisa Gorbachev and I'd be back in about a week, it was a little bit extraordinary, and a little strange. I go to a rather academically intense college, and you are supposed to be there every day. I don't even know if all of my teachers believed that I was going to Moscow because it came up so fast. Once there was some media about the trip, though, most of my professors were really supportive.

A friend and I raised about $600 to pay for the ticket. I was so surprised at how willing people were to support me. When we told people what I was doing and what my commitment is and what would come out of the trip, people were just incredible about giving money to me. It never took selling — just honesty and asking. There was even a person in the college administration who donated $100 for my trip and I got help from the student travel agency in getting a cheap ticket.

> **HINTS**
>
> Airlines overbook and so do politicians. Expect scheduling snafus with just about any bigwig. Don't be discouraged if a meeting is postponed. The flexibility shown by the Peace in Ethiopia delegation demonstrates that it really pays off to try to accommodate a busy leader's calendar.

I left in March of 1990 and went to London where I was supposed to meet up with the other participants from other countries. Our original meeting was postponed so I waited in London a week and a half, and then the meeting with Mrs. Gorbachev got put off for another two weeks. I couldn't spend that much time away from school, so I flew back to Oregon and took my mid-terms. I returned to London about a week later.

INSIDE THE KREMLIN

Soon we wound up in Moscow for a three-day visit and I can't believe how much we got done. We didn't just meet with Raisa Gorbachev. We were invited to speak during a live television broadcast from a performing arts school we visited. I spoke and was told that my words reached over five million people on Soviet TV. Over one thousand children were in the audience of that show, too.

We also talked to people wherever we went, handing out cards that were printed up in English and Russian describing our mission for peace and the end of hunger. We talked to several large organizations in the Soviet Union and we had meetings with organizers of youth activities to try to get Youth Ending Hunger set up in the Soviet Union. People were so receptive!

We walked into the Kremlin carrying huge stacks of letters. I think Raisa Gorbachev was really in awe that we had collected all these letters. We showed her a few in particular that we especially liked, and some members of our delegation brought presents from their countries to give to her.

I really expected to walk in and have it be a meeting with a distant politician. I expected Mrs. Gorbachev to shake our hands and all the press to take our pictures and then to be quickly ushered out. There was a lot of press there and she did shake our hands but there was so much more. She hugged us and held us and showed us around the Kremlin, her home. She talked about ending hunger by the year 2000.

The internal strife in the USSR was beginning to be a severe problem and Mrs. Gorbachev told us how hard it was to look outward when it was so hard in her own country. She actually invited us back to the Kremlin when hunger is ended.

It was really a wonderful meeting. I know that Mrs. Gorbachev heard our message and took it back to her husband. Maybe the Russians would have pulled out of Ethiopia within the next few months or within the next year anyway, because they could no longer stand it economically. But by giving Mr. Gorbachev our message, we let him know that children around the world care about his actions.

I think our trip opened up new options. People who heard about it know that they can start a small project like collect $5 for UNICEF or a large project that effects the world like meeting with an incredible world leader.

PREDICTIONS

Heidi Hattenbach, who admits to being both naive and cynical, knows the Peace in Ethiopia delegation will not return to the Kremlin any time soon. She remains cautiously optimistic, however, that the Youth Ending Hunger organization she helped set up in Moscow will survive this volatile period in Russian history.

Perhaps the most lasting legacy of Heidi's mission is her sense of connection with a global community, rather than thinking of herself as an American first and foremost. "Now with almost any place that comes on the news, I can associate some project or some person I know of and it makes the rest of the world matter so much more to me."

Heidi's ambitious plans include studying hunger in India for a semester. After she graduates with a degree in international studies, she may go on to law school or explore working at the United Nations or with a non-governmental hunger organization. One of Heidi's fears, she concedes, is growing up, "because I don't want to suddenly become an adult and stop reaching for my dreams like a lot of adults I know."

INFORMATION STARTERS

Additional organizations concerned with international policy are listed in Part IV.

★ **Campaign to End Childhood Hunger**
   Food Research and Action Center
   1875 Connecticut Avenue NW #540
   Washington, DC 20009
   (202) 986-2200 Fax: 202-986-2525
Concentrates primarily on domestic hunger.

★ **CARE**
   660 First Avenue
   New York, NY 10016
   (800) 242-GIVE (212) 686-3110 in NY Fax: (212) 696-4005
Provides food, disaster aid, and health training overseas.

★ **Oxfam America**
   115 Broadway
   Boston, MA 02116
   (617) 482-1211
Promotes self-reliance in food production.

★ **Population Crisis Committee**
   1120 19th Street NW #550
   Washington, DC 20036
   (202) 659-1833 Fax: (202) 293-1795
Encourages those activities that promise to have the greatest impact on reducing world population growth.

★ **RESULTS**

236 Massachusetts Avenue NE

Washington, DC 20002

(202) 543-9340

Supports grassroots campaigns, like the international letter-writing initiative in which Heidi participated.

★ **United Nations' Children's Fund (UNICEF)**

Three United Nations Plaza

New York, NY 10017

(212) 326-7000

Serves as the coordinating hub for the 1995 mid-decade review on the World Summit for Children.

★ **Youth Ending Hunger**

The Hunger Project

1388 Sutter Street

San Francisco, CA 94109-5952

(415) 928-8700 Fax: (415) 928-8799

Operates youth clubs in more than fifty cities. YEH also has an active presence in twenty countries around the world. The group's emphasis is on raising awareness about global hunger.

★ **Zero Population Growth**

1400 16th Street NW #320

Washington, DC 20036

(202) 332-2200 Fax: (202) 332-2302

Works to mobilize public support for a sustainable balance of people, resources, and the environment.

TRACK ME TO FREEDOM
*The Struggle for Equal Education
Continues*

*I think Alabama has one of the worst drop-out rates in the United States. The
tracking system we have is just terrible. Think if you are a twelfth grade
student, but they classified you as a ninth grader. I was taking a ninth grade
English class, tenth grade geometry, eleventh grade biology. Think about peer
pressure. Tell me — would you want to continue to go to school when you
see all your friends graduating and you're down here in the ninth grade
homeroom? You're supposed to be a twelfth grader, but nine times out of ten
it is not your fault.*

— Richard Walker
Kendrick High School '92

*It really bothers me, especially when adults criticize: "Look at that bad child;
how dare they do this; they are just wild." I've even heard teachers call their
students "monkeys." The students are in the lowest Level Three class where
their peers laugh about them being there. The teachers don't care. If you live
with that on a day-to-day basis, to me if you graduate you're doing extremely
well. From what I've seen, most students in Level Three do drop out of
school.*

— Malika Sanders
Selma High School '91

In the winter of 1990, black youth and adults took to the streets in Selma,
Alabama. They demanded an end to the persistent second-class treatment
of African-American students; specifically, to racial tracking in the schools.
Their acts of civil disobedience, so reminiscent of the civil rights movement
of the sixties, were met with police brutality, illegal arrests, and even bomb
threats. The mayor of Selma, Joseph Smitherman, who has been running
City Hall for more than a quarter of a century, tried to undermine this
non-violent movement just as he tried in 1965 to break the spirit of the
voting rights marchers led by Dr. Martin Luther King, Jr.

Two student leaders, Malika Sanders, who now is at Spellman
College, and high school senior Richard Walker, who was fifteen at the
time of the protests, describe a disturbing situation that has changed little

in the past twenty-five years. The school board members still are appointed by the white-majority city council, and legislation that would make these critical policy makers elected by a majority of the voters remains stymied in the Alabama Statehouse.

These young people achieved a small but significant victory and their efforts for equal education continue. As long-time civil rights activist J. L. Chestnut reminds us in *Black in Selma*, "What's wrong with confront-ation? That's how Selma's progressed."

Malika, a junior at Selma High School when the student movement formed, believes she was destined to be an activist because of the influence of both her parents. Hank Sanders is a state senator and a key figure in the New South Coalition, a broad-based civil rights organization. Malika's mother, Rose Sanders, is a prominent civil rights lawyer and leader whose political involvement began three decades ago when she was a student.

Richard, on the other hand, has no roots in political activism. "There would have to be a storm for me to protest!" says Richard who, for the first few months, paid no attention to the student movement in Selma. But when he came to realize how the tracking system shattered his future dreams, his involvement was unstoppable. Even Richard's grandmother could not persuade him to simmer down when the protests moved to city hall.

Malika and Richard predict that the civil rights movement in Selma has many more hard years of work ahead. Their own firsthand accounts provide a chilling perspective on racism in the 1990s. Although these two young activists were interviewed separately, their stories are interwoven.

IN THEIR OWN WORDS . . .

MALIKA: The Best Education Support Team [BEST] got started two years before the young people began to organize themselves into the student movement. BEST had a steering committee that was made up of adults who dealt with the public school system in general and who looked at the tracking system. During that time, BEST began talking with Dr. Roussell, the Superintendent, about the tracking system and got him to make some criteria besides teacher recommendations. Basically you were placed in the tracking system according to what your teacher said. Tests, scores, grades weren't involved. I have a friend who's at Tuskegee University right now, carrying an A average in engineering and the school system tried to put him in Levels Two and Three.

The way some of these young people got out of the lower levels is if their parents had a certain kind of position. I have a friend and her father is a doctor and her mother is a teacher in the public school system. The school administration didn't know that when she was enrolled in Selma High, because she came from Michigan. They automatically put her in Level Three. It wasn't until her mother came down and told them all that her husband was a doctor and she was a teacher that they moved that child [out of the bottom track].

So, BEST was working with the superintendent. Dr. Roussell got the board of education to vote on a plan based on test scores. This outraged many in the white community, and from that moment on we think they started to plot to make sure Dr. Roussell was out. I remember it being extremely emotional. We immediately went to the church to discuss a plan of action and the next day we were on the picket lines with BEST.

BEST started to call for boycotts; for students not to go to school. Then my little sister's friend told me that they had called off the boycott. We thought the adults were just backing down and we became outraged and decided that the young people needed to organize on their own. It was at that point that we decided to have the "Student March for Dreams," which was our first action. We carried a casket and we tied in other problems of the community like drug abuse. Our message was "Don't take away our dreams. Instead, kill racism; eliminate teen pregnancy."

The march was just the beginning of the students making their own agenda and developing some leaders. It wasn't extremely big but it was just enough to let people know that there were young people who were really involved and it kind of took off from there.

When the movement first began with the March for Dreams, I remember Richard was in the crowd saying, "Look at these crazies." He went from not liking me at all, to following me everywhere I go — always being there for me. I tease him about it all the time. At this point he's someone I could ask to do anything for me and he would. It's so funny to me. Once he got involved, his commitment surpassed many people who had been involved for a long time. I'm sure it was very hard for him to adjust.

THE CONSEQUENCES OF PASSING OUT LEAFLETS

MALIKA: One day we were outside of school and we were putting up a tent to give parents leaflets about what was going on in the school system about the tracking system. The literature described what criteria they used to level the young people and what parents could do to make sure that their children didn't fall into a level that would not help them in any way. The first time the police came we just took the tent down. If they asked us, we would take it down and when they left, we would put it back up again. The next time, they didn't ask us. They just came in and took it down. There were some people in the tent, and they just took it down over them. There were a lot of policemen. They had a truck. They started grabbing people. They were saying that having the tent on school property was a problem. My mother [Rose Sanders] was speaking to the students. She wasn't even near the tent but they went after her and handcuffed her. Then they went after Richard. Richard is a big young man and he is very dark and that made him — all throughout the movement — more of a target than a lot of other young people. I have a picture of at least ten policemen trying to get this one fifteen-year old young man down.

RICHARD: I wanted to be put in the same police car with attorney Rose Sanders, so I could be a witness. During another protest when Rose Sanders went to speak with the Mayor about his critical involvement with the school board, police beat her and she spent a week or more in the hospital. So, when the police came and took our tent down, I approached Rose Sanders and about six cops came behind me and picked me up and body-slammed me hard. I fell on a piece of thick Coke bottle glass and I still have a scar.

MALIKA: When I look back at stuff like that I cannot really believe that it happened. Especially being out of Selma now, it just amazes me that I even witnessed that. That was the first time all of us got arrested.

BEYOND HEADLINES

The media, especially photographers and television camera crews, make a local protest visible to the entire community, sometimes even reaching a national audience. In this case, the presence of reporters actually helped protect protestors. Malika Sander explains: "During all this, we had the Selma-to-Montgomery March 25th Anniversary where you were having national leaders come to Selma anyway. Jesse Jackson came and spoke at our school. As long as the media was there the police weren't as brutal. But once the media left Selma after the 25th Anniversary, our personal lives became even more difficult."

THE TAKEOVER

MALIKA: When we called a mass meeting at First Baptist, the church looked like what I would have thought it looked like in the sixties. People were standing up, kids were running around everywhere. It was just packed to capacity.

People would ask, "What are you doing tonight?" I'd answer "Oh, I'm going to the church." It took the place of any social life. That was the place to be. Everybody went to the church to find out the next plan of action.

A group of adults went down to city hall and asked to speak to the mayor. Words were exchanged and something happened where people had been hurt. Once that news got to the school, people who were in support of the movement, just kind of got fed up to the point that it made some of them violent. Two or three fights broke out at school and our school board was very nervous about that and they called off school. The school would resume that Friday. It was a perfect opportunity to take over the school.

We told the BEST steering committee that we were going to march to city hall and have a sit-in there. We figured that some of the students might tell their mothers and fathers. A lot of the kids were worried. As we were lining up, we told everyone that we were going to Selma High and we sent some young men to make sure that they didn't lock the doors 'cause policemen were always following us around. At the end, policemen came in droves. People broke out into a run from this march, some jumped and climbed up the gate, and others were just frantic to get inside the building. This part really reminded me of the civil rights movement of the sixties.

Everyone wanted to make sure this plan worked well. I thought it was just so wonderful because the adults knew nothing about what we were doing. We asked people to bring their sleeping bags and that's all they knew. They thought we were going to city hall. I would have thought more people would have felt like, "You didn't tell us what was going on," but then we explained that we were afraid that our real destination would be leaked.

We have one main building at Selma High. There was an old janitor; he's retired now. We walked in through the doors and the object was to try to figure out how we were going to make sure that the teachers and no one else could get into the school. We thought about how to keep the doors locked. But I think the janitor just locked it for us so we could go out but no one could come in. I really think it was him. It's still a mystery. None of the administration knows how the doors remained locked. They just adore him [the janitor] to death; even the most racist whites adore him. They have no idea that he was the one who made our protest work!

One night turned into another night. We went to some college students who had been involved in actions that had been done before. They went back to their respective schools and brought other college students. By the time they got there that night, they had a system of how they were going to protect us and guard the outside all night long so things just sort of fell into place wonderfully. We didn't plan out each detail, like how we were going to get food, but the community came with grocery bags.

After a while, everyone decided they were staying until some concrete things were done about tracking. Then the board of education replaced Dr. Roussell. We really expected the police to raid the building and take us out. This one man came in and showed us how to resist arrest. People would scream, "Lock Up!" We ran to our positions and locked arms so no one could take us out unless they really got violent and then we knew we would just stop. People thought we would have to use this tactic because we felt they were determined to have school start that Monday.

On Sunday night a lot of people kind of got frantic. The college students began to think about what the consequences of an arrest would be. They might not be able to get their scholarships or their tuition and once they began questioning that, the [high school] seniors began questioning what would happen to them. If we had been expelled, we would have had to go live with relatives in another city. It was a very real possibility.

My mother was one of the people who came in and raised the question to everyone. The reason she did that is she felt a lot of people were saying they didn't care about being expelled. At that moment, our emotions were so mixed up. We were at the point where we weren't leaving, come explosion or anything. Many of the people who were involved were not people who grew up with this [sit-ins and other acts of civil disobedience]. To make sure they had thought about the consequences, we ended up doing some talking about it and taking a vote.

Right before the vote, Dr. Roussell came in and said he was leaving the school system even before his contract ended and a lot of students reacted, "Why, why?" He said, "The school board has told me that either I have to expel you or I have to leave." And he said, "You have been so committed that I know I cannot expel you; so I'm just leaving."

Many of the young people could not fully understand the problems of the tracking system, but they could clearly see the injustice that was being done to Dr. Roussell. So that's what they grabbed on to. For many of them that became their reason for being there. Those of us who understood the tracking issue and what it was doing to black people in Selma and to our people as a whole, were torn. I think the reason we ended up leaving was that many of the young people were there because of Dr. Roussell.

The majority of the people voted to leave but it was really dramatic because even as they voted, people were crying about not really wanting to leave. In a situation like that we bonded with each other and became brothers and sisters and it was really hard to leave. We have pictures of us coming out of the building, everybody in tears.

We truly felt a bonding that had become so powerful that even our adult leaders could not understand. There was a sense of commitment to our struggle . . . a new sense of who we were as African-American youth.

CITY HALL

MALIKA: The adults were in city hall the same time we were at school during the takeover. They stayed in city hall. It seemed like forever.

RICHARD: I mixed in mainly with the adults at the city hall. We were members of the Best Education Support Team [BEST]. We were at city hall to let them know we wanted tracking ended and that we knew that the mayor was controlling the school board as well as the schools because he had the power. We weren't going to take it any more and we demanded justice.

I stayed in city hall several days at a time before I'd go home. Night and day, night and day. We had tents outside. The sit-in lasted a month and two-and-a-half weeks. During the whole time, we probably had three to four thousand teenagers and adults.

We had people come from Washington, Vermont, New Orleans, and California. We had some whites in Selma backing us — the nuns. When we were at city hall they came down to pray for us.

During the day we would go around the building singing our chants. They sent down a court order saying we had to leave city hall or we'd have to go to jail. A few of us decided we weren't going to listen to this. That's when they tried to charge me as an adult and sentenced me to five days in jail. I am talking about jail — *jail.*

They were going to lock us in. Then BEST realized I was a student and told me, "You go to school so we can help you learn." I slipped in the lockup anyway.

I was the only one in my family involved. They were trying to persuade me not to participate, saying that the best thing was to step down for a while. I had to let my family know that I didn't disrespect them, but I had to go ahead. If I don't stand up for my rights, then no one else will. So I told my grandmother that I loved her and respected her and I didn't want to hurt her but I felt it was my duty to go out and help myself. She sort of went along with it and she started reading stuff about tracking and she found out there was really something to this movement.

MALIKA: When we went out to picket in front of city hall, mostly it was adults. But some days it would be nothing but young people and the number of policemen dramatically changed. If it was just the adults picketing, there would be one or two police but if it was young people, it seemed like most of the police force was driving around or sitting near us. By seeming so much afraid of the youth they gave us power and fed our drive.

RICHARD: People were scared to give support. So we decided to tell people: Don't be scared; if you support us just honk your horn for equal education when you pass by city hall. People started honking their horns, and the police started pulling them over and giving them tickets and then it went so far that they arrested people for blowing their horns. We went back to court and the judge said to me that if I holler "Honk Your Horn For Equal Education" again that I would be given up to five days in jail for each time I said it.

They thought I was a major figure in the movement. They had five or ten different charges against me. I was sixteen at the time but I was being charged as an adult. The judge was saying, "I'm in power here, and the Constitution states that when a judge is in power, whatever he rules, goes." Our lawyers said "You have to treat him as a minor." All the charges got dropped.

When everything else failed, we decided that we had to negotiate with the powers-that-be. The city broke negotiations with BEST and we had to go back to the drawing board. The majority of Selma's population and the Selma public school system is black so we wanted majority representation on the school board.

We finally came up with a rotating school board. Every six months, blacks are in the majority and then the whites are the majority for the next six months. When the school board rotates, the white school board cannot overrule anything that the black board members ruled on.

Even though we got the school board to agree to a rotating system, Selma still has some of the same basic problems. We are trying to figure out another way to go about solving these problems other than starting up another movement.

MALIKA: I think what I would do in Selma, if I could, is to have a mass education project because I think if people had been more educated about the issues before the movement started, it would have helped so much. A lot of people stayed at home and remained complacent because they were ignorant of the issues. Yes, they heard about it on the news or in the newspapers, but many people didn't get the facts.

Even though I think it was an achievement to have a majority black school board, many other things need to happen. There is still an unelected school board whose allegiance is to the mayor and the city council, not to the people of Selma.

RICHARD: One thing that I've learned is getting angry ain't going to do but one thing and that's get you or someone else hurt. You've got to learn to deal with the problem. We are headed in a better direction when we can deal with the racism which revolves around tracking. We still have whites in Selma saying, "Well, at least you have freedom," but you can't call it freedom if you aren't free to grow. There's a huge amount of racism in Selma.

PREDICTIONS

Progress in Selma is slow. "We had our first Black History Month program in the history of the school but students are still not allowed to wear a shirt with Martin Luther King or any other symbol of black pride," reports Malika.

The core organization of black parents, BEST, continues to try to work with the school board but more confrontation and civil disobedience seem inevitable in this southern city. Cries for justice by African Americans still ring out. The rap from "Track Me To Freedom," a musical written by Rose Sanders, says it all:

> *Track me to excel, don't track me to fail;*
> *Track me to hope, don't track me to dope;*
> *Track me to work, don't track me to crime,*
> *Track me to fame, don't track me to gangs;*
> *So let me hear the freedom bells ring.*

Richard Walker and Malika Sanders, who you might expect would be battle-weary, continue to reflect on the movement and consider how they can contribute in the future.

Richard is an active volunteer with 21st Century Youth Leadership Training Project, a national multicultural organization founded by Rose Sanders, where the main mission is to build confidence and promote community involvement and an entrepreneurial spirit in the next generation. Following the Selma protests, Richard moved to Georgia to live with his father and complete his senior year there. Richard's future plans include majoring in history and then perhaps going to law school.

Malika, who expected to pursue a career as a lawyer, now plans to major in education. She dreams of a school system that "challenges the minds of students and teaches Americans how to think, rather than what to think."

INFORMATION STARTERS

Other organizations that concentrate on racism are listed in "Issues A to Z" in Part IV.

★ **Center for Youth Development and Policy Research**
   Academy for Educational Development
   1255 23rd Street NW
   Washington, DC 20037
   (202) 862-1842
Disseminates information on exemplary youth programs and policies, with a special focus on minorities and the poor.

★ **Education Research Information Clearinghouse [ERIC]**
   U.S. Department of Education
   555 New Jersey Avenue NW #300
   Washington, DC 20208-5641
   (800) USE-ERIC (202) 626-9854 in DC
Provides information on tracking as well as many other educational issues and can refer you to other ERIC centers.

★ **Massachusetts Advocacy Center**
    76 Summer Street
    Boston, MA 02110
    (617) 357-8431
Studies tracking and alternatives.

★ **National Association for the Advancement of Colored People**
    NAACP Youth Division
    4805 Mount Hope Drive
    Baltimore, MD 21215-3297
    (301) 358-8900
The NAACP was involved with the landmark 1954 *Brown v. Board of Education* case when the Supreme Court ruled that segregated public schools violated the equal protection clause of the 14th Amendment to the U.S. Constitution.

★ **National Black Youth Leadership Council**
    250 West 54th Street #800
    New York, NY 10019
    (212) 541-7600
Promotes minority student leadership and works to reduce the number of minority students who do not graduate from high school. The Council provides information on problems of bigotry and racism.

★ **National Coalition of Education Activists**
    PO Box 405
    Rosedale, NY 12472
    (914) 658-8115
Focuses on how the long history of racism, class, and gender discrimination has undermined our educational system.

★ **National School Boards Association**
    Resource Center/Library
    1680 Duke Street
    Alexandria, VA 22314
    (703) 838-6722
Provides information about policy decisions of school boards in neighboring counties or states, which may provide you with useful information when trying to get your own school board to consider specific educational reforms.

★ 21st Century Youth Leadership Training Project
PO Box 2516
Selma, AL 36702
(205) 874-0065

Sponsors many conferences, leadership training sessions, and summer camps, all aimed at developing young leaders. This multicultural organization has chapters in thirteen states including Louisiana, Mississippi, New Jersey, New York, Pennsylvania, and Washington, D.C.

PART III:

IN THEIR OWN WORDS
Getting A Law On The Books

IN THEIR OWN WORDS
Getting A Law on The Books

Our answer is the world's hope; it is to rely on youth. The cruelties and obstacles of this swiftly changing planet will not yield to obsolete dogmas and outworn slogans. It cannot be moved by those who cling to a present which is already dying, who prefer the illusion of security to the excitement of danger. It demands the qualities of youth: not a time of life but a state of mind, a temper of the will, a quality of imagination, a predominance of courage over timidity, of the appetite for adventure over the love of ease.
— Senator Robert F. Kennedy
Speech at University of Capetown, South Africa 1966

Most Americans assume that the business of crafting new laws is confined to legislators, lobbyists, and the experts. For the most part, that's true. It is rare for ordinary citizens to participate in such policy making. It is even more extraordinary when young people are the catalysts for getting a law on the books.

These citizens, who lack political clout because they are not yet old enough to vote, enjoy special leverage. At first it is their honesty that stuns decision makers. When lawmakers begin to listen to the proposals of these teenagers, they are jolted with the realization that these Americans — unlike the usual influence-peddlers or hired guns seen in the halls of the legislature — are beholden to no one. It is apparent that these young leaders are gripped with a sense that this is a critical point in their lives when they should be working for change.

It obviously takes more than naive idealism to produce laws. Any proposal must withstand an enormous amount of criticism, and in every one of these oral histories, young activists meet with opposition. They also express how it feels when politicians ignore or intimidate them. They relive those bruising moments in their campaigns when they felt discouraged or questioned their own positions. When faced with out-and-out defeat, they only become more determined to try harder.

The perseverance of these young activists is a powerful signal to lawmakers that they aren't kidding around. It takes many trips to the statehouse, often testifying more than once, to begin to sway public opinion and a politician's vote. An ongoing publicity campaign is critical to keep a legislative initiative from being pushed to the back burner. Many months or even years may pass before legislative decisions are made.

The real message which runs through these success stories is that everyone can have an impact in the political arena, even when it sometimes seems as if government is a private club that's closed to the general public. These young activists have paid their dues, learned how to win, and expect to do it again!

I THOUGHT YOU SAID THIS WAS *FAST* FOOD.

OUTLAWING STEEL ANIMAL TRAPS
Five Teens
Sway the Statehouse

Animal trapping is still a way of life in many parts of America. Some proponents argue that steel traps are necessary to stop the overpopulation of raccoons, foxes and other wild animals.

Spring-loaded steel jaw traps, often called leg-hold traps, snap down on an animal's leg. The even more gruesome snare traps catch animals by the neck with a piece of steel wire, and usually kills them instantly. Steel-jaw traps are outlawed in New Jersey and only a few other states. At last count sixteen states prohibit snare traps and eight other states have enacted partial bans.

A group of students at the Severn School in Annapolis, Maryland became convinced that a more humane trapping device, the box trap, should be the only trap permitted in the state. Bridget Berger, Dabney Boye, Amy Hackman, Sarah Long, and their leader, Jessica Early, took their concerns to the State Capitol building, which is located just a stone's throw away from their school. These five friends entered the Statehouse as untested thirteen-year old students and left as successful lobbyists.

IN THEIR OWN WORDS . . .

JESSICA: What happened was I saw an ad in the newspaper with a picture of a cat with its leg in a steel jaw trap. I believe it was printed by the SPCA — Society for the Prevention of Cruelty to Animals. I saw Delegate Marsha Perry's name on the ad. She is with the Maryland General Assembly.

I thought about it all night long. Leg-hold traps have teeth. They are made of steel. When an animal gets caught in one, it cannot free itself. It usually ends up biting or gnawing its legs or whatever is caught in the trap, to free itself.

I had been an animal rights activist before that. I am a vegetarian. I don't buy leather. I just feel very strongly about animal rights. When I saw that ad, it was such a sad picture that I had to do something.

So what I did was put together a folder of sheets of paper and wrote a little paragraph about banning traps on the first page. The next day I brought it to school and I got almost everyone in the middle school to sign it — about 155 students.

Then I just sent the petition to Marsha Perry and told her I was from Severn School. I really had no idea how to get a bill passed. I didn't go to my parents because I knew I would get a three-hour lecture. My parents think I go a little overboard sometimes, especially because of my vegetarianism and my refusal to buy leather. My parents thought it was a stage I was going through, but it is something that I will believe in forever.

I think Marsha Perry called Severn School and asked to talk with someone in reference to the petition I sent to her. They put Mr. Hoage on the phone because he was in charge of the Key Club and the Environment Club. Later that day he came up to me and said he'd like to see me after school. I didn't know him because he taught in the upper school and so I was a little worried. After school he showed me a letter from Delegate Perry. She had already been working on the legislation [to extend the Maryland law banning traps to their county which is adjacent to the Chesapeake Bay and other ecological resources].

After I talked with Ms. Perry, she told me about some of the counties in the state that already did ban the traps, about some that didn't, and about some that they were trying to work on. Ms. Perry wanted me to go before the committee and speak about the traps. If I had gone by myself, I would have been so nervous. I couldn't have done it by myself because I had no idea what it would be like or how many people were going to be there. So I first asked Amy, Dabney, and Sarah if they would help me. Then we realized Bridget had had a dog that had been killed by one of these traps.

SARAH: Jessica and I have been friends for a long time and I knew she stood by all this stuff. When she asked me, I was really willing to get involved and also I really love animals. So I was happy to help her out.

DABNEY: I've always loved animals, even though I am not a vegetarian. I was willing to do anything. I wasn't sure if the petition was going to make a difference, but I was willing to help.

AMY: I had seen the petition and Jessica asked all of us if we wanted to do something with this. She explained about how the traps were still legal and still being sold. I remembered Bridget and how her dog died in a trap.

BRIDGET: I cannot remember how old I was, but my brother came up from the woods and he was holding something and I wasn't quite sure what it was. He was crying. My mom told me and my sister to go to my room and later she told me our dog, Mandy, was dead. My brother told me he had found her on the ice on the pond with a trap around her neck. After that, my dad called our neighbor and told him to get the traps out of there. Even though the neighbor said he had gotten all the traps out, my dad went back into the woods and collected another twenty-five traps.

HINTS

MAKE EACH MINUTE COUNT!

When you speak before a legislative committee, each witness is usually limited to two or three minutes. At this hearing, the five girls delivered concise speeches. Jessica gave the opening plea supporting the trap bill, which lasted about a minute. Dabney completed the second half of the speech. Sarah and Amy split their two-minute speech which zeroed in on the "killer amendment" that would have made the ban useless. They didn't mince words: "We are against elected officials getting credit in an election year for passing what looks like an animal rights bill but really isn't." Once they had the senators' attention, Bridget concluded with her account of how her dog died.

JESSICA: I wrote the speech for Dabney and me. Mr. Hoage helped us by putting it into more complex words. He had many ideas and we all talked about them together. We didn't really know all of the details. I think Delegate Perry told Mr. Hoage about the amendment that five senators supported that would allow people to own and sell traps but not use them. [The justification for this "killer" amendment was to give individuals an opportunity to sell their traps to people in rural counties where this law would not apply. The girls suggested an amendment to this amendment allowing owners only one year to get rid of their traps.]

SARAH: When we first got in, there were five women talking in front of us and saying "These girls are just doing this to get out of school." That was before we spoke.

DABNEY: Marsha Perry spoke before we did and introduced us. We were really nervous. The only other people testifying were a hunter and an old lady who had lost several cats to these traps.

JESSICA: When I first got to the podium I was so nervous. I looked at all of the senators and they were whispering to each other and grinning, which was very intimidating. But once we started they *really* tuned in.

BRIDGET: After I spoke I was fine but then a hunter testified. He wore khaki pants and a shirt and was very mean. He started saying, "I believe this little girl but there is no way her dog could have died that way." As the hunter was talking, I was crying. My dog didn't die right away. When the snare grabbed Mandy's neck it didn't hit the places where she would have died instantly so she suffered all through the night.

The women in front of us who had said "These girls are here just to get out of school" were trying to comfort me. Mr. Hoage was trying to comfort me. All the reporters were looking at me and they got the idea that what the hunter was saying was very upsetting.

AMY: The hunter also talked about how we wear leather shoes rather than canvas. But I think all of the senators thought that what we were saying was true.

SARAH: Plus the fact that we were *so young* made a big difference to them. Wow! If people this young realize what is going on, these traps *must* be a problem.

JESSICA: I had my doubts that we would win. Even though the hunter's speech wasn't very convincing, we wondered if the senators really believed him. He brought in a plastic snare trap and put it right on his arm and pulled it off to show that there was no pain. We weren't sure if the senators had really seen a snare trap and whether they believed that was what it would look and feel like. The traps are made of steel, not plastic. He spoke after we did so we didn't have a chance to make any comments about what he said.

AMY: I remember Sarah and I handed out copies of our testimony to reporters. At first they didn't even look at it. Afterwards, they asked us a lot of questions. It was Mr. Hoage's idea to have enough copies of the speeches for the newspapers.

SARAH: I remember after we came back from the Statehouse, all of us were saying "I want to do that again!"

JESSICA: The next day there was a newspaper article. That's when we found out that the vote was unanimous. The first thing I did was call Bridget because her story affected me the most. I said, "We won! We won!" I left a message with most of the girls' parents just saying, "Tell her we won!"

BRIDGET: Everyone said, "Oh you must be so proud. I cannot believe you did this." The article was posted up on the bulletin board in school. Our names were underlined but I wasn't mentioned in the newspaper. [Bridget probably did not get her name in the story because she spoke extemporaneously; since reporters had received copies of the written speeches, they only had the full names of the other girls to include in the article.]

JESSICA: I remember some of the boys were making fun of us before we went to the Statehouse but they were *amazed* when we won.

HINTS

Make sure to make copies of your speech! Pass out a copy of your statement to every committee member and if a legislator is absent, leave a copy in front of his or her nameplate. Don't wait for reporters to ask you for a copy; hand your statement out before it is your turn to testify. Reporters are easy to spot because they often sit at a designated "Press" table and use steno pads to take notes.

Distributing copies increases the chance that your speech will get the attention it deserves, especially by those lawmakers or reporters who might arrive after you have spoken.

AMY: It made me feel that we can make a difference even though we are young. We were just five girls and we realized that just a few people can make a difference.

DABNEY: It seemed so easy. Anybody could do it, so if anybody could do it, then why aren't people doing it? If five eighth graders can do it, anyone can. If we had not been as young as we were, maybe they would have ignored us. If someone feels strongly about something, nothing can get in the way of acting on a concern and making a difference.

BRIDGET: After doing that, I think that we could go back and do anything. We did it when we were only thirteen years old. My brother wishes he had done this himself after Mandy died. I think more kids need to start going out and doing more things for animals.

PREDICTIONS

This new law went into effect July 1992. In the words of the students' faculty advisor, Jim Hoage, "The people in Anne Arundel County who care about animals owe a debt to five Severn eighth graders. Without their lobbying effort, there would have been no time limit at all on possessing and selling the cruel traps. And the law, for that reason, would have become a dead-letter. It would appear to work but really would not."

These animal rights activists seem to have changed the attitude of some of their peers. Boys who used to tell stories about feeding Alka-Seltzer to sea gulls and watching the birds blow up have stopped. Jokes about vegetarians have ceased, too. Sarah remembers how supportive many of her classmates were after their victory at the General Assembly.

Jessica Early has her eye on another project: "Before I graduate I am hoping to combat cosmetic research on animals. It is wrong and unnecessary!" Dabney chimes in, "Animals don't need to be dying for mascara. If animals need to die, let it be for the curing of diseases, not for testing facial products!" A new animal rights campaign will no doubt be underway before these sophomores move on to college.

INFORMATION STARTERS

First, to learn about existing laws and regulations, contact the local animal control agency or the state department of natural resources. Each of the animal welfare organizations listed below has a unique perspective and philosophy about animal rights.

★ **American Society for the Prevention of Cruelty to Animals**
   441 East 92nd Street
   New York, NY 10128
   (212) 876-7700   Fax: (212) 348-3031
Monitors pending legislation.

★ **Animal Welfare Information Center**
   National Agricultural Library
   Room 304
   Beltsville, MD 20705
   (301) 344-3704
Provides information about the federal government's responsibility for animal protection.

★ **Animal Welfare Institute**
   PO Box 3650
   Washington, DC 20007
   (202) 337-2333
Tracks legislation and also provides information on box traps, leg-hold, and cable-coated snare traps and other alternative trapping devices.

★ **Fish and Wildlife Service**
   U.S. Department of Interior
   4401 North Fairfax Drive
   Arlington VA 22203
   (703) 343-5333
Enforces federal rules and regulations on trapping.

★ **Fur Takers of America**
Route 3, Box 211A1
Aurora, IN 47001
(812) 926-1049

Seeks to educate trappers in humane methods of trapping and conservation ethics.

★ **Humane Society of U.S.**
2100 L Street NW
Washington, DC 20037
(202) 452-1100

Provides information on the status of legislation nationwide. The Humane Society's Youth Education Division, 67 Salem Road, East Haddam, CT 06423-0362 (203) 434-8666, offers a free copy of "HSUS Student Action Guide."

★ **National Trappers Association**
PO Box 3667
Bloomington, IL 61702
(309) 829-2422

Provides the perspective of "harvesters of furbearers."

★ **People for the Ethical Treatment of Animals**
PO Box 42516
Washington, DC 20015
(301) 770-7444

Embraces perhaps the most radical animal rights view, opposing all forms of animal abuse and experimentation.

SMOKE-FREE GENERATION
*A Two-Year Campaign
That Refused
To Be Snuffed Out*

About an hour outside of Boston in the town of Sandwich, nearly thirty students launched what turned out to be a two-year campaign of lobbying Massachusetts lawmakers. Eventually these determined teenagers transformed their idea for tobacco-free public schools into law by overcoming opposition and many setbacks. Since this statute was enacted in 1987, many other states have adopted similar laws.

Now in their final year of high school, seven seniors reminisced about the campaign they conducted four years earlier, but which still ranks as a milestone for each of them. One night after school, Jeff Curry, Cindy DeNaples, Amanda Helfen, Aaron Hobart, Jenn Pistone, Ryan Tedeschi, and Lynn Terrill sat around eating pizza and sharing memories.

INITIAL SPARK

William Sangster, a health education teacher at Sandwich Junior/Senior High School, was the spark that ignited this campaign. He kept the flame burning for two years. The previous year, Mr. Sangster's class was the driving force behind a new state law which increased fines levied on merchants for selling cigarettes and chewing tobacco to kids under eighteen.

Impressed by the accomplishment of their older classmates, dozens of seventh graders wanted to do more than just take a field trip to the state capitol. They formed a group called Sandwich Students Against Smoking and started meeting after school with Mr. Sangster.

Their idea was to ban smoking on public school grounds throughout Massachusetts as a way to discourage younger students from taking up the habit. State Representative Peter Morin, who had been the sponsor of the law restricting over-the-counter tobacco sales to minors, introduced the smoke-free schools legislation. State Senator Paul Doane agreed to shepherd the bill through the Senate. Here's how it all began.

IN THEIR OWN WORDS . . .

JEFF: Mr. Sangster always emphasized that smoking is a privilege, not a right. What gives you the right to make someone else inhale your smoke if it hurts someone else's health? It is not a constitutional right. We were not trying to stop people who were already smoking but we were trying to keep people from starting. My father had quadruple bypass heart surgery two times. He used to smoke a lot. That was part of the reason I got involved. It wasn't something we had to do but something we wanted to do.

RYAN: My grandmother was a heavy smoker so I kind of wanted to get involved to learn more about it. Also, when we were in sixth grade, the older kids were working on the bill and it looked exciting going to Boston and I wanted to be on TV. That was half the reason, but once I got involved I really got involved in the issues at hand. I didn't expect I'd get into it as much as I did. Some of the questions were tough. Obviously, kids who are smoking at sixteen or seventeen aren't going to easily quit, but we wanted to stop smoking on school grounds so by the time kids who now are three or four get to be our age they won't smoke.

JENN: People would ask us, "Why get rid of the smoking area if there is smoking in the bathrooms and stuff?" We thought if you cannot buy cigarettes until you are eighteen, how can you allow smoking in the schools? It was totally contradictory.

[Early on in the campaign, students picked their "area of expertise," which meant letter-writing, speech-making, interviews with the media, lobbying, or working behind-the-scenes. The meetings were brainstorming sessions.]

JEFF: Mr. Sangster would throw out an idea and we would all bring up our own ideas and end up changing it completely. For instance, he would give us an idea of writing a letter to a sports player and then he would suggest what information we could put down — basic facts and figures such as numbers of deaths from cigarettes, and we'd get pretty creative.

JENN: We divided the House of Representatives into who Mr. Sangster thought would oppose us, who was kind of in the middle, and who would definitely support us. Then we went forward writing certain types of letters to certain types of representatives.

AARON: It wasn't a form letter. Each letter that we wrote was different, and in our own handwriting.

LYNN: The letter writing was a stressful time. We needed a boost in confidence, which came when we finally got feedback from the legislators. This was only the beginning of a long road, and we were unaware of how hard and how difficult it would be.

RYAN: It wasn't all work. Mr. Sangster made it fun for us, too. We got together after school and the meetings were attended by a bunch of kids that we all knew.

AMANDA: I think we had a good combination. I mean there were go-getters like Lynn Terrill and Lori Beth Lind and they were the ones that could snag legislators. Then we had the effective writers. Those thirty people really blended. We've been told that we are a very special class and we are unique. But every class has its unity that it can build on. And if you catch those kids at the right time, then *every class* might be able to. A lot of kids let it slip by or they don't have the oomph to go out and try to do something.

TESTIFYING . . . ROUND ONE

Once the committee scheduled hearings on Rep. Morin's bill, the students, who were twelve years old at the time, prepared for center stage.

A favorite was Mr. Sangster's anti-anxiety technique:

> *I told them that they were going to be uncomfortable, and to wear loafers or shoes they could take on and off. When you're up there and get nervous, you take your loafers off. Rub the bottom of your feet, and before you put your shoes back on, switch them around and put them on the wrong feet. Then say to yourself, you've got to turn them around. Then you won't feel nervous anymore.*

AMANDA: Besides a crash course in lobbying, we knew all our statistics; what the tar in cigarettes would do to you. We knew all the definitions — we knew what we were talking about. We had been discussing it in class and we'd stay after school and have meetings.

RYAN: All the hard questions we got asked, Mr. Sangster went over. He covered everything with us, often on the bus ride to Boston. If we weren't sure about a question, Mr. Sangster would suggest how to answer it the way a politician does.

AMANDA: I don't think Mr. Sangster would have let anyone testify who didn't know what they were doing. I don't think he would have put anyone there who would have felt threatened. I remember when I was speaking and someone got up and left, I didn't blurt out "Hey, where are you going?" but I knew enough to give him the eye. You learn about double talk and whom to look at and whom not to look at, not to speak quickly, and to emphasize what you really want.

JENN: Mr. Sangster would say, "Expect this, expect that." It helped us as seventh and eighth graders to deal with the rudeness. When you are actually talking to the committee members and they are talking to the person next to them, you learn just to keep going by speaking louder and keeping their attention.

LYNN: For example, in my statement I testified about the white shoe analogy: "Think a moment about a brand new pair of white shoes a young kid would get. Think of those shoes as your lungs. Every day the shoes get a tiny speck of dirt on them. After a while they will get worn and torn. Think of a ten-year old kid with clear lungs. If he or she smokes, they are contaminating themselves a little bit each day just like the shoe. There is only one problem: the shoe can be replaced but what about the ten year old kid?"

More hard-hitting testimony was offered. April Swartz, a soft-spoken member of the Students Against Smoking, challenged committee members with this argument: "If someone came to you asking to stop teen suicide, everyone would be in favor of that idea. Our bill is the first step in slowing down a form of teen suicide. We need your help. Vote in favor of our bill for the children of tomorrow." Such moral reasoning, however, lost out to the arguments posed by those opposing the smoke-free school legislation.

OPPOSITION WHERE YOU LEAST EXPECT IT

The powerful tobacco industry was able to watch this battle from the sidelines because opposition surfaced from unexpected quarters. Although the Massachusetts Department of Public Health supported the legislation, the Massachusetts Department of Education argued that local school boards should decide such policies. Student governments across the state took the position that it was unfair to deny students eighteen years of age the right to smoke and at the same time allow the school faculty to smoke. Perhaps the most significant roadblock was the committee chairman in the House.

Mr. Sangster remembers talking with the kids after school the day he found out their bill was never going to get past the Committee Chairman, who insisted that the legislation prohibit faculty as well as students from smoking on school grounds. The Massachusetts Federation of Teachers had made it clear that such an amendment infringed on the rights of teachers as adults in the workplace and they would lobby strenuously against it. The students' reaction to defeat was amazing.

JEFF: We got defeated but I think it was better for us. In a way we would have been happy if our bill hadn't died but it gave us more of a sense of the real world. I didn't look at it like a soccer game; I didn't think it was a loss. I felt maybe it was the wrong time and maybe if we worked harder that they might pass it. It wasn't the end of the world.

JENN: It was all part of the entire experience — just realizing not everyone was going to be for us. It really helped to set our minds as far as what we were actually going to have to do, all the convincing and selling we were going to have to do in order to get our point across in order to win. This was our community and we wanted everyone to know that we were here and we wanted to be heard. We knew what politics was about. We wanted to be understood. It strengthened our resolve.

RYAN: After the black period we just gave up after awhile. During the summer I remember we were at a baseball game and this reporter caught us off guard. It wasn't like an interview where she called to talk with us. Her article in the newspaper was about how we were frustrated with the smoking campaign.

AARON: It was basically local gossip and the reporter from *Broadsider* misquoted us to make it sound like we were wasting our time and we were bunch of little kids trying to do something that we knew couldn't be done. We were really mad.

LYNN: It was a ploy to divide us even further. For a while I guess it seemed to do just that. That summer, I got the letter from Channel 4 saying they decided they wanted to have us on. I remember saying "Mom, Mom, Mom, We're going to be on TV!" I had tried many times to get in touch with Channel 4's *People Are Talking*, a big daytime show in the Boston area like *Oprah Winfrey*. It's on right before the soaps. It had been a year and a half since Channel 4 had been in touch with us and we finally had somewhere to start again. I called Mr. Sangster at his home.

CINDY: I remember Mr. Sangster coming up to us and just making sure we wanted to do it. He was really excited and wanted to know who he still had with him and then we just started work all over again.

Mr. Sangster recalls, "It was a very, very long summer. I don't know what spark it was. It might have been the reporter talking to the kids or the call from the TV station, but whatever, it was kid-motivated. It wasn't me. About eight of them came in after school and said: "Mr Sangster, we really want to keep going on it. Can we re-file that bill?" I said, "I'll go home and write one tonight and you guys take a look at it. If you want to re-file, you call Representative Morin and you ask him if he will re-file it." Mr. Sangster told the group, "We learned a lesson in life. We've got to give them what they want."

THE COMEBACK

The students' new proposal, sponsored again by Representative Morin, a Republican, included teachers and met the objections of the committee chairman. Mr. Sangster remembers how these eighth graders rehearsed for the second round before the House committee. In a classroom, each of the students got comfortable sitting in front of a microphone and Mr. Sangster grilled them.

During the hearing, Representative Paleologos, the committee chairman, questioned the students repeatedly about why they now favored including teachers in the tobacco-free school legislation. The students knew they had to compromise and told him so: "Our whole campaign has been for kids. We don't want kids to smoke at school. Your problem is with the adults. If you want to put teachers back in the bill go ahead."

JEFF: I didn't feel that the committee was trying to trip us up but they were seeing if we were really knowledgeable. They wanted to see if we really believed in what we were doing and I think we did real well. I think what really got their attention was our persistence. We wouldn't take 'no' for an answer. But Representative Paleologos really tried to intimidate us by asking us questions.

LYNN: It was amazing how we all reacted because it was obvious that we felt deeply; otherwise we would not have gone against such tough opposition. I must say, that day every one of us grew up a little.

JENN: A lot of teachers at our school smoked and they didn't enjoy the fact that we kids were trying to prevent them from smoking in their school. But they did appreciate what we were doing and that we had the guts to do something like that. Mr. Sangster was so proud of us and had so much confidence in us, and that really helped us to deal with obstacles.

AARON: Being attacked by people you know is a lot worse than being attacked by politicians. We had opposition by our own community, our friends' parents and our friends' older brothers and sisters. Once you get past that, it doesn't faze you as much. We got totally shutdown and we came back to the Statehouse knowing exactly what we did wrong and we were 100% more efficient. What sticks out in my mind, and still does, is the testifying that we did. We were little kids. Our age was probably a factor against us but we still went up and we said what was on our minds without thinking about how other people were going to react to it.

AMANDA: I remember a comment from one of the women legislators after I was done testifying. She was really impressed that a girl was testifying and talked about the progress of women in politics. I remember her saying, "I'm curious why the four officers of Sandwich Students Against Smoking are women and I'm glad to see you here." I am glad that she listened and I could tell that the committee understood. And they did take us seriously because after each of us spoke there was a silence, not necessarily an empty silence but a moment for reflecting. That made me very, very proud.

MORE PARLIAMENTARY MANEUVERS

By the time the tobacco-free schools bill landed in the Senate after clearing the House committee and the full House, senators were being pressured to remove teachers from the legislation. Tricky procedural maneuvering developed. The proposal was sent to a joint conference committee that serves as a sort of final court of appeals to iron out all the differences between the House and Senate versions of the bill. Often legislation dies in the conference committee. With a big assist from Senator Doane, the bill emerged stripped of the controversial provision to include teachers.

This trip to the state capitol didn't involve testifying before the committee, but meant face-to-face lobbying. Again, the students were prepared for rough sledding. They were ready for the inevitable question: "What are you going to say when they ask why aren't the teachers in the bill any more?" Their response: "Our whole campaign was for kids. All we wanted to do was to keep students from smoking. Teachers are adults and they can decide for themselves."

Mr. Sangster paired up the students and set them free in the Statehouse to talk with every legislator they could find. The impact was evident. Two of the kids wound up having lunch with the Speaker of the House and the next thing that happened was the Speaker jumped on the bandwagon and became a co-sponsor of the bill — a very unusual move for the leader of the House. The Speaker told Mr. Sangster in jest: "You'd better register these lobbyists!" As a result, the student initiative originally sponsored by two Republican legislators, Representative Morin and Senator Doane, won bipartisan support from the powerful Democratic leadership.

THE FINAL ROUND

"The kidpower was incredible," says William Sangster. The outcome was unprecedented. The House overruled its own committee chairman and passed the legislation. As if it were only yesterday, Mr. Sangster remembers seeing "the board light up almost all green" as he watched the vote being tallied on television. The vote was 112-27. After final Senate approval, the students basked in victory at the Governor's bill-signing ceremony amid the whir of photographers' cameras.

Since this Massachusetts law went into effective in 1987, many other states including Kansas, New Jersey, and Wisconsin have passed smoke-free school legislation. Some laws prohibit tobacco use by both students and teachers on school grounds.

Jeff Curry believes their efforts also had a real impact on their own high school: "Especially in our class, the number of people who smoke is far less. There aren't many smokers at all."

Lynn Terrill knows her efforts have paid off — not just at school, but at home. "I yelled at my Mom from the first day when we started the campaign. I'd say that smoking is real bad and she used to get really annoyed with me. She made a New Year's resolution not to smoke inside the house and she's cut down her smoking quite a bit."

PREDICTIONS

Four years later Mr. Sangster's enthusiasm has not waned but he is disappointed that "the kids didn't get the publicity they deserved. It was the only major piece of legislation ever passed in the history of the Massachusetts legislature by kids — sponsored directly by kids."

Even if the students deserved more recognition, Aaron Hobart suggests this experience has made an indelible imprint. "Because we've done this, it is probably easier for us to get up and say what's on our minds rather than sit back and say that we cannot do anything about it. I don't think like that too often." Cindy DeNaples realizes the benefits of what she calls applied learning. "Just looking back at it, we were so prepared and so mature compared to what's going on now [in school]."

The campaign seems to have pushed two of the seven students to consider a career in government. Lynn Terrill says, "I think it was real neat to lobby. That's what started me to really like politics and that interest hasn't stopped. It hasn't stopped for a lot of us. Hopefully, if I ever get in the economics department up in the Statehouse I would listen to a kid who comes in, and listen more to the common person rather than the people who think that they know all statistics but don't have any feelings." Amanda Heflen also plans to pursue public service.

Jenn Pistone adds: "If you believe in your cause and you truly believe in yourself, then you shouldn't be afraid of any obstacles that you meet. You have to believe in yourself and have confidence. Even if you don't have confidence in other people around you, still realize it is up to you to express yourself. It is just the most important thing you can ever do."

INFORMATION STARTERS

Check with the local chapter of the American Lung Association, American Heart Association, American Cancer Society, or March of Dimes. Some of these health organizations concentrate on education and prevention rather than political action. Check also with the local chapter of Group Against Smokers' Pollution (GASP) which usually takes a lead at the state and local level in monitoring pending legislation.

★ **Advocacy Institute**
   1730 Rhode Island Avenue NW #600
   Washington, DC 20036
   (202) 659-8475 Fax: (202) 659-8484
Serves as a clearinghouse on several public health issues, including tobacco control, with an emphasis on media strategies to counter industry advertising.

★ **Americans for Nonsmokers' Rights**
   2530 San Pablo Avenue #J
   Berkeley, CA 94702
   (510) 841-3032 Fax: (510) 841-7702
Works with activists of all ages in pursuit of a smoke-free environment. It sponsors many teen advocacy workshops.

★ **Smokefree Educational Services**
   375 South End Avenue #32F
   New York, NY 10280
   (212) 912-0960 Fax: (212) 488-8911
Sponsors a national counter-tobacco advertisement poster contest. Joe Cherner's organization has produced "Ten Reasons for Tobacco-Free Schools" and other information on ongoing initiatives in the state of New York as well as news about what is happening nationwide.

★ **Smokers' Rights Alliance**
   20 East Main Street #710
   Mesa, AZ 85201
   (602) 461-8882
Concentrates on preserving "the right to smoke" without unnecessary interference by the government.

★ **Stop Teenage Addiction Today (STAT)**
  121 Lyman Street #210
  Springfield, MA 01103
  (413) 732-STAT

Advocates minimizing minors' access to tobacco products. It also works to raise public awareness of the role of tobacco advertisements in influencing children to smoke. STAT conducts research and maintains a library and a speakers' bureau.

★ **Tobacco Institute**
  1875 Eye Street NW #800
  Washington, DC 20006
  (202) 457-4800

Provides the industry's perspective.

STEERING CLEAR OF DRUNK DRIVERS
Hollywood Stars
Shine in Student-led Drive

You hear about gang violence or freeway slayings and all these things that are deep-rooted problems and very complicated. Solutions are so simple for this problem: sober driving. Drunk driving is the biggest waste.
— Lisa Goldsmith

For over six years, a North Hollywood, California, high school group has taken a leading role to change public attitudes about drunk driving. One of the reasons for the students' ongoing success is their ability to tap a community resource unique to North Hollywood — celebrities. This collaboration of students and stars, as well as the involvement of many parents, continues to produce results.

The Oakwood School organization formed back in 1986 after seventeen-year old Alexandra Vincent was "murdered," as the students say, by a drunk driver. Fred Mednick, now the principal, was determined to turn the students' mourning into a constructive long-term commitment and that is precisely what happened.

A recap of all the rallies and other initiatives organized by this group over the years could fill a book. Oakwood Students Against Drunk Driving (OSADD) is still the most popular elective offered at school, with over 30% of the students applying. The fifteen teenagers who get in this Special Studies class form the leadership core. Participation by the entire student body is encouraged.

Shortly after she graduated from this small private school, Lisa Goldsmith reminisced about her OSADD involvement, which began in ninth grade and did not let up. Lisa served as co-president of the group during both her junior and senior years, and on the following pages shares her fondest memories of and disappointments in what she depicts as the "war on an epidemic that is a threat to everyone's life."

IN HER OWN WORDS . . .

I heard one of the juniors was killed. She was hit by a drunk driver. I cannot quite explain why but Alex's murder really grabbed me. I remember looking in the newspaper that day when I got home and they had a picture of the accident. It's like a nightmare when you look at it.

From the time Alex was killed in February through the end of that year, it was very intense how the school was responding. Many of Alex's friends and the older students were going to the trial and were writing letters to the newspapers and city councilmembers to try to get some penalties for the man who killed her. I don't remember what the sentencing was, but the drunk driver will be out of jail soon. It hasn't been even six years.

They started this group called OSADD. They held rallies and school assemblies but I didn't get involved then. In ninth grade I started working on OSADD and wasn't really sure of how the whole process worked. That year we were really targeting public awareness. I did a lot of phone calls and follow up letter-writing, and did a lot of the leg-work. We had T-shirts printed that we sold, trying to make people more aware. It was really successful and we got a lot of media coverage.

The ideas come from the students. Fred Mednick, our principal, has been the advisor as long as I've been involved. He sort of helps us focus but he doesn't really make any decisions. When big shots want to talk to an adult, which happens very often, he takes care of it. But mostly he has trained us in all aspects of community organizing so that we take full responsibility.

I think one of the reasons that we are effective is we don't tell people not to drink because right away you turn off a lot of party types. In general when you just drink — if you're not an alcoholic — you really are not hurting anybody but yourself. But if you get behind the wheel, you are putting everybody at risk and that is not fair. We're saying you can have your good time, but don't drive home.

GAINING MOMENTUM

We organized a rally on April 30th. Abbey, the co-president of OSADD that year, went to the Screen Actors Guild to get addresses of celebrities. We got Henry Winkler to come and speak at the rally. We wrote the mayor and asked him to come. He couldn't but his office declared April 30th "Sober Driving Day" in Los Angeles and someone came and presented us with an official plaque. It was good because it gave us some sort of public validation.

Rhea Perlman [of the television sitcom *Cheers*] said something so true at one of our press conferences: "No one is in favor of drinking and driving, but the problem is, not enough people are against it." In some states, people think you're infringing on their rights but people don't think that they are infringing other peoples' rights when they get behind the wheel.

We had done just about as much as we possibly could do as far as public awareness. Then we started legislative action. We got a lot of information from MADD (Mothers Against Drunk Driving) and the highway patrol. We got all sorts of statistics about blood-alcohol level.

The American Medical Association is one of the organizations that wants to lower the legal blood-alcohol concentration (BAC) level to .05 because you are still very impaired if you are at .08. If you see the statistics, it is so inane that people don't change the law. Many states don't even have .08 already. Some states like Georgia have it at 1.2. It is so amazing to me why it hasn't been adopted nationwide but it has to go state-by-state.

First we were going to try to introduce legislation lowering the BAC from .10 to .08 on our own, but we needed three hundred thousand signatures to get a bill for a referendum. It was going to take forever, and Alex's mom knew State Senator Bill Leonard who had introduced Senate Bill 408 calling for .08 legislation.

> ### HINTS
>
> Notice the attention-getting bill number (408 = For .08). Lawmakers can reserve a relevant or catchy number so if you have an idea, pass it along to your inside ally in the legislature.

This is when we hooked up with the national office of SADD (Students Against Drunk Driving). We asked them for a list of all SADD chapters in California and then we went to all local schools. We wrote them each a letter, told them who we were and what we were doing, and asked them to support this bill. We asked them to write to the state legislature saying, "We want this bill passed." We got this huge letter-writing campaign and we had petitions.

Then we had a press conference and some people came from Northern California and other places. We had the head of the California Highway Patrol speak, a national spokesperson of MADD, and the district attorney for the city of Los Angeles. Again, you've got to have a celebrity or some very prominent political figure to get at the top of the news. I remember Jennifer Grodin, OSADD co-president at the time, spoke and showed this stack of petitions and said, "This is how many students want this law passed." It was kind of a trick — we had each person sign one piece of paper so there was tons of paper.

We wrote to every news person and I remember personally calling every news station that morning and saying, "Are you coming? Are you coming?" I know we really annoyed them, but we just kept calling and calling them. I remember after the press conference, going to my geometry class and writing a list of all the news and radio stations we had. We had seven networks out of nine, thirteen radio stations and a lot of press there. It was really exciting. We just wanted people to do something. We had a big sign behind all the speakers saying: "Write your state legislator!" We were pleading for people to write. That was our most successful event so far.

I don't know how effective the press conference was or how instrumental we were, but that January the law was passed. The Governor of California sent us his congratulations. Only three other states have .08 legislation — Maine, Oregon, and Utah — and we became the fourth. It was the biggest rush when we found out that the BAC had passed.

The best feeling is that you have accomplished something. When someone writes and says, "We saw your press conference or read about what you are doing and it's wonderful," or when someone takes notice or gets involved, you feel like you've accomplished something and it kind of keeps you going. We worked really hard and we were definitely a part of this huge campaign. The fact that students were taking an interest drew the media's attention. I think it was that same year that the Governor declared April 30th "Sober Driving Day" in California. So we had success in L.A. and in all of California, and that was pretty exciting. We felt we were on a roll.

Within the first five months that the law was in effect, the number of arrests of intoxicated drivers rose by 12% and the number of fatal alcohol-related crashes dropped by 10%. It also had to do with another new state law called the Administrative License Revocation, where your license is taken away right then and there by the arresting police officer. You are issued a temporary license before your court hearing. I think drivers are more aware of losing their license than they are worrying about their blood-alcohol level, but the .08 limit allows more people to be convicted of drunk driving.

DRIVING THE MESSAGE ACROSS THE COUNTRY

Fred Mednick, Oakwood School principal and OSADD faculty advisor, describes the expansion of their campaign:

Students contacted celebrities and political figures throughout the country to lend their name to a board of supporters. We flew to Chicago, the mid-point of the country, and gathered various SADD chapters together to organize the campaign to lower the legal blood-alcohol limit. It was important for us to organize the campaign around a single issue rather than general consciousness-raising.

The mayors' offices in Los Angeles, Chicago, and New York agreed to hold rallies on April 30th. The national news agencies covered the story in detail. And we understand there is a bill being drafted in Illinois that will support the goal of a lower blood-alcohol limit.

After OSADD launched the National Sober Driving Campaign calling for .08 legislation nationwide, students explored other ways to publicize their cause in cities across the country.

LISA GOLDSMITH continues . . .

We wanted to do some sort of commercial — a public service announcement (PSA). The PSA was our idea. Sarah's dad had a production company, Angel City Productions. He said he would produce it and get in touch with an award-winning director and an advertising guy. Sarah worked with him on the script. I think the idea behind the script came from what I had seen on TV that said sixty-five people were killed every day by terrorists.

> ### EXECUTION
>
> *If a foreign government executed sixty-five Americans today, we'd declare war tomorrow. Yet, that's how many of us will be put to death today and every day this year by drunk drivers.*
>
> *It's time to lower the legal blood-alcohol limit. It's time to stop the killing.*
>
> - OSADD Public Service Announcement

I remember the shoot was on May 6th, the day after the SAT's. We went to this place at four in the morning, at least most of us. We went downtown to this warehouse that was being torn down. We got permission to use the property. Sarah's dad arranged for all these extras who donated their time, which was great. We got free catering for all the production staff. We made sure everyone had enough water because it was so hot. It was really fun. We spent the whole day there. We saw how the sets were designed. Basically we learned to do a PSA for .08 legislation. There were some donkeys and mules in the shoot. They used all this junk that was around to make it look like a war zone. Then the actor, Edward James Olmos, a parent at Oakwood School who's been very supportive of us, said he'd do the narration.

We started mailing the public service announcement to NBC, ABC, etc. We thought the PSA was professionally done and it wasn't just kids' stuff. It had an important message and was the kind of thing that people would be interested in and it would appeal to their emotions. We sent two or three tapes to a network. It was very expensive, even though a lot of this cost was absorbed by Sarah's dad. We never heard back from them. It was very disconcerting when we spent all this time doing it. We just wanted them to look at it and tell us what they thought.

We wanted to get the PSA aired so we tried the networks again. I assigned each person a network. We called the station, found out who was in charge of it, mailed it to them, and never heard from them. I wrote this letter saying: "We are Oakwood Students Against Drunk Driving and we, along with this production company, produced this thirty-second public service announcement called Execution. It is very timely because of the whole Persian Gulf situation. We want people to think before they drink and we think this will prompt them to do it."

The tragic thing is that one of the people who volunteered on the production staff was killed by a drunk driver. He was in charge of the wiring. I even put that in the letter to try to appeal to these people to get this aired. I remember when Fred told me, I sat down and was hysterical because it keeps happening over and over again. It was a most difficult year. At times I felt very hopeless and very frustrated.

CELEBRITIES CHIME IN

Today, we ask for the support of other high school students across the nation, students who do not want to see their friends die as a result of drunk driving. Each day, nine 15- to 19-year olds die in alcohol-related crashes. We ask you, as students, to do something. We ask you to join our campaign to promote sober driving and to save lives.
— Lisa Goldsmith

We got connected with the head of Recording Artists Against Drunk Driving. He told us "Wilson Phillips" was chosen as our honorary group. The band happens to be affiliated with Oakwood because Carnie and Wendy Wilson went to Oakwood and wanted to do something for the school.

We decided we'd have a press conference and Wilson Phillips would be there and that would attract the media. Wilson Phillips finally agreed to come two weeks before the scheduled press conference and it was one of those rushed things.

That year OSADD was the biggest it's ever been. There were about twenty-five people who were really involved. Each person kept track of who the contact was at the station and what time the PSA would run. Then a few people who felt comfortable working with the celebrities were put in charge of the speakers. Someone else was in charge of getting food. Another person was in charge of calling everyone at the last minute to make sure they were coming; and someone was supposed to get all the equipment set up — the mikes and video. When it came down to it, everyone was really involved and helpful.

I never like to speak in public — it's like my biggest fear. But when I talk about OSADD I'm not nervous. The press conference [with three hundred people and TV cameras] was pretty successful. NBC aired our PSA with clips from the press conference. The Entertainment Network was airing it every hour for a while. In *TV Guide*, there's a picture of Wilson Phillips and underneath it says, "Carnie and Wendy Wilson of the pop trio return to their high school . . . to support Oakwood Students Against Drunk Driving."

Personally, I've learned a lot. I never would have known how to get a law passed, how to contact people, how to talk and appeal to certain people, and how to get what you need to get done. I remember calling the media and saying that we were having this press conference and they said, "We don't cover those kinds of things." When I said that Wilson Phillips was going to be there, then they said, "Where is it?"

PREDICTIONS

The Oakwood Students Against Drunk Driving and their principal have not slowed down for six years; they're in for the long haul. They've learned how to pace themselves so their energy and enthusiasm don't flag. Despite a changing of the guard, new student leaders appear determined to pursue the unfinished agenda left by their immediate predecessors and many other OSADD alumni. The public service announcement "Execution" has been widely shown and has earned the Gold Plaque Award at the 26th Chicago International Film Festival and also won third place in the Community Action Network's Media Awards.

At a recent press conference, OSADD made announcements about plans for the next six years. First, they plan to develop an outreach program for elementary schools and travel around to local public and private schools to demonstrate through drama, art, and discussion the dangers of drinking and driving. Secondly, Oakwood is working to persuade the Governor not reduce state funds to enforce the law which prohibits selling liquor to minors.

OSADD will not be satisfied until drunk drivers are off the road. Disappointments occur in their campaign but it doesn't stem their drive. Lisa Goldsmith, who served two exhausting years as co-president of OSADD, says, "My college essay that got me into Duke University was about disillusionment. No matter how much work OSADD does, no matter how much work MADD, SADD, and other groups do, drunk driving is a back-burner issue. The President has made no effort — nothing that I have read about — to see it as a crisis and to make it a priority. There is no government leadership." But Lisa's "disillusionment" has not caused her to give up. Shortly before she departed for college she spoke energetically about forging ahead: "I found out that North Carolina isn't one of the states that has .08; so when I get to Duke, one of the things I want to do is start writing letters and try get something going there."

INFORMATION STARTERS

★ **Advocacy Institute**
1730 Rhode Island Avenue NW #600
Washington, DC 20036
(202) 659-8475 Fax: (202) 659-8484
Serves as a clearinghouse on several health issues including alcohol, with a specific focus on the advertising practices of the liquor industry.

★ **Beer Institute**
   1225 Eye Street NW
   Washington, DC 20005
   (202) 737-BEER
Provides the industry's perspective.

★ **Distilled Spirits Council of the U.S.**
   1250 Eye Street NW
   Washington, DC 20005
   (202) 628-3544
Offers the industry's perspective.

★ **Governor's Highway Safety Office**
Serves as the central hub to collect and analyze state and local statistics pertaining to drunk driving. Contact your governor's office and most likely you will be routed to the Youth Highway Traffic Safety Coordinator.

★ **Mothers Against Drunk Drivers (MADD)**
   511 East John Carpenter Freeway
   Irving, TX 75062
   (214) 744-6233
Works both in the political arena on legislation and the courts on sentencing convicted drunk drivers.

★ **National Clearinghouse for Alcohol and Drug Information**
   PO Box 2345
   Rockville, MD 20852
   (800) 729-6686 (301) 468-2600 in MD
Provides referral service and offers a free resource catalog.

★ **National Commission on Drunk Driving**
   1910 K Street NW #810
   Washington, DC 20006
   (202) 452-6004   Fax: (202) 223-7012
Compiles reports such as "A Comparison of State Drunk Driving Countermeasures" and also serves as a central clearinghouse.

★ **National Highway Traffic Safety Administration (NHTSA)**
   400 Seventh Street SW #5232
   Washington, DC 20590
   (202) 366-2540   Fax: (202) 366-5962
Provides statistics on injuries and deaths caused by drunk driving.

★ **National Sober Driving Campaign**
Oakwood School
11600 Magnolia Boulevard
North Hollywood, CA 91601
(818) 766-5177
Fred Mednick, the school principal, coordinates the National Sober Driving Campaign, formerly called OSADD.

★ **Public Interest Video Network**
1642 R Street NW
Washington, DC 20009
(202) 797-8997
Produces public service announcements and news stories on behalf of public interest organizations.

★ **Recording Artists Against Drunk Driving (R.A.D.D.)**
1308 Factory Place #3B
Los Angeles, CA 90013
(213) 624-9398
Matches musicians with sober driving campaigns nationwide.

★ **Students Against Drunk Drivers (SADD)**
Box 800
Marlboro, MA 01752
(508) 481-3568
Concentrates on education and believes that political action could detract from its message. A recognized SADD chapter can speak out about proposed laws if "the individual makes it clear that he or she is expressing individual views and does not speak for SADD National."

★ **StarServe**
701 Santa Monica Boulevard #220
Santa Monica, CA 90401
(800) 888- 8232 (213) 452-STAR in CA   Fax: (213) 576-0592
Links celebrities with specific causes and community service campaigns.

MAKING HEADWAY
School Effort
Responsible for
Landmark Bicycle Helmet Law

The first law in the United States requiring bicyclists under sixteen years of age to wear safety helmets can be traced to a coordinated campaign headed up by Brian Meshkin and his classmates and their teachers at Glenwood Middle School in Howard County, Maryland. Spurred into action by the tragic death of a student, this coalition of students and teachers succeeded at getting a helmet law put on the books.

The school's multi-faceted bike safety initiative got off to a fast start. Bike rodeos and a video on bike safety produced by the students received widespread community support. The proposed legislation, however, hit roadblocks. When the school year ended, debate intensified against the mandatory helmet bill. A second round of hearings was scheduled and Brian insisted that his family postpone their summer vacation so he could testify for a second time before the county council. He turned out to be the only witness who represented his school at the subsequent hearings. By a narrow margin, the legislation passed. Then opponents, who argued that the proposal backpedals away from fundamental personal rights, sought to overturn it by means of a referendum but failed to get the required four thousand five hundred signatures within sixty days of the enactment of the law.

Looking back at this victorious campaign of 1990, Brian says this political training "has made a difference for the rest of my life." He sees a future career in politics and clearly has the ambition it takes to run for office.

IN HIS OWN WORDS . . .

Because this is a rural area, we have a lot of people around here who like to bicycle on our scenic roads. Nobody would wear helmets because most people don't think defensively. There are all these advertisements by MADD about drunk driving, so you know it is stupid to drive after drinking. But there are no warnings about proper safety precautions and the dangers of cycling without a helmet.

It was a mistake that anyone could have made. Chris Kelly was riding down the road on his bike and he got hit by a car. It was something you couldn't believe happened. It was not fair because he had not been warned of the dangers of cycling without a helmet and the proper safety precautions.

I found out from Chris Kelly's mom that they had planned to buy a helmet that weekend. The police believe that in Chris's case, a helmet may not have helped him. Chris was riding on the wrong side of the road into traffic.

There had been another fatal bike accident in the county farther out in the boonies and another one in this area about six months before Chris was killed. I wanted to make sure that Chris did not die in vain. Because of his death, I felt somebody must make a difference in preventing this from happening again. I did not want him to be another statistic. I just thought it had to be done and I felt that I was obligated to do this for Chris.

Chris had a lot of friends; he was a real character. He was the kind of guy who made you laugh but he didn't get in trouble. A lot of the teachers opened their heart to Chris. Both Diane Wells, the gifted and talented coordinator, and Suzie Sullivan, a teacher at Glenwood Middle School, were the ones who orchestrated the entire campaign.

The faculty came out with an actual plan in which we would attack different aspects of bike safety. We formed a group responsible for legislation, a group for editorials, a bicycle safety group, a public awareness group, and a bike rally group.

Out of 230 kids in the eighth grade, most everyone was in support of our efforts. The principal, Robert Childers, and social studies teacher Mark Vinje, also gave us a lot of help. It was like a family — everybody uniting for one cause.

The chairs and co-chairs of each group were all students. You had all types of kids working together; the disruptive students, the equivalent of the nerds, and the 'popular' crowd were all working mutually for one cause. It worked out pretty well.

Because my heart has always been in legislation, I was placed as chair of the legislation group. I have always read the newspapers and watched the news on television, but I had never really been involved. Most of my friends were the chairs of the other groups so we all kept in contact over the phone. It was a lot of fun.

People with the editorials group contacted all the local TV and radio stations and newspapers. The bike video group was in charge of making a film for local elementary schools. We also conducted a bike safety rodeo.

The legislation group met every other day. The choice was between mandatory bike helmets or mandatory registration. We decided to go the route of bike helmets. Our main objective was to promote bike safety and along with that to pass the bike helmet law. The law would be the only permanent and *concrete* result of our work that would always be with us.

MOBILIZING SUPPORT

Legislative work centered around writing letters to county legislators. Because Glenwood is not a municipality, we contacted our county councilman, Charles Feaga, about introducing legislation. Ms. Wells had sent a letter to Mr. Feaga, and his special assistant, Peter Beck, came over to our school and met with us.

Drafting the legislation was in the hands of Mr. Feaga. We were contacted once the bill was drafted and were informed of the date of the public hearing. The original County Bill 28 required all children under the age of sixteen to wear a bike helmet. I have stated in the past that the basic point of the bill was not to punish offenders but to influence and educate law-abiding citizens. The use of bike helmets is a vital part of the new focus on bicycle safety.

I called a lot of the parents and asked them to write letters in support of the bill. We thought parents would be angry because we were interfering with their decisions, but we were wrong. They agreed with us. I spent a lot of time in the student lounge where I'd make phone calls and write letters. Because of the large number of letters I was forced to type, I learned to use a computer really well.

Ms. Wells would give me this long list of people to contact, such as the superintendent of middle schools in the county, the superintendent of physical education in the county, and the owner of a local sporting goods store. I would first write a letter asking for their testimony, and then follow up with a phone call.

The teachers asked for volunteers for public testimony. Besides me, between four and six other kids volunteered. It was primarily the legislative and editorial members of our group who were planning to testify. We tried to bring in numbers because numbers are powerful with politicians. We were able to get approximately ten people from Glenwood to testify. My mom gave me pointers on my testimony; she's really good at that. She is a great coach and my biggest fan!

Shane Pendergrass, the council chairman at the time, was totally against the bill from the get-go. At the public hearing she listened. I believe we were given more attention because kids have never come out and taken a stand before Howard County. It really set a precedent for the future.

The council passed our bill with a significant amendment proposed at the last minute by Councilwoman Angela Beltram that would require the use of helmets for all ages. Her rationale was that her friend, a twenty-year old, wasn't wearing a helmet and she was hit head-on. Ironically, Ms. Beltram voted against the bill with her amendment.

We received a load of negative responses to the amended bill. I became outraged. In my first article that was published in the newspaper I wrote:

> I believe that Ms. Beltram used this amendment to shoot down the bill.
> As a result, Glenwood Middle School should not be held responsible for
> the actions of Angie Beltram.

Because of all the opposition to the amendment, another bill was introduced that would return the law back to its original form [requiring helmets for bikers under sixteen]. I was only one from Glenwood Middle School who testified on the new bill. I don't know why, because everyone got a letter about the hearing. It was later on in the summer and I guess they were all on vacation.

The council passed the new Bill 58. It was known as our law, Glenwood Middle School's Eighth Grade Bill. We were the spinal cord of that bill in that we could make or break it. The campaign gave a purpose to school. Middle school was really a drag until then.

The deaths and injuries have decreased so I would assume that we did the right thing. I just wish someone had thought of this last summer before Chris's death.

PREDICTIONS

Capitalizing on the momentum generated by this victory, Brian took his lobbying efforts to a more congested county just outside of Washington, D.C., where traffic poses an even greater threat to bicyclists than on the winding country roads of his rural community. Once again, his persuasive letter to the editor and testimony helped convince the Montgomery County government to follow the lead of Howard County.

At fifteen, this politicized teenager landed a summer internship working with Councilmember Charles Feaga, the author of the precedent-setting helmet law in Howard County. No doubt Brian's firsthand government experience makes him more effective now as the student representative for his high school on the board of education. His leadership continues to be recognized, and in the spring of 1992 Brian was chosen as the Student Volunteer of the Year for Howard County. This is one activist who's moved beyond single-issue politics to broader public policy concerns, including education reform and congressional redistricting.

INFORMATION STARTERS

★ **American Academy of Pediatrics**
114 Northwest Point Boulevard
Elk Grove Village, IL 60009
(800) 433-9016
Maintains statistics on injuries and also tracks federal and state legislation.

★ **American Association of State Highway & Transportation Officials**
444 North Capitol Street NW #225
Washington, DC 20001
(202) 624-5800
Publishes *Guide for the Development of New Bicycle Facilities* ($8.00).

★ **Bicycle Federation of America**
1818 R Street NW
Washington, DC 20009
(202) 332-6986 Fax: (202) 332-6989
Concentrates on bicycle safety but does not take a position on mandatory bike helmets legislation.

★ **Bicycling Forum**
Box 1776
Missoula, MT 59807
(406) 721-1776
Offers a free four-page pamphlet, "Improving Local Conditions for Bicycling."

★ **Bicycle Manufacturers Association of America**
3050 K Street NW #400
Washington, DC 20007
(202) 944-9297
Compiles statistics and monitors legislation.

★ **National Safe Kids Campaign**
111 Michigan Avenue NW
Washington, DC 20010-2970
(202) 939-4993   Fax: (202) 939-4838

Provides information packets, videos, and other materials regarding bicycle helmets. This umbrella organization can tell you if one of the 110 active "Safe Kids" coalitions exists in your community.

★ U.S. Consumer Product Safety Commission
5401 Westbard Avenue
Bethesda, MD 20207
(800) 638-CPSC

Compiles accident statistics. This government agency monitors the voluntary standards set by bike helmet manufacturers; at this time there are no federal minimum safety specifications.

★ U.S. Department of Transportation
National Highway Traffic Safety Administration
Office of Crashworthiness Research
400 Seventh Street SW
Washington, DC 20590
(202) 366-4862

Maintains statistics and data on bike safety headgear.

PART IV:

INFORMATION RESOURCES

INFORMATION
RESOURCES

Americans of all ages, all stations in life, and all types of disposition are forever forming associations in the United States.
— Alexis de Tocqueville

This section of *No Kidding Around!* is designed to help steer you in the direction of organizations and groups which can supply your campaign with facts, figures, and opinions. Part IV begins with a menu of issues that especially affect young people. Other pressing problems that concern citizens of all ages, such as the environment, are also included here. Once your appetite for information has been whetted by something you've heard or read about, consult the organizations listed below that may be able to fill in some of the gaps in your knowledge.

Since every government agency, industry organization, trade association, and public interest group — even non-partisan ones — has its own slant on a given issue, your safest best is to rely on a variety of information sources. Don't be afraid of discovering facts that don't bolster your own arguments; seeing an issue through the eyes of your opponents is essential. You'll find a mix of organizations: liberal and conservative, pro and con, *ad hoc* and well-established.

Don't despair if this list doesn't contain a source you're looking for. It is meant to be an intriguing, rather than exhaustive, sampling of all the information resources you have at your command. For example, the comprehensive three-volume source, Gale's *Encyclopedia of Associations,* is available at most public libraries. By using its keyword index, you can discover hundreds of organizations, especially trade associations, which are usually happy to supply you with relevant information.

In addition to statistics, reports, and other documents, many state and federal government departments and private non-profit associations operate speakers' bureaus and offer videotapes and other audiovisual materials.

Another way to track down source material is to contact the Information Central at the American Society of Association Executives at 1575 Eye Street NW, Washington, DC 20005 (202) 626-2723, which can direct you to those trade associations actively concerned with your specific issue. Also, over two dozen Federal Information Centers exist nationwide which can put you in touch with U.S. government experts who may be studying the topic you're interested in. (Check the blue pages of your phone book or write to Federal Information Program, KJF, U.S. General Services Administration, Washington, DC 20405.)

Since new groups pop up every day while others fold, it's a good idea to verify telephone numbers. To avoid long-distance calls, first check with the "800" operator at (800) 555-1212 to see if a particular organization offers a toll-free number.

Finally, it's important to note that most of the information centers listed here are national organizations which can help you get a sense of the big picture. State government agencies can provide a more focused snapshot. However, for a detailed, local viewpoint, your best resources will be city and county government agencies as well as community-based organizations.

The real key to successful information-gathering is to ask everyone with whom you talk for suggestions of other individuals and organizations to contact. Not only will you acquire a broad perspective on your issue by doing this, but you'll be learning the value of "networking" at the same time. Good luck!

Issues from A to Z

This list represents, quite literally, the tip of the iceberg. Every information source you contact can lead you to dozens of other organizations. Keep in mind that telephone numbers and addresses change as frequently as the weather.

ADVERTISING & CONSUMER CONCERNS

★ **American Advertising Federation**
1400 K Street NW #100
Washington, DC 20005
(202) 898-0089

★ **Badvertising Institute**
(counter tobacco ads)
25 Boyd Street #2
Portland, ME 04101
(207) 773-3275

★ **Consumers Union**
101 Truman Avenue
Yonkers, NY 10703
(914) 378-2000

★ **Public Citizen**
PO Box 19404
Washington, DC 20036
(202) 833-3000

★ **Scenic America**
(billboard control)
216 Seventh Avenue SE
Washington, DC 20003
(202) 546-1100

★ **U.S. Consumer Product Safety Commission**
5401 Westbard Avenue
Bethesda, DC 20207
(800) 638-CPSC (301) 492-8104 in MD

★ **U.S. Federal Trade Commission**
Advertising Practices
Sixth and Pennsylvania Avenue NW
Washington, DC 20580
(202) 326-3131

★ **U.S. Public Interest Research Group (PIRG)**
215 Pennsylvania Avenue SE
Washington, DC 20003
(202) 546-9707

AIDS (Acquired Immune Deficiency Syndrome) & HIV VIRUS

★ **AIDS Action Council**
2033 M Street NW #802
Washington, DC 20036
(202) 293-2886

★ **Citizens Commission on AIDS**
121 Sixth Avenue Sixth Floor
New York, NY 10013
(212) 925-5290 Fax: (212) 925-5675

★ **National AIDS Information Clearinghouse**
Centers for Disease Control
PO Box 6003
Rockville, MD 20850
(800) 458-5231 TTY/TTD: (800) 243-7012

★ **Ryan White National Fund**
c/o Athletes and Entertainers for Kids
PO Box 191, Building B
Gardena, CA 90248-0191
(213) 768-8493

★ **Teens Teaching AIDS Prevention**
3030 Walnut Street
Kansas City, MO 64108
(800) 234-TEEN (816) 561-8784 in MO

ALCOHOL
(see DRUGS & ALCOHOL)

ANIMALS
(see also WILDLIFE; ZOOS)

★ **American Society for the Prevention of Cruelty to Animals**
441 East 92nd Street
New York, NY 10128
(212) 876-7700 Fax: (212) 348-3031

★ **Animal Legal Defense Fund**
1363 Lincoln Avenue
San Rafael, CA 94901
(800) 922-FROG

★ **Animal Welfare Information Center**
National Agricultural Library #304
Beltsville, MD 20705
(301) 344-3704

★ **Humane Society of the U.S.**
2100 L Street NW
Washington, DC 20037
(202) 452-1100

★ **Institute of Laboratory Animal Resources**
National Research Council
2101 Constitution Avenue NW
Washington, DC 20418
(202) 334-2590 Fax: (202) 334-1639

★ **National Association for Biomedical Research**
818 Connecticut Avenue NW #303
Washington, DC 20006
(202) 857-0540

★ **People for the Ethical Treatment of Animals**
PO Box 42516
Washington, DC 20015
(301) 770-7444

★ **Student Action Corps for Animals**
PO Box 15588
Washington, DC 20003
(202) 543-8983

BILINGUAL EDUCATION
(see also EDUCATION)

★ **ASPIRA Association**
1112 16th Street NW #340
Washington, DC 20036
(202) 835-3600

★ **English First**
8001 Forbes Place
Springfield, VA 22151
(703) 321-8818

★ **ERIC Clearinghouse for Bilingual Education**
8737 Colesville Road #900
Silver Spring, MD 20910
(800) 647-0123

★ **Intercultural Development Research Association**
5835 Callaghan Road #350
San Antonio, TX 78228
(512) 684-8180

★ **National Association for Bilingual Education**
810 First Street NE, Third Floor
Washington, DC 20002
(202) 898-1829 Fax: (202) 289-8173

★ **National Clearinghouse for Bilingual Education**
1118 22nd Street NW #217
Washington, DC 20037
(800) 321-NCBE (202) 467-0867 in DC

CAREERS
(see JOBS)

CENSORSHIP
(see also FIRST AMENDMENT; TELEVISION & MEDIA)

★ **American Civil Liberties Union**
132 West 43rd Street
New York, NY 10036
(212) 944-9800

★ **American Library Association**
Office of Intellectual Freedom
50 East Huron Street
Chicago, IL 60611
(312) 944-6780

★ **Focus on Family**
801 Corporate Center Drive
Pomona, CA 91768
(714) 620-8500

★ **National Coalition Against Censorship**
2 West 64th Street
New York, NY 10023
(212) 724-1500

★ **Parents' Music Resource Center**
1500 Arlington Boulevard
Arlington, VA 22209
(703) 527-9466

★ **People for the American Way**
Freedom to Learn Project
2000 M Street NW
Washington, DC 20036
(800) 326-PFAW (202) 467-4999 in DC

★ **Student Press Law Center**
1735 Eye Street NW
Washington, DC 20006-2402
(202) 466-5242

CHILD ABUSE AND RUNAWAYS
(see also FAMILY)

★ **Adam Walsh Child Resource Center**
3111 South Dixie Highway #244
West Palm Beach, FL 33405
(407) 833-9080

★ **Clearinghouse on Child Abuse and Neglect**
PO Box 1182
Washington, DC 20013
(703) 821-2086

★ **National Center for Missing and Exploited Children**
2101 Wilson Boulevard #550
Arlington, VA 22201
(800) 843-5678

★ **National Coalition of State Juvenile Justice Advisory Groups**
1211 Connecticut Avenue NW #3414
Washington, DC 20036
(202) 467-0864 Fax: (202) 887-0738

★ **National Network of Runaway and Youth Services**
1400 Eye Street NW #330
Washington DC 20005
(202) 682-4114

CIGARETTES & CHEWING TOBACCO
(see TOBACCO)

COMMUNITY SERVICE
(see DRAFT & NATIONAL SERVICE)

CONFLICT RESOLUTION
(see PEACE)

CRIME & VIOLENCE
(see also GUNS & WEAPONS)

★ **Congressional Crime Caucus**
SH-303 Hart Senate Office Building
Washington, DC 20510
(202) 224-4254

★ **Clearinghouse on Family Violence Information**
PO Box 1182
Washington, DC 20013
(703) 385-7565

★ **Cult Awareness Network (CULTS)**
2421 West Pratt Boulevard #1173
Chicago, IL 60645
(312) 267-7777

★ **Justice Statistics Clearinghouse**
Bureau of Justice Statistics
U.S. Department of Justice
Box 6000
Rockville, MD 20850
(800) 732-3277 (301) 251-5500 in MD

★ **Kids Against Crime**
PO Box 22004
San Bernandino, CA 92406
(714) 882-1344

★ **National Crime Prevention Council**
1700 K Street NW, Second Floor
Washington, DC 20006
(202) 466-NCPC

★ **Police Foundation**
1001 22nd Street NW #200
Washington, DC 20037
(202) 833-1460

DISABILITIES

★ **Clearinghouse on Disability Information Programs**
U.S. Department of Education
Mary Switzer Building, Room 3132
Washington, DC 20202-2524
(202) 732-1241

★ **National Easter Seal Society**
70 East Lake Street
Chicago, IL 60601
(312) 726-6200 Fax/TTD: (312) 726-1494

★ **National Information Center for Children and Youth with Handicaps**
PO Box 1492
Washington, DC 20013
(703) 893-6061 TDD: (800) 999-5599

DISCRIMINATION
(see PREJUDICE & RACISM; SEXISM; DISABILITIES)

DRAFT & NATIONAL SERVICE

★ **ACTION Student Community Service Projects**
1100 Vermont Avenue NW
Washington, DC 20525
(202) 606-4824

★ **National Association of Service and Conservation Corps**
1001 Connecticut Avenue NW #827
Washington, DC 20036
(202) 331-9647

★ **Office of National Service**
The White House, Room 100
Washington, DC 20500
(202) 456-6266

★ **Selective Service System**
National Headquarters
Washington, DC 20435
(202) 724-0435

★ **U.S. Student Association**
1012 14th Street #207
Washington, DC 20005
(202) 347-8772

★ **Youth Service America**
1319 F Street NW
Washington, DC 20004
(202) 783-8855 Fax: (202) 341-2603

DRUGS & ALCOHOL
(see also HEALTH; TOBACCO)

★ **ACTION Drug Alliance Office**
806 Connecticut Avenue NW
Washington, DC 20525
(202) 606-4857

★ **Advocacy Institute**
1730 Rhode Island Avenue NW
Room 600
Washington, DC 20036
(202) 659-8475 Fax: (202) 659-8484

★ **Bacchus of the U.S.**
PO Box 100430
Denver, CO 80210
(303) 871-3068

★ **Beer Institute**
1225 Eye Street NW
Washington, DC 20005
(202) 737-BEER

★ **Distilled Spirits Council of the U.S.**
1250 Eye Street NW
Washington, DC 20005
(202) 628-3544

★ **Drug Abuse Prevention Office**
U.S. Department of Education
400 Maryland Avenue SW
Room 4145
Washington, DC 20202
(202) 401-1599

★ **Drugs and Crime Data Center and Clearinghouse**
1600 Research Boulevard
Rockville, MD 20850
(800) 666-3332 (301) 251-5500 in MD

★ **Drug Policy Foundation**
4801 Massachusetts Avenue NW
Room 400
Washington, DC 20016-2087
(202) 895-1634

★ **Mothers Against Drunk Drivers (MADD)**
511 East John Carpenter Freeway
Irving, TX 75062
(214) 744-6233

★ **National Clearinghouse for Alcohol and Drug Abuse Information**
5600 Fishers Lane
Rockville, MD 20857
(800) 729-6686 (301) 468-2600 in MD

★ **National Commission on Drunk Driving**
1140 Connecticut Avenue NW #804
Washington, DC 20036
(202) 452-6004 Fax: (202) 223-7012

★ **Students Against Drunk Drivers (SADD)**
Box 800
Marlboro, MA 01752
(508) 481-3568

EATING DISORDERS
(see also FOOD)

★ **American Anorexia/Bulimia Association**
418 East 76th Street
New York, NY 10021
(212) 734-1113

★ **National Association of Anorexia Nervosa and Associated Disorders**
Box 7
Highland Park, IL 60035
(708) 831-3438

EDUCATION
(see also STUDENT RIGHTS; GUNS & WEAPONS; BILINGUAL EDUCATION; HIGHER EDUCATION & STUDENT AID; VOCATIONAL EDUCATION)

★ **American Council on Education**
1 Dupont Circle NW #800
Washington, DC 20036
(202) 939-9300

★ **Educational Research Information Clearinghouse (ERIC)**
Office of Educational Research and Improvements Information Service
U.S. Department of Education
555 New Jersey Avenue NW #300
Washington, DC 20208-5641
(800) USE-ERIC (202) 626-9854 in DC

★ **ERIC Clearinghouse on Urban Education**
Teachers College Columbia University
Institute for Urban and Minority Education
525 West 120th Street #303
New York, NY 10027-9998
(212) 678-3433

★ **ERIC Clearinghouse on Rural Education and Small Schools**
Appalachia Educational Laboratory, Inc.
1031 Quarrier Street
Charleston, WV 25325-1348
(800) 624-9120 (800) 344-6646 in WV

★ **ERIC Clearinghouse for Science, Mathematics, and Environmental Education**
1200 Chambers Road, Third Floor
Columbus, OH 43212
(614) 292-6717

★ **ERIC Clearinghouse for Social Studies/Social Science Education**
Social Studies Development Center
Indiana University Smith Research Center
2805 East Tenth Street #120
Bloomington, IN 47405
(812) 855-3838

★ **ERIC Clearinghouse on Tests, Measurement, and Evaluation**
American Institutes for Research
3333 K Street NW
Washington, DC 20007-3893
(202) 342-5060

★ **National Coalition of Education Activists**
PO Box 405
Rosedale, NY 12472
(914) 658-8115

★ **National School Boards Association**
Resource Center/Library
1680 Duke Street
Alexandria, VA 22314
(703) 838-6722

★ **National Society for Internships and Experimental Education**
3509 Haworth Drive
Raleigh, NC 27609
(919) 787-3263

ELDERLY

★ **American Association of Retired Persons**
1909 K Street NW
Washington, DC 20049
(202) 434-2277

★ **Americans for Generational Equity**
608 Massachusetts Avenue NE
Washington, DC 20002
(202) 686-4196

★ **Generations United**
c/o Child Welfare League of America
440 First Street NW
Room 310
Washington, DC 20001
(202) 638-2952

★ **Gray Panthers**
1424 16th Street NW #602
Washington, DC 20036
(202) 387-3111

★ **National Council of Senior Citizens**
925 15th Street NW
Washington, DC 20005
(202) 347-8800

★ **Retired Senior Volunteer Program**
1100 Vermont Avenue NW
Washington, DC 20525
(202) 634-9353

EMPLOYMENT
(See JOBS; VOCATIONAL EDUCATION)

ENERGY
(see also ENVIRONMENT)

★ **Americans for Nuclear Energy**
2525 Wilson Boulevard
Arlington, VA 22201
(703) 528-4430

★ **Conservation and Renewable Energy Inquiry and Referral Service (CAREIRS)**
U.S. Department of Energy
Box 8900
Silver Spring, MD 20907
(800) 523-2929

★ **Consumer Energy Council of America Research Foundation**
2000 L Street NW
Room 802
Washington, DC 20036
(202) 659-0404

★ **Energy Conservation Coalition**
Environmental Action
1525 New Hampshire Avenue
Washington, DC 20036
(202) 745-4874

★ **National Energy Information Center**
U.S. Department of Energy
1000 Independence Avenue SW
Room 1H-093
Washington, DC 20585
(202) 586-1094

★ **Safe Energy Communications Council**
1717 Massachusetts Avenue NW
Washington, DC 20036
(202) 483-8491

★ **World Resources Institute**
1735 New York Avenue NW #400
Washington, DC 20006
(202) 638-6300

ENVIRONMENT
(see also ENERGY; FORESTS; OCEANS; OZONE; TOXICS)

★ **Children's Alliance for Protection of the Environment**
PO Box 307
Austin, TX 78767
(512) 476-2273

★ **Environmental Defense Fund**
1616 P Street NW
Room 150
Washington, DC 20036
(202) 387-3500

★ **Friends of the Earth**
218 D Street SE
Washington, DC 20003
(202) 544-2600

★ **Global Tomorrow Coalition**
1325 G Street NW
Room 915
Washington, DC 20005-3104
(202) 628-4016

★ **Greenpeace USA**
1436 U Street NW
Washington, DC 20009
(202) 462-1177

★ **Kids Against Pollution (KAP)**
275 High Street
Closter, NJ 07624
(201) 784-0668

★ **Kids For Saving Earth (KSE)**
PO Box 47247
Plymouth, MN 55447
(612) 525-0002

★ **Mothers and Others For A Livable Planet**
40 West 20th Street
New York, NY 10011
(212) 727-4474

★ **National Home Builders Association**
Environmental Regulation
15th & M Streets NW
Washington, DC 20005
(202) 822-0484

★ **National Science Foundation**
1800 G Street NW
Washington, DC 20550
(202) 357-9498

★ **Natural Resources Defense Council**
40 West 20th Street
New York, NY 10011
(212) 727-2700

★ **Renew America**
1400 16th Street NW #710
Washington DC 20036
(202) 232-2252

★ **Student Environmental Action Coalition**
University of North Carolina
Campus Y, Building #1514A, CB #5115
Chapel Hill, NC 27599
(919) 962-2333

★ **United Nations Conference on**
Environment and Development (UNCED)
U.N. Room S-3060
New York, NY 10017
(212) 963-5959 Fax: (212) 963-1010

★ **U.S. Army Corps of Engineers**
Regulatory Branch
20 Massachusetts Avenue NW
Washington, DC 20314-1000
(202) 272-1785

★ **U.S. Environmental Protection Agency**
Public Information Reference Unit
401 M Street SW
Room 2904
Washington, DC 20460
(202) 260-2080

★ **World Resources Institute**
1735 New York Avenue NW
Washington, DC 20006
(202) 638-6300

★ **Worldwatch Institute**
1776 Massachusetts Avenue NW
Washington, DC 20036
(202) 452-1999

★ **Youth Earth Action**
Box 485
Barre, VT 05461
(802) 476-7757

★ **Youth For Environmental Sanity (YES)**
706 Frederick Street
Santa Cruz, CA 95062
(408) 459-9344

FAMILY
(see also CHILD ABUSE & RUNAWAYS)

★ **Administration for Children and Families**
U.S. Department of Health & Human Services
370 L'Enfant Promenade SW
Washington, DC 20447
(202) 401-9275

★ **Association of Child Advocates**
PO Box 5873
Cleveland, OH 44101
(216) 881-2225

★ **Children's Advocacy Institute**
1160 Battery Street #340
San Francisco, CA 94111
(415) 544-8832

★ **Children's Defense Fund**
122 C Street
Washington, DC 20001
(202) 628-8787 Fax: (202) 783-7324

★ **Child Welfare League**
440 First Street NW #310
Washington, DC 20001-2085
(202) 638-2952 Fax: (202) 638-4004

★ **Coalition on Human Needs**
1000 Wisconsin Avenue NW
Washington, DC 20007
(202) 342-0726

★ **Family Information Center**
National Agricultural Library
10301 Baltimore Boulevard #304
Beltsville, MD 20705
(301) 504-5719

★ **House Select Committee on Children,**
Youth and Families
U.S. Congress
Washington, DC 20515
(202) 226-7660

★ **International Child Resource Institute**
1810 Hopkins Avenue
Berkeley, CA 94707
(415) 644-1000 Fax: (415) 845-1115

FIRST AMENDMENT & FREE SPEECH
(see also CENSORSHIP; TELEVISION & MEDIA)

★ **American Civil Liberties Union**
132 West 43rd Street
New York, NY 10036
(212) 944-9800

★ **Constitutional Rights Foundation**
601 South Kingsley Drive
Los Angeles, CA 90005
(213) 487-5590

★ **First Amendment Congress**
1250 14th Street #840
Denver, CO 80202
(303) 556-4522

★ **The Media Institute**
3017 M Street NW
Washington, DC 20007
(202) 298-7512

FOOD
(see also HUNGER; EATING DISORDERS)

★ **Center for Science in the Public Interest**
1875 Connecticut Avenue NW
Washington, DC 20009
(202) 332-9110

★ **Coalition for Food Irradiation**
1401 New York Avenue #4
Washington, DC 20005-2101
(202) 639-5935

★ **Food and Nutrition Information Center**
National Agricultural Library
U.S. Department of Agriculture
Beltsville, MD 20705
(301) 504-5719

★ **Public Voice for Food and Health Policy**
1001 Connecticut Avenue NW #522
Washington, DC 20036
(202) 659-5930

FORESTS
(see also ENVIRONMENT; OZONE)

★ **Biological Institute of Tropical America**
PO Box 2585
Menlo Park, CA 94025
(415) 593-9024

★ **Congressional Forestry 2000 Task Force**
431 Cannon House Office Building
Washington, DC 20515
(202) 225-5831

★ **Forest Industries Council**
1250 Connecticut Avenue NW #320
Washington, DC 20036
(202) 463-2460

★ **Forest Service**
U.S. Department of Agriculture
PO Box 96090
Washington, DC 20090-6090
(202) 205-1760

★ **Light Hawk**
418 Montezuma Avenue
Santa Fe, NM 87501
(505) 982-9656

★ **National Forest Products Association**
1250 Connecticut Avenue NW #200
Washington, DC 20036
(202) 463-2700

★ **Rainforest Action Network**
301 Broadway
Suite A
San Francisco, CA 94133
(415) 398-4404

★ **The Children's Rainforest**
PO Box 936
Lewiston, ME 04240
(207) 784-1069

GUNS & WEAPONS
(see also CRIME & VIOLENCE; EDUCATION; FAMILY)

★ **Bureau of Alcohol, Tobacco and Firearms**
U.S. Department of Treasury
650 Massachusetts Avenue
Washington, DC 20226
(202) 927-7777

★ **Handgun Control Inc.**
1225 Eye Street NW
Room 1100
Washington, DC 20005
(202) 898-0792

★ **National Rifle Association**
1600 Rhode Island Avenue NW
Washington, DC 20036
(202) 828-6000

★ **National School Safety Association**
Pepperdine University
4165 Thousand Oaks Boulevard #290
Westlake, CA 91362
(805) 373-9977

GOVERNMENT REFORM
(see also VOTE)

★ **Center for Public Integrity**
1910 K Street NW
Washington, DC 20036
(202) 223-0299

★ **Citizens Against Government Waste**
1301 Connecticut Avenue NW #400
Washington, DC 20036
(202) 467-5300

★ **Committee for the Study of
the American Electorate**
421 New Jersey Avenue SE
Washington, DC 20003
(202) 546-3221

★ **Common Cause**
2030 M Street NW
Washington, DC 20036
(202) 833-1200

★ **Congress Watch**
215 Pennsylvania Avenue SE
Washington, DC 20003
(202) 546-4996

★ **Public Citizen**
PO Box 19404
Washington, DC 20036
(202) 833-3000

HATE CRIMES
(see PREJUDICE & RACISM)

HAZARDOUS WASTES
(see also ENVIRONMENT; TOXICS)

HEALTH
(See also AIDS; DRUGS &
ALCOHOL; TOBACCO; TOXICS)

★ **American Medical Association**
515 North State Street
Chicago, IL 60610
(312) 464-5000

★ **Citizen Action**
1300 Connecticut Avenue NW
Washington, DC 20036
(202) 857-5153

★ **National Center for Health Statistics**
3700 East-West Highway
Hyattsville, MD 20782
(301) 486-8500

★ **National Health Information Center**
PO Box 1133
Washington, DC 20013-1133
(800) 336-4797 (301) 565-4167 in MD

HIGHER EDUCATION
& STUDENT AID
(see also STUDENT RIGHTS)

★ **ERIC Clearinghouse on Higher Education**
George Washington University
One Dupont Circle
Washington, DC 20036-1183
(202) 296-2597

★ **ERIC Clearinghouse on Junior Colleges**
University of California
Mathematical Sciences Building Room 8118
405 Hilgard Avenue
Los Angeles, CA 90024-1564
(310) 825-3931

★ **U.S. Department of Education**
Postsecondary Education Staff
Office for Minorities and Women
400 Maryland Avenue SW
Room 3915/MS3325
Washington, DC 20202
(202) 708-5656

★ **U.S. Student Association**
1012 14th Street NW
Room 207
Washington, DC 20005
(202) 347-8772

HOMELESSNESS

★ **Community for Creative Non-Violence**
425 Second Street NW
Washington, DC 20001
(202) 393-4409

★ **Families for the Homeless**
National Mental Health Association
1021 Prince Street
Alexandria, VA 22314
(703) 684-7782

★ **Homelessness Information Exchange**
1830 Connecticut Avenue NW
Washington, DC 20009
(202) 462-7551

★ **National Alliance to End Homelessness**
1518 K Street NW #206
Washington, DC 20005
(202) 638-1526

★ **National Coalition for the Homeless**
1621 Connecticut Avenue NW #400
Washington, DC 20009
(202) 265-2371

★ **National Network on the Homeless**
1319 F Street NW
Room 401
Washington, DC 20004
(202) 783-7949

★ **National Student Campaign Against Hunger and Homelessness**
29 Temple Place
Boston, MA 02111
(617) 292-4823

★ **Shooting Back**
(Photographs taken by homeless kids)
1901 18th Street NW
Washington, DC 20008
(202) 232-5169

★ **Trevor's Campaign for the Homeless**
Box 21
Gladwyne, PA 19035
(215) 325-0640

★ **U.S. Department of Housing and Urban Development**
Library and Information Services
451 Seventh Street SW
Washington, DC 20410
(202) 708-1420

HUMAN RIGHTS - International
(see also PREJUDICE & RACISM)

★ **Amnesty USA**
322 Eighth Ave
New York, NY 10001
(212) 807-8400

★ **Children of the Earth Coalition**
PO Box 217
Newfane, VT 05345
(802) 365-7616 Fax: (802) 365-7798

★ **Congressional Human Rights Caucus**
H2-552 House Office Building, Annex 2
Washington, DC 20515
(202) 226-4040

★ **Human Rights Advocates International**
230 Park Avenue #460
New York, NY 10169
(212) 986-5555

★ **U.S. Department of State**
Bureau of Human Rights and Humanitarian Affairs
2201 C Street NW
Washington, DC 20520
(202) 647-2126

HUNGER

★ **Campaign to End Childhood Hunger**
Food Research and Action Center
1875 Connecticut Avenue NW #540
Washington, DC 20009
(202) 986-2200 Fax: (202) 986-2525

★ **CARE**
660 First Avenue
New York, NY 10016
(800) 242-GIVE (212) 686-3110 in NY

★ **House Select Committee on Hunger**
U.S. Congress
507 House Annex 2
Washington, DC 20515
(202) 226-5470

★ **Oxfam America**
115 Broadway
Boston, MA 02116
(617) 482-1211

★ **Population Crisis Committee**
1120 19th Street NW #550
Washington, DC 20036
(202) 659-1833 Fax: (202) 293-1795

★ **RESULTS**
236 Massachusetts Avenue NE
Washington, DC 20002
(202) 543-9340

★ **United Nations' Children's Fund (UNICEF)**
3 United Nations Plaza
New York, NY 10017
(212) 326-7000

★ **U.S. Committee for UNICEF**
333 East 38th Street
New York, NY 10016
(212) 922-2508

★ **Youth Ending Hunger**
The Hunger Project
1388 Sutter Street
San Francisco, CA 94109-5952
(415) 928-8700 Fax: (415) 928-8799

★ **Zero Population Growth**
1400 16th Street NW #320
Washington, DC 20036
(202) 332-2200

JOBS
(see also VOCATIONAL
EDUCATION)

★ **Child Labor Programs**
Employment Standards Administration
U.S. Department of Labor
200 Constitution Avenue NW
Washington, DC 20210
(202) 523-7579

★ **National Center for Careers in Public Life**
1225 15th Street NW
Washington, DC 20005
(202) 232-6800

★ **U.S. Department of Labor**
Office of Strategic Planning
200 Constitution Avenue NW #S2322
Washington, DC 20210
(202) 523-0660

★ **U.S. Equal Employment Opportunity Commission**
1801 L Street NW
Washington, DC 20507
(800) 669-3362 (202) 663-4900 in DC

JUVENILE DELINQUENCY
(see CRIME & VIOLENCE)

LIBRARIES

★ **American Library Association**
Young Adult Services Division
50 East Huron Street
Chicago, IL 60611
(312) 944-6780

★ **Library of Congress**
101 Independence Avenue SE
Washington, DC 20540
(202) 707-5522

★ **National Commission on Libraries & Information Science**
1111 18th Street NW #310
Washington, DC 20036
(202) 254-3100

MEDIA
(see TELEVISION & MEDIA)

MUSIC & VIDEOS
(see CENSORSHIP)

NUCLEAR DISARMAMENT
(see also PEACE)

★ **Arms Control Association**
11 Dupont Circle NW
Washington, DC 20036
(202) 797-6450

★ **Center for Innovative Diplomacy**
17931 Sky Park Circle #F
Irvine, CA 92714
(714) 250-7340

★ **SANE/Freeze**
1819 H Street NW #640
Washington, DC 20006
(202) 862-9740

★ **U.S. Arms Control and Disarmament Agency**
320 21st Street NW
Washington, DC 20451
(202) 647-8677

OCEANS
(see also ENVIRONMENT; WATER)

★ **Center for Marine Conservation**
1725 DeSales Street NW
Room 500
Washington, DC 20036
(202) 429-5609 Fax: (202) 872-0619

★ **Cousteau Society**
930 West 21st Street
Norfolk, VA 23517
(804) 627-1144

★ **National Oceanic and Atmospheric Administration**
U.S. Department of Commerce
Washington, DC 20230
(202) 377-2985

★ **Save The Whales**
PO Box 2000
Washington, DC 20007
(202) 337-2332

OZONE
(See also ENVIRONMENT; FORESTS)

★ **Carbon Dioxide Campaign**
Children's Earth Fund
40 West 20th Street
New York, NY 10011
(212) 727-4493 Fax: (212) 727-1773

★ **Global ReLeaf Program**
American Forestry Program
PO Box 2000
Washington, DC 20013
(800) 368-5748 (202) 667-3300 in DC

★ **International Ozone Association**
Pan American Commission
83 Oakwood Avenue
Norwalk, CT 06850
(203) 847-8169

PARKS & RECREATION
(see also FORESTS)

★ **National Parks and Conservation Association**
1776 Massachusetts Avenue NW #200
Washington, DC 20036
(202) 223-6722

★ **National Park Service Clearinghouse**
Technical Information Center
12795 West Alameda Parkway
Denver, CO 80225-0287
(303) 969-2130

★ **Sierra Club**
730 Polk Street
San Francisco, CA 94109
(415) 776-2211

★ **U.S. Department of Interior**
Bureau of Land Management
1849 C Street NW
Washington, DC 20240
(202) 208-5717

★ **U.S. Department of Transportation**
Environment Division
400 7th Street, SW #9217
Washington, DC 20590
(202) 366-4366

PEACE
(see also NUCLEAR DISARMAMENT)

★ **Children of War**
85 South Oxford Street
Brooklyn, NY 11217
(718) 858-6882 Fax: (718) 237-3193

★ **Cumberland Center for Justice and Peace**
PO Box 857
Sewanee, TN 37375
(615) 598-5369

★ **Educators for Social Responsibility**
23 Garden Street
Cambridge, MA 02138
(617) 492-1764

★ **Peace Development Fund**
PO Box 270
Amherst, MA 01007
(413) 256-8306

★ **U.S. Institute for Peace**
1550 M Street NW
Washington, DC 20005-1708
(202) 457-6063

★ **Young and Teen Peacemakers**
37 Lebanon Street
Hamilton, NY 13346
(315) 824-4332

POPULATION
(see HUNGER)

PREJUDICE & RACISM
(see also PEACE; SEXISM)

★ **American-Arab Anti-Discrimination Committee**
4201 Connecticut Avenue NW #500
Washington, DC 20008
(202) 244-2990

★ **Anti-Defamation League of B'nai B'rith**
823 United Nations Plaza
New York, NY 10017
(212) 490-2525 Fax: (212) 867-0779

★ **Asian-American Legal Defense and Education Fund**
99 Hudson Street
New York, NY 10013
(212) 966-5932

★ **Congressional Black Caucus**
H2-344 House Office Building Annex 2
Washington, DC 20515
(202) 226-7790

★ **Congressional Hispanic Caucus**
H2-557 House Office Building Annex 2
Washington, DC 20515
(202) 226-3430

★ **League of United Latin American Citizens**
400 First Street NW #716
Washington, DC 20001
(202) 628-0717

★ **National Association for the Advancement of Colored People/Youth and College Division**
4805 Mount Hope Drive
Baltimore, MD 21215-3297
(301) 358-8900

★ **National Institute Against Prejudice and Violence**
31 South Greene Street
Baltimore, MD 21201
(301) 328-5170

★ **National Urban League**
Youth Services Department
500 East 62nd Street
New York, NY 10021
(212) 310-9000

★ **Students and Youth Against Racism**
PO Box 1819
New York, NY 10159
(212) 741-0633

★ **U.S. Commission on Civil Rights**
Clearinghouse Division
1121 Vermont Avenue NW
Washington, DC 20425
(202) 376-8113

★ **U.S. Department of Justice**
Community Relations Service
5550 Friendship Boulevard #330
Chevy Chase, MD 20815
(800) 347-4283

RAIN FORESTS
(see FORESTS; ENVIRONMENT)

RECYCLING
(see also ENVIRONMENT)

★ **American Paper Institute**
1250 Connecticut Avenue NW
Washington, DC 20036
(800) 878-8878

★ **Environmental Action**
1525 New Hampshire Avenue NW
Washington, DC 20036
(202) 745-4870

★ **Institute for Local Self-Reliance**
2425 18th Street NW
Washington, DC 20009
(202) 232-4108

★ **National Recycling Coalition**
1101 30th Street NW #305
Washington, DC 20009
(202) 625-6406

RUNAWAYS
(see FAMILY;
CHILD ABUSE & RUNAWAYS)

SCHOOL SAFETY
(see CRIME & VIOLENCE;
GUNS & WEAPONS)

SEXISM

★ **American Association of University Women**
2401 Virginia Avenue NW
Washington, DC 20037
(202) 785-7700

★ **Institute for Women's Policy Research**
1400 20th Street NW #104
Washington, DC 20036
(202) 785-5100

★ **National Organization for Women (NOW)**
1000 16th Street NW #700
Washington, DC 20036
(202) 331-0066

SMOKING
(see TOBACCO)

SPORTS

★ **National Association for Girls and Women in Sports**
1900 Association Drive
Reston, VA 22091
(703) 476-3450

★ **President's Council on Physical Fitness and Sports**
450 Fifth Street NW #7103
Washington, DC 20001
(202) 272-3421

STUDENT RIGHTS
(see also EDUCATION;
CENSORSHIP)

★ **American Civil Liberties Union (ACLU)**
132 West 43rd Street
New York, NY 10036
(212) 944-9800

★ **American Student Council Association**
National Association of Elementary School Principals
1516 Duke Street
Alexandria, VA 22314
(703) 684-3345

★ **Family Rights and Privacy Office**
U.S. Department of Education
400 Maryland Avenue SW
Washington, DC 20202
(202) 732-1807

★ **National Association of Student Councils**
National Association of Secondary School Principals
Division of Student Activities
1904 Association Drive
Reston, VA 22091
(703) 860-0200

SUICIDE PREVENTION

★ **National Committee on Youth Suicide Prevention**
65 Essex Road
Chestnut Hill, MA 02167
(617) 738-7800

★ **National Mental Health Association**
1021 Prince Street
Alexandria, VA 22314
(703) 684-7722

★ **Youth Suicide National Center**
445 Virginia Avenue
San Mateo, CA 94402
(415) 347-3961

TEEN PREGNANCY

★ **Adolescent Pregnancy Program**
U.S. Department of Health and Human Services
200 Independence Avenue SW #736E
Washington, DC 20201
(202) 245-7473

★ **American Civil Liberties Union**
132 West 43rd Street
New York, NY 10036
(212) 944-9800

★ **American Life League**
PO Box 1350
Stafford, VA 22554
(202) 546-5550

★ **Congressional Coalition on Adoption**
Room SH-331 Hart Senate Office Building
Washington, DC 20510
(202) 224-2752

★ **National Abortion Rights Action League**
11101 14th Street NW Fifth Floor
Washington, DC 20005
(202) 408-4600

★ **National Right to Life Committee**
419 Seventh Street NW #500
Washington, DC 20004
(202) 626-8800

★ **Planned Parenthood Federation of America**
810 Seventh Avenue
New York, NY 10019
(212) 541-7800

TELEVISION & MEDIA
(see also ADVERTISING & CONSUMER CONCERNS)

★ **Accuracy in Media**
1275 K Street NW #1150
Washington, DC 20005
(202) 371-6710

★ **Cable Television Information Center**
PO Box 1205
Annandale, VA 22003
(703) 941-1770

★ **Center for Investigative Reporting**
530 Howard Street, Second Floor
San Francisco, CA 94105-3007
(415) 543-1200

★ **Corporation for Public Broadcasting**
901 E Street NW
Washington, DC 20004
(202) 879-9600

★ **Fairness and Accuracy in Reporting**
130 West 25th Street
New York, NY 10001
(212) 633-6700

★ **Federal Communications Commission**
Mass Media Bureau
1919 M Street NW
Washington, DC 20554
(202) 632-7048

★ **National Association of Broadcasters**
1771 N Street NW
Washington, DC 20036
(202) 429-5300

★ **National Council for Families & Television**
3801 Barham Boulevard #300
Los Angeles, CA 90068
(213) 876-5959

TOBACCO
(see also HEALTH)

★ **Advocacy Institute**
1730 Rhode Island Avenue NW #600
Washington, DC 20036
(202) 659-8475 Fax: (202) 659-8484

★ **American Cancer Society**
1599 Clifton Road NE
Atlanta, GA 30329
(404) 320-3333

★ **American Heart Association**
7320 Greenville Avenue
Dallas, TX 75231
(214) 373-6300

★ **American Lung Association**
1740 Broadway
New York, NY 10019
(212) 315-8700

★ **Americans for Nonsmokers' Rights**
2530 San Pablo Avenue #J
Berkeley, CA 94702
(510) 841-3032 Fax: (510) 841-7702

★ **Coalition on Smoking or Health**
1607 New Hampshire Avenue NW
Washington, DC 20009
(202) 785-3355

★ **Doctors Ought To Care (DOC)**
1423 Harper Street
Augusta, GA 30912
(404) 721-2269

★ **National Cancer Institute**
9000 Rockville Pike
Bethesda, MD 20892
(800) 4-CANCER

★ **Smokefree Educational Services**
375 South End Avenue #32F
New York, NY 10280
(212) 912-0960 Fax: (212) 488-8911

★ **Smokeless Tobacco Council**
2550 M Street NW #300
Washington, DC 20037
(202) 452-1252

★ **Smokers' Rights Alliance**
20 East Main Street #710
Mesa, AZ 85201
(602) 461-8882

★ **Stop Teenage Addiction Today (STAT)**
121 Lyman Street #210
Springfield, MA 01103
(413) 732-7828

★ **Tobacco Divestment Project**
143 Newbury Street
Boston, MA 02116
(617) 266-6130

★ **Tobacco Institute**
1875 Eye Street NW #800
Washington, DC 20006
(202) 457-4800

TOXICS

★ **Alliance to End Childhood Lead Poisoning**
600 Pennsylvania Avenue SE #100
Washington, DC 20003
(202) 543-1147

★ **Center for Safety in the Arts**
5 Beekman Street
New York, NY 10038
(212) 227-6220

★ **Citizens Clearinghouse for Hazardous Wastes**
PO Box 926
Arlington, VA 22216
(703) 276-7070

★ **National Agricultural Chemicals Association**
1155 15th Street NW #900
Washington, DC 20005
(202) 296-1585

★ **National Institute of Environmental Health Sciences**
PO Box 12233
Research Triangle Park, NC 27709
(919) 541-3345

★ **National Pesticide Telecommunications Network**
Texas Tech University Health Sciences Center
Department of Preventative Medicine
Lubbock, TX 79430
(800) 858-PEST Fax: (806) 743-3091

★ **Office of Hazardous Materials**
U.S. Department of Transportation
400 Seventh Street SW
Washington, DC 20590
(202) 366-0656

★ **Toxic Substances and Disease Registry**
U.S. Department of Health and Human Services
1600 Clifton Street NE
Atlanta, GA 30333
(404) 452-4111

VOCATIONAL EDUCATION

★ **Career College Association**
750 First Street NE
Washington, DC 20002
(202) 336-6700

★ **ERIC Clearinghouse on Adult, Career and Vocational Learning**
Ohio State University on Education
1960 Kenny Road
Columbus, OH 43210-1090
(800) 848-4815 (614) 292-4353 in OH

★ **National Center for Research in Vocational Education**
Graduate School of Education, Tolman Hall
University of California
Berkeley, CA 94720
(415) 642-4004

VOTE
(see also GOVERNMENT REFORM)

★ **League of Women Voters**
1730 M Street NW
Washington, DC 20036
(202) 429-1965

★ **Project Vote**
1424 16th Street NW
Room 101
Washington, DC 20036
(202) 328-1500

★ **Rock The Vote**
PO Box 5434
Beverly Hills, CA 90209
(310) 276-8364

★ **Youth Action**
2335 18th Street NW
Washington, DC 20009
(202) 483-1432

WATER
(see also ENVIRONMENT; OCEANS)

★ **Clean Water Action**
317 Pennsylvania Avenue
Washington, DC 20003
(202) 457-1286

★ **Safe Drinking Water Hotline**
U.S. Environmental Protection Agency
401 M Street SW
Washington, DC 20460
(800) 426-4791

★ **Save Our Streams (SOS)**
Izaak Walton League of America
1401 Wilson Boulevard
Level B
Arlington VA 22209
(703) 528-1818

★ **Water Pollution Control Federation**
601 Wythe Street
Alexandria, VA 22314-1994
(703) 684-2400

WILDLIFE
(See also ANIMALS; ZOOS)

★ **Defenders of Wildlife**
1244 19th Street NW
Washington, DC 20036
(202) 659-9510

★ **National Audubon Society**
950 Third Avenue
New York, NY 10022
(212) 832-3200

★ **National Wildlife Federation**
1400 16th Street NW
Washington, DC 20036-2266
(202) 797-6800

★ **U.S. Fish and Wildlife Service**
Office of Endangered Species
4401 North Fairfax Drive
Arlington, VA 22203
(703) 358-1711

★ **Wilderness Society**
900 17th Street NW
Washington, DC 20036
(202) 833-2300

★ **World Wildlife Fund**
1250 24th Street NW
Washington, DC 20037
(202) 293-4800

ZOOS
(see also ANIMALS; WILDLIFE)

★ **American Association of Zoo Keepers**
Topeka Zoological Park
635 Gage Boulevard
Topeka, KS 66606
(913) 272-5821

★ **American Association of Zoological Parks and Aquariums**
Oglebay Park, Route 88
Wheeling, WV 26003
(304) 242-2160

U.S. Congressional Committees

There is virtually *no* subject that some legislative aide on Capitol Hill isn't following. Many congressional committees have overlapping authority on particular issues; for example, twenty-one Senate and fifty-four House panels have responsibility for some aspect of the "War on Drugs." The staff members on the committees and subcommittees listed below can share their expertise over the phone, refer you to other specialists, and send you published hearings and other documents free-of-charge. Congress tends to be particularly responsive to information requests because legislators want your vote.

If, for some reason, a congressional employee initially does not take your request seriously, explain the reasons behind your query and make sure they realize you aren't kidding around!

SENATE COMMITTEES

★ Senate Special Committee on Aging

41-G Dirksen Senate Office Building
Washington, DC 20510   (202) 224-5364
Topics covered: elderly Americans. This committee has no legislative authority but it conducts investigative hearings in Washington, D.C. and around the country.

★ Senate Committee on Agriculture, Nutrition and Forestry

328 Russell Senate Office Building
Washington, DC 20510   (202) 224-2035
Topics covered: agriculture; forestry and forest reserves; farm credit; school nutrition; and food stamp programs.

SUBCOMMITTEES:
Agricultural Credit
Agricultural Production and Stabilization of Prices
Agricultural Research, and General Legislation
Conservation and Forestry
Domestic and Foreign Marketing and Product Promotion
Nutrition and Investigations
Rural Development and Rural Electrification

★ Senate Committee on Appropriations

S-128 Capitol Building
Washington, DC 20510   (202) 224-7282

Topics covered: appropriations of revenues for executive agencies and federal programs.

SUBCOMMITTEES:
Agriculture and Related Agencies/(202) 224-7240
Commerce, Justice, State, and Judiciary/(202) 224-7277
Defense/(202) 224-7255
District of Columbia/(202) 224-2731
Energy and Water Development/(202) 224-7260
Foreign Operations/(202) 224-7284
HUD-Independent Agencies/(202) 224-7231
Interior and Related Agencies/(202) 224-7214
Labor, Health and Human Services, Education/(202) 224-7288
Legislative Branch/(202) 224-7338
Military Construction/(202) 224-7276
Transportation and Related Agencies/(202) 224-0330
Treasury, Postal Service, and General Government/(202) 224-6280

★ Senate Committee on the Armed Services

228 Russell Senate Office Building
Washington, DC 20510   (202) 224-3871
Topics covered: military and defense matters.

SUBCOMMITTEES:
Strategic Forces and Nuclear Deterrence
Conventional Forces and Alliance Defense

Projection Forces and Regional Defense
Defense Industry and Technology
Readiness, Sustainability, and Support
Manpower and Personnel

★ Senate Committee on Banking, Housing, and Urban Affairs

534 Dirksen Senate Office Building
Washington, DC 20510   (202) 224-7391

Topics covered: banks and other financial institutions; public and private housing; federal monetary policy; urban development; mass transit; and certain foreign trade matters.

SUBCOMMITTEES:
Housing and Urban Affairs/(202) 224-6348
International Finance and Monetary Policy
Securities
Consumer and Regulatory Affairs
[The rest of the subcommittees can be reached at (202) 224-7391.]

★ Senate Committee on the Budget

621 Dirksen Senate Office Building
Washington, DC 20510   (202) 224-0642

Topics covered: coordination of appropriations and revenues in federal budget. This committee has no subcommittees.

★ Senate Committee on Commerce, Science, and Transportation

Suite SD-508 Dirksen Senate Office Building
Washington, DC 20510   (202) 224-5115

Topics covered: regulation of interstate transportation, including railroads, buses, trucks, ships, pipelines, and civil aviation; Coast Guard; Merchant Marine; science and technology research policy; communications; non-military aeronautical and space sciences; coastal zone management; and oceans policy.

SUBCOMMITTEES:
Aviation
Communications
Consumer
Foreign Commerce and Tourism
Merchant Marine
Science, Technology, and Space
Surface Transportation
National Ocean Policy Study

★ Senate Committee on Energy and Natural Resources

364 Dirksen Senate Office Building
Washington, DC 20510   (202) 224-4971

Topics covered: regulation, conservation, and research and development of all forms of energy; mining; national parks; wilderness areas and historical sites; and territorial possessions of the U.S.

SUBCOMMITTEES:
Energy Regulation and Conservation
Energy Research and Development
Mineral Resources Development and Production

Public Lands, National Parks and Forests
Water and Power

★ Senate Committee on Environment and Public Works

458 Dirksen Senate Office Building
Washington, DC 20510   (202) 224-6176

Topics covered: environmental protection; water resources; flood control; public works and buildings; highways; noise pollution.

SUBCOMMITTEES:
Environmental Protection
Nuclear Regulation
Superfund, Ocean and Water Protection
Toxic Substances, Environmental Oversight, Research and Development
Water Resources, Transportation and Infrastructure

★ Senate Committee on Finance

205 Dirksen Senate Office Building
Washington, DC 20510   (202) 224-4515

Topics covered: taxes; tariffs; import quotas; old-age and survivors insurance; Medicare; unemployment insurance; general revenue sharing.

SUBCOMMITTEES:
Energy and Agricultural Taxation
Health for Families and the Uninsured
International Debt
International Trade
Medicare and Long-Term Care
Private Retirement Plans and Internal Revenue Service
Social Security and Family Policy
Taxation and Debt Management

★ Senate Committee on Foreign Relations

419 Dirksen Senate Office Building
Washington, DC 20510   (202) 224-4651

Topics covered: foreign policy; treaties; diplomatic affairs; United Nations.

SUBCOMMITTEES:
African Affairs
East Asian and Pacific Affairs
European Affairs
International Economic Policy, Trade, Oceans and Environment
Near Eastern and South Asian Affairs
Terrorism, Narcotics, and International Communications
Western Hemisphere and Peace Corps Affairs

★ Senate Committee on Governmental Affairs

340 Dirksen Senate Office Building
Washington, DC 20510   (202) 224-4751

Topics covered: budget and accounting matters; organization and reorganization of executive branch; intergovernmental relations; municipal affairs of the District of Columbia; civil service; postal service; and the census.

SUBCOMMITTEES:
Federal Services, Post Office, and Civil Service/(202) 224-2254
General Services, Federalism, and DC/(202) 224-4718
Government Information and Regulation/(202) 224-9000
Oversight of Government Management/(202) 224-3682
Permanent Subcommittee on Investigations/(202) 224-3721

★ Senate Select Committee on Indian Affairs
838 Hart Senate Office Building
Washington, DC 20510   (202) 224-2251
Topics covered: Native Americans. This Committee does not have legislative power but studies and investigates such issues as education, health care, housing and career opportunities.

★ Senate Select Committee on Intelligence
211 Hart Senate Office Building
Washington, DC 20510   (202) 224-1700
Topics covered: FBI, Central Intelligence Agency and other intelligence gathering and surveillance operations.

★ Senate Committee on the Judiciary
224 Dirksen Senate Office Building
Washington, DC 20510   (202) 224-5225
Topics covered: federal courts and judges; civil rights and civil liberties; constitutional amendments; legislative apportionment; antitrust and monopoly; immigration and naturalization.

SUBCOMMITTEES:
Antitrust, Monopolies and Business Rights/(202) 224-5701
Constitution/(202) 224-5573
Courts and Administrative Practice/(202) 224-4022
Immigration and Refugee Affairs/(202) 224-7878
Patents, Copyrights, and Trademarks/(202) 224-8178
Technology and the Law/(202) 224-3406

★ Senate Committee on Labor and Human Resources
428 Dirksen Senate Office Building
Washington, DC 20510   (202) 224-5375

Topics covered: education, labor, health, and public welfare.

SUBCOMMITTEES:
Aging
Children, Family, Drugs and Alcoholism
Education, Arts, and Humanities
Employment and Productivity
Handicapped
Labor

★ Senate Committee on Rules and Administration
305 Russell Senate Office Building
Washington, DC 20510   (202) 224-6352
Topics covered: rules governing the Senate; Senate employees; management of the Senate; federal elections; Presidential succession; the Smithsonian Institution; Library of Congress. There are no subcommittees.

★ Senate Committee on Small Business
428-A Russell Senate Office Building
Washington, DC 20510   (202) 224-5175
Topics covered: measures relating to small businesses generally, and to the Small Business Administration.

SUBCOMMITTEES:
Competition and Antitrust Enforcement
Export Expansion
Government Contracting and Paperwork Reduction
Innovation, Technology, and Productivity
Rural Economy and Family Farming
Urban and Minority-Owned Business Development

★ Senate Committee on Veterans' Affairs
414 Russell Senate Office Building
Washington, DC 20510   (202) 224-9126
Topics covered: veterans' affairs, including pensions, medical care, life insurance, education, and rehabilitation. No subcommittees.

HOUSE OF REPRESENTATIVES COMMITTEES

★ House Committee on Agriculture
1301 Longworth House Office Building
Washington, DC 20515   (202) 225-2171
Topics covered: agriculture and forestry measures, including farm credit, crop insurance, soil conservation, rural electrification, domestic marketing, and nutrition.

SUBCOMMITTEES:
Conservation, Credit, and Rural Development
Cotton, Rice, and Sugar
Department Operations, Research, and Foreign Agriculture

Domestic Marketing, Consumer Relations, and Nutrition
Forests, Family Farms, and Energy
Livestock, Dairy, and Poultry
Tobacco and Peanuts
Wheat, Soybeans, and Feed Grains

★ House Committee on Appropriations
H-218 Capitol Building
Washington, DC 20515   (202) 225-2771

SUBCOMMITTEES:
Commerce, Justice, State, The Judiciary/(202) 225-3351
Defense/(202) 225-2847
District of Columbia/(202) 225-5338
Energy and Water Development/(202) 225-3421
Foreign Operations, Export Financing/(202) 225-2041
Interior and Related Agencies/(202) 225-3081
Labor, Health and Human Services, Education/(202) 225-3508
Legislative/(202) 225-5338
Military Construction/(202) 225-3047
Rural Development, Agriculture/(202) 225-2068
Transportation/(202) 225-2141
Treasury, Postal Service, and General Government/(202) 225-5834
VA, HUD, and Independent Agencies/(202) 225-3241

★ House Committee on Armed Services
2120 Rayburn House Office Building
Washington, DC 20515   (202) 225-4151
Topics covered: defense matters, including procurement practices, weapons systems, manpower, military intelligence, naval petroleum reserves, and military applications of nuclear energy.

SUBCOMMITTEES:
Investigations
Military Installations and Facilities
Military Personnel and Compensation
Procurement and Military Nuclear Systems
Readiness
Research and Development
Seapower and Strategic and Critical Materials

★ House Committee on Banking, Finance, and Urban Affairs
2129 Rayburn House Office Building
Washington, DC 20515   (202) 225-4247
Topics covered: banking and currency legislation; international financial organizations; public and private housing.

SUBCOMMITTEES:
Consumer Affairs and Coinage
Domestic Monetary Policy
Economic Stabilization
Financial Institutions Supervision, Regulation, and Insurance
General Oversight and Investigations
Housing and Community Development
International Development, Finance, Trade, and Monetary Policy
Policy Research and Insurance

★ House Committee on the Budget
214 House Office Building Annex I
Washington, DC 20515   (202) 226-7200
Topics covered: coordination of spending and revenues in federal budget.

SUBCOMMITTEES:
Budget Process, Reconciliation, and Enforcement
Community Development and Natural Resources
Defense, Foreign Policy and Space
Urgent Fiscal Issues
Human Resources

Economic Policy, Projections, and Revenues

★ House Committee on the District of Columbia
1310 Longworth House Office Building
Washington, DC 20515   (202) 225-4457
Topics covered: municipal affairs and administration of the District of Columbia.

SUBCOMMITTEES:
Fiscal Affairs and Health
Government Operations and Metropolitan Affairs
Judiciary and Education

★ House Committee on Education and Labor
2181 Rayburn House Office Building
Washington, DC 20515   (202) 225-4527
Topics covered: education and labor legislation, including vocational rehabilitation, minimum wage legislation, and school lunch programs.

SUBCOMMITTEES:
Elementary, Secondary, and Vocational Education
Employment Opportunities
Health and Safety
Human Resources
Labor-Management Relations
Labor Standards
Postsecondary Education
Select Education

★ House Energy and Commerce Committee
2125 Rayburn House Office Building
Washington, DC 20515   (202) 225-2927
Topics covered: national energy policy; interstate commerce; communications; securities and exchanges; health care; biomedical research; railroads and railroad labor; and consumer affairs and protection.

SUBCOMMITTEES:
Consumer Protection, and Competitiveness/(202) 226-3160
Energy and Power/(202) 226-2500
Health and the Environment/(202) 225-4952
Oversight and Investigations/(202) 225-4441
Telecommunications and Finance/(202) 226-2424
Transportation and Hazardous Materials/(202) 225-9304

★ House Committee on Foreign Affairs
2170 Rayburn House Office Building
Washington, DC 20515   (202) 225-5021
Topics covered: foreign relations; international trade and economic policy; Food For Peace; international commodity agreements.

SUBCOMMITTEES:
Africa/(202) 226-7807
Arms Control, International Security, and Science/(202) 225-8926

Asian and Pacific Affairs/(202) 226-7801
Europe and the Middle East/(202) 225-3345
Human Rights and International Organizations/(202) 226-7825
International Economic Policy and Trade/(202) 226-7820
International Operations/(202) 225-3424
Western Hemisphere Affairs/(202) 226-7812

★ House Committee on Government Operations

2157 Rayburn House Office Building
Washington, DC 20515   (202) 225-5051
Topics covered: executive branch reorganization, intergovernmental relations, and revenue sharing.

SUBCOMMITTEES:
Commerce, Consumer, and Monetary Affairs/(202) 225-4407
Employment and Housing/(202) 225-6751
Environment, Energy, and Natural Resources/(202) 225-6427
Government Activities and Transportation/(202) 225-7920
Government Information, Justice, and Agriculture/(202) 225-3741
Human Resources, Intergovernmental Relations/(202) 225-2548
Legislation and National Security/(202) 225-5147

★ House Committee on House Administration

H-326 Capitol Building
Washington, DC 20515   (202) 225-2061
Topics covered: House administration and management; federal election legislation; Library of Congress; Smithsonian Institution.

SUBCOMMITTEES:
Accounts/(202) 226-7540
Elections/(202) 226-7616
Libraries and Memorials/(202) 226-2307
Office Systems/(202) 225-1608
Personnel and Police/(202) 226-7641
Procurement and Printing/(202) 225-4568
Task Force on Legislative Service Organizations/(202) 225-2061

★ House Committee on Interior and Insular Affairs

1324 Longworth House Office Building
Washington, DC 20515
Topics covered: public lands; national parks; military cemeteries; irrigation; reclamation; U.S. territories and possessions; Native Americans; domestic nuclear energy industry.

SUBCOMMITTEES:
Energy and the Environment/(202) 225-8331
General Oversight and Investigations/(202) 226-4085
Insular and International Affairs/(202) 225-9297
Mining and Natural Resources/(202) 226-7761
National Parks and Public Lands/(202) 226-7736
Water, Power, and Offshore Energy Resources/(202) 225-6042
Indian Affairs Office/(202) 226-7393

★ House Committee on the Judiciary

2137 Rayburn House Office Building
Washington, DC 20515   (202) 225-3951

Topics covered: federal courts; constitutional amendments; immigration and naturalization; presidential succession; antitrust and monopolies; impeachment resolutions; and patents, trademarks, and copyrights.

SUBCOMMITTEES:
Administrative Law and Governmental Relations/(202) 225-5741
Civil and Constitutional Rights/(202) 226-7680
Courts, Intellectual Property, Justice/(202) 225-3926
Crime/(202) 225-1695
Criminal Justice/(202) 226-2406
Economic and Commercial Law/(202) 225-2825
Immigration, Refugees, and International Law/(202) 225-5727

★ House Committee on the Merchant Marine and Fisheries

1334 Longworth House Office Building
Washington, DC 20515   (202) 225-4047
Topics covered: regulation and protection of fisheries and wildlife; Coast Guard; merchant marine; and the Panama Canal.

SUBCOMMITTEES:
Coast Guard and Navigation/(202) 226-3587
Fisheries, Wildlife Conservation, Environment/(202) 226-3533
Merchant Marine/(202) 226-3500
Oceanography/(202) 226-3504
Oversight and Investigations/(202) 226-3508
Panama Canal and Outer Continental Shelf/(202) 226-3514

★ House Committee on the Post Office and Civil Service

309 Cannon House Office Building
Washington, DC 20515   (202) 225-4054
Topics covered: postal service; civil service; and federal statistics.

SUBCOMMITTEES:
Census and Population/(202) 226-7523
Civil Service/(202) 225-4025
Compensation and Employee Benefits/(202) 226-7546
Human Resources/(202) 225-2821
Investigations/(202) 225-6295
Postal Operations and Services/(202) 225-9124
Postal Personnel and Modernization/(202) 226-7520

★ House Committee on Public Works and Transportation

2165 Rayburn House Office Building
Washington, DC 20515   (202) 225-4472
Topics covered: public buildings and roads; bridges and dams; flood control; rivers and harbors; watershed development; mass transit; surface transportation excluding railroads; and civil aviation.

SUBCOMMITTEES:
Aviation/(202) 225-9161
Economic Development/(202) 225-6151
Investigations and Oversight/(202) 225-3274
Public Buildings and Grounds/(202) 225-9961
Surface Transportation/(202) 225-9989
Water Resources/(202) 225-0060

★ House Committee on Rules

H-312 Capitol Building
Washington, DC 20515   (202) 225-9486
Topics covered: schedule for House debate on legislation and which amendments can be considered by the full House.

SUBCOMMITTEES:
Rules of the House/(202) 225-9091
The Legislative Process/(202) 225-1037

★ House Committee on Science, Space, and Technology

2321 Rayburn House Office Building
Washington, DC 20515   (202) 225-6371; Fax 225-8280
Topics covered: astronautical research and development; energy research and development; space; and scientific research and development.

SUBCOMMITTEES:
Energy Research and Development/(202) 225-2884
Investigations and Oversight/(202) 225-2891
International Scientific Cooperation/(202) 226-3636
Natural Resources, Agriculture, Environment/(202) 226-6980
Science, Research, and Technology/(202) 225-1060
Space Science and Applications/(202) 225-7858
Transportation, Aviation, and Materials/(202) 225-8105

★ House Committee on Small Business

2361 Rayburn House Office Building
Washington, DC 20515   (202) 225-5821
Topics covered: measures related to small business, and the U.S. Small Business Administration (SBA).

SUBCOMMITTEES:
Antitrust, Impact of Deregulation and Privatization/(202) 225-6026
Environment and Labor/(202) 225-7673
Exports, Tax Policy, and Special Problems/(202) 225-8944
Procurement, Tourism, and Rural Development/(202) 225-9368
Regulation, Business Opportunity, and Energy/(202) 225-7797
SBA, Minority Enterprise Development/(202) 225-5821

★ House Committee on Standards of Official Conduct

HT-2, Capitol Building
Washington, DC 20515   (202) 225-7103
Topics covered: rules and ethics for members of the House.

★ House Committee on Veterans' Affairs

355 Cannon House Office Building
Washington, DC 20515   (202) 225-3527
Topics covered: veterans' affairs, including pensions, medical care, life insurance, education, and rehabilitation.

SUBCOMMITTEES:
Hospitals and Health Care/(202) 225-9154

Compensation, Pension, and Insurance/(202) 225-3569
Oversight and Investigations/(202) 225-3541
Education, Training and Employment/(202) 225-9166
Housing and Memorial Affairs/(202) 225-9164

★ House Committee on Ways and Means

1102 Longworth House Office Building
Washington, DC 20515   (202) 225-3625
Topics covered: taxation, social security, tariffs, and health care programs financed through payroll taxes.

SUBCOMMITTEES:
Health/(202) 225-7785
Human Resources/(202) 225-1025
Oversight/(202) 225-5522
Select Revenue Measures/(202) 225-6649
Social Security/(202) 225-3943
Trade/(202) 225-3943

★ House Permanent Select Committee on Intelligence

Room H-405, The Capitol Building
Washington, DC 20515   (202) 225-4121

SUBCOMMITTEES:
Legislation/(202) 225-7311
Oversight and Evaluation/(202) 225-5658
Program and Budget Authorization/(202) 225-7690

★ House Select Committee on Aging

House Office Building Annex I, Room H1-712,
Washington, DC 20515   (202) 226-3375
Topics covered: no legislative power but conducts investigative hearings on such issues as housing and health care for the elderly.

★ House Select Committee on Children, Youth, and Families

House Office Building Annex 2, H2-385
Washington, DC 20515   (202) 226-7660
Topics covered: conducts investigative hearings but has no legislative authority.

★ House Select Committee on Hunger

House Office Building Annex 2, H2-507
Washington, DC 20515   (202) 226-5470
Topics covered: surveys both domestic and global hunger and proposes laws but has no legislative authority.

★ House Select Committee on Narcotics Abuse and Control

Room H2-234, House Office Building Annex 2
Washington, DC 20515   (202) 226-3040
Topics covered: conducts investigative hearings only.

State Legislatures

You will find more than fifty information offices listed here because some statehouses do not have one centralized office for legislative information. The toll-free "800" numbers are for in-state residents.

ALABAMA

Senate Bill Status, New Statehouse, 11 South Union Street, Montgomery, AL 36130 (205) 242-7800 Fax: (205) 242-8819. This office can respond to questions about all Senate bills and refer you to the appropriate committee, document room, etc.

House of Representatives, Fifth Floor, Bill Status, Statehouse, 11 South Union Street, Montgomery, AL 36130 (205) 242-7600 Fax: (205) 242-4759. This office can provide information on all bills pending before the Senate or the House of Representatives and can refer you to the appropriate committees, document rooms, etc.

ALASKA

Legislative Information, PO Box Y, Juneau, AK 99811 (907) 465-4648 Fax: (907) 465-2865. This office can provide information on the status of House and Senate bills. It can do subject searches by accessing a database and can provide computer printouts. Copies of bills and laws will be sent out by this office.

ARIZONA

Information Desk, Arizona House of Representatives, State Capitol House Wing, 1700 West Washington Street, Phoenix, AZ 85007 (602) 542-4221 Fax: (602) 542-5411. This information desk is the best starting point to learn the status of all bills pending before the House of Representatives. Information is given out over the phone. Bills, but not printouts, can be mailed out. This office will refer you to the appropriate committees, document room, etc.

Senate Information Desk, Arizona State Senate, Capitol Senate Wing, 1700 West Washington Street, Phoenix, AZ 85007 (602) 542-3559 Fax: (602) 542-3429. This information desk maintains current information on all bills pending before the Senate. Minutes are available by mail, in person, or by fax. This office will refer you to the appropriate committees, document rooms, etc.

ARKANSAS

Office of Legislative Counsel, Bureau of Legislative Research, State Capitol Building, Room 315, Little Rock, AR 72201 (501) 682-1937 Fax: (501) 682-1936. Separate fax for Senate: (501) 682-2917. This office can provide status information on all legislation pending before the House of Representatives and the Senate. It also has scheduling information and can refer you to the

appropriate committees, document rooms, etc. This office will mail copies of bills. For copies of acts, they will refer you to the Secretary of State's Office at (501) 682-1010.

CALIFORNIA

Office of the Chief Clerk, State Assembly, State Capitol, Room 3196, Sacramento, CA 95814 (916) 445-3614. This office can respond to questions regarding legislation pending before the State Assembly and Assembly committees. This office can refer you to the appropriate offices in the State Capitol such as the document rooms.

Secretary of the Senate, State Capitol, Room 3044, Sacramento, CA 95814 (916) 445-4251. This office can provide information about bills pending before the Senate and the Senate committees. The Secretary of the Senate will also refer you to appropriate offices where you can obtain copies of Senate bills.

COLORADO

Legislative Information Center, Legislative Services Building, 200 East 14th Ave, Bill Room, Denver, CO 80203 (303) 866-3055. This office can provide information on the status of both House and Senate bills. The Legislative Information Center can also send you copies of bills as well as mail out status sheets which list bills pertaining to a specific subject.

CONNECTICUT

Legislative Bill Room, Law & Legislative Reference Dept., Connecticut State Library, 231 Capitol Avenue, Hartford, CT 06106 (203) 566-5736. This office can provide information about both House and Senate bills and send you copies of bills. Besides doing a key word or subject search, this office can mail you a printout of all legislation pertaining to one topic. No charge unless copies must be made. Fee for photocopies is 25¢ per page, plus postage.

DELAWARE

Division of Research, Legislative Counsel, Legislative Hall, PO Box 1401, Dover, DE 19903 (302) 739-4114 (800) 282-8545 Fax: (302) 739-3895. This office can provide status information on both House and Senate bills and send you copies of bills. It can access a legislative computerized database and do searches for free. The toll-free number operates year-round. No charge for mailed copies of bills or for the first five pages of faxed copies.

FLORIDA

Legislative Information Division, 704 Claude Pepper Bldg., 111 West Madison Street, Tallahassee, FL 32399-1400 (904) 488-4371 (800) 342-1827. This office can provide status information on all House and Senate bills. It can send you single copies of up to ten bills and mail out printouts of all House and Senate bills pertaining to a specific subject.

GEORGIA

Clerk of the House, House of Representatives, Room 309, State Capitol Building, Atlanta, GA 30334 (404) 656-5015 (800) 282-5803. This office can provide up-to-date information on all House bills and send you copies of House bills. The Clerk of the House will also search a computerized database to tell you all legislation that has been introduced on a specific topic for the current year.

Secretary of the Senate, Room 352, State Capitol Building, Atlanta, GA 30334 (404) 656-5040 (800) 282-5803. This office can respond to questions about all bills pending before the Georgia Senate. The Secretary of the Senate can send you copies of Senate bills and search a computerized database for legislation pertaining to a specific subject.

HAWAII

Clerk of the House, State Capitol of Hawaii, Honolulu, HI 96813 (808) 586-6400 House Fax: (808) 586-6401. This office can respond to questions about bills pending before the House and refer you to the appropriate offices in the State Capitol, such as the document room.

Clerk of the Senate, State Capitol of Hawaii, Honolulu, HI 96813 (808) 548-4675 or 586-6720 Senate Fax: (808) 586-6719. This office can provide status information on all legislation pending before the Hawaii Senate. It can refer you to the appropriate offices in the State Capitol, such as the document room.

IDAHO

Legislative Counsel, State Capitol (Basement East Wing), Boise, ID 83720 (208) 334-2475 Fax: (208) 334-2125. While in session, information and copies of bills are also available from the Legislative Information Center, Statehouse Room 301, Boise, ID 83720 (208) 334-3175. This office can give you information on the status of all House and Senate bills. It also can send you copies of bills, as well as a printout of all legislation pertaining to a specific topic.

ILLINOIS

Clerk of the House, State Capitol Building, Room 424, Springfield, IL 62706 (217) 782-6010 (800) 252-6300. This office can respond to questions about House bills. It can provide you with copies of bills. For example, the Clerk's office is able to send you printouts, a list of all bills sponsored by one legislator, or will refer you to the House Enrolling and Engrossing Office, Room 420 (217) 782-7192. Cost of printouts is 10¢ per page.

Senate Journal Room, Room 407, State Capitol Building, Springfield, IL 62706 (217) 782-4517. This office can respond to questions about Senate bills. For copies, it will refer you to the Senate Enrolling and Engrossing Room, Room 405 (217) 782-6970. Cost is 10¢ per page.

INDIANA

Legislative Information, Legislative Services Agency, 302 Statehouse, Indianapolis, IN 46204 (317) 232-9856. Mr. Jeff Porter can give you bill status information and do searches by key word, subject or legislator. Legislative Information can send you copies of bills but charges 15¢ per page.

IOWA

Legislative Information Office, East 9th and Grand Ave., Room 16, Iowa State Capitol, Des Moines, IA 50319 (515) 281-5129. This office can provide information on all House and Senate bills and send you copies of bills. It can access a computerized database and mail you a printout of all legislation pertaining to a specific subject.

KANSAS

Legislative Reference, Kansas State Library, Third Floor, Statehouse, Room 343 North, Topeka, KS 66612 (913) 296-2149 (800) 432-3924 Fax: (913) 296-6650. This office can tell you the status of all current House and Senate legislation as well as provide bill histories. Legislative Reference can send you copies of bills and voting records.

KENTUCKY

Bill Status, State Capitol Annex Building, Room T-1, Capitol Ave., Frankfort, KY 40601 (502) 564-8100 (800) 633-4171 Fax: (502) 223-5094. This office can provide information on House and Senate bills pending before the legislature. It can also send you copies of bills.

LOUISIANA

Legislative Research Library, House of Representatives, PO Box 94012, Baton Rouge, LA 70804-9012 (504) 342-2431 (800) 272-8186. During the session, call toll-free PULS Line [if out-of-state, (504) 342-2456] for bill status information and they will send you copies of House and Senate bills for a nominal fee. When the legislature is not in session, contact the Legislative Research Library, (504) 342-2431 for bill number. They will then refer you for copies of bills to: The House Docket Office, PO Box 44486, Baton Rouge, LA 70804 (504) 342-6458; or The Senate Docket Office, PO Box 94183, Baton Rouge, LA 70804 (504) 342-2365.

MAINE

Legislative Information Office, Statehouse, Room 314, Station 100, Augusta, ME 04333 (207) 289-1692 Fax: (207) 289-1580. This office can respond to questions about House and Senate bills and do key word or subject searches of its database. Copies of bills are obtained from the Document Room (207) 289-1408. Copies of public laws are available from the Engrossing Room: (207) 289-1324. No charge.

MARYLAND

Legislative Information Desk, Dept. of Legislative Reference, 90 State Circle, Annapolis, MD 21401 (301) 841-3886 (800) 492-7122 Fax: (301) 858-3850. This office can provide status information on all House and Senate bills and send you copies of bills. It can also provide you with a printout of all bills which pertain to a specific subject area. There is no charge.

MASSACHUSETTS

Citizen Information Service, Office of the Secretary of State, 1 Ashburton Place, Room 1611, 16th Floor, Boston, MA 02018 (617) 727-7030 Fax for Senate: (617) 367-8658. This office can provide bill status information and supply copies of bills but you must know the bill number. To obtain bill numbers and other information, contact the Clerk of the Senate: (617) 722-1276 or the Clerk of the House, which is listed below.

Clerk of the House, House of Representatives, Statehouse, Boston, MA 02133; (617) 722-2356; no fax for House. This office can respond to questions about House and Senate bills and will refer you to the document room and other appropriate offices within the Statehouse.

MICHIGAN

Clerk's Office, House of Representatives, PO Box 30014, Lansing, MI 48909 (517) 373-0135 Fax: (517) 373-5791. This office can provide information on the status of House bills and can do searches of its database to identify legislation which pertains to a specific subject. It will refer you to the House document room for copies of bills. For most recent status of House bills, call Bill Clerk for the House, (517) 373-0136.

Secretary of the Senate, PO Box 30036, Lansing, MI 48933 (517) 373-2400. This office can provide Senate bill status information and can also send you copies of bills. For most recent status of Senate bills, call Bill Clerk for the Senate (517) 373-0514.

For copies of bills in either House or Senate, if you have the bill number, call the Document Room, (517) 373-0169.

MINNESOTA

House Index Office, State Capitol Building, Room 211, St Paul, MN 55155 (612) 296-6646. This office can tell you the status of all House bills but will refer you to the Chief Clerk's office at (612) 296-2314 for copies of all House bills. It can search its computerized database to identify all bills that pertain to a specific subject. Fax: (612) 296-9441.

Senate Index Office, State Capitol Building, Room 231, St. Paul, MN 55155 (612) 296-2887 Fax: (612) 296-6511. This office can provide bill copies and status information on all Senate legislation and will refer you to the Secretary of the Senate if you want to obtain copies of bills. It can search its computerized database and identify all bills pertaining to a specific subject.

MISSISSIPPI

House Docket Room, PO Box 1018, New Capitol Room 305, Jackson, MS 39215-1018 (601) 359-3358 Fax: (601) 359-3728. This office can tell you the status of all House bills and send you copies of proposed laws pending before the House.

Senate Docket Room, PO Box 1018, 400 High Street, New Capitol Room 308, Jackson, MS 39215-1018 (601) 359-3229 Fax: (601) 359-3935. This office can respond to questions about bills pending before the Mississippi Senate and send you copies of Senate bills.

MISSOURI

House Information Bill Status, State Capitol, Room 307B, Jefferson City, MO 65101 (314) 751-3659. This office can provide information on bills pending before the House and will refer you to the appropriate offices within the State Capitol, such as the document room.

Senate Research, State Capitol Room B-9, Jefferson City, MO 65101 (314) 751-4666. This office can respond to questions about bills pending before the Senate and will refer you to the appropriate offices such as the document room. No fax capability.

MONTANA

Legislative Counsel, State Capitol, Room 138, Helena, MT 59620 (406) 444-3064 (800) 333-3408 Fax: (406) 444-3036. The in-state toll-free number may change in subsequent sessions of the Montana legislature. The Legislative Counsel office can respond to inquiries year-round and send you copies of bills for 15¢ per page if they photocopy it.

NEBRASKA

Hotline, Office of the Clerk of the Legislature, State Capitol, Room 2018, Lincoln, NE 68509 (402) 471-2609 (800) 742-7456 Fax: (402) 471-2126. This office operates an in-state hotline during the session that can provide information on all bills pending before this unicameral legislature. The Clerk can respond to questions year-round. Requests for bills are directed to the Bill Room, Room 1102, State Capitol Building.

NEVADA

Chief Clerk of the Assembly, Legislative Building, Room 102, 401 S. Carson St., Carson City, NV 89710 (702) 687-5739 Fax: (702) 687-5962. This office can provide information about the status of bills pending before the Assembly. The Chief Clerk will refer you to the appropriate offices in the State Capitol, such as the Publications Department of the Legislature Counsel Bureau, Room 107 (702) 687-6835, or the Secretary of the Senate, Room 123, (702) 687-5742.

NEW HAMPSHIRE

State Library Government, Government Information Bureau, 20 Park Street, Concord, NH 03301 (603) 271-2239 Fax: (603) 271-2205. This office can respond to questions about House and Senate bills pending before the legislature. It can send you copies of bills and search its computerized database for bills pertaining to specific subject areas. The charge is 20¢ per photocopy page and 35¢ per faxed page.

NEW JERSEY

Office of Legislative Services, Bill Room, The Executive Statehouse CN068, Trenton, NJ 08625 (609) 292-6395 (800)

792-8630 Fax: (609) 777-2440. This office can provide information about House and Senate legislation and send you copies of bills by Fax or mail. Office requests that you list bills in numerical order and separate out Assembly from Senate bills. It will refer you to other offices within the Statehouse if necessary.

NEW MEXICO

Legislative Counsel, State Capitol, PERA Building, Room 363, Santa Fe, NM 87503 (505) 984-9600 Fax: (505) 984-9610. This office can provide bill status information on House and Senate legislation. It will refer you to the appropriate offices within the State Capitol, such as the document room.

NEW YORK

New York State Assembly Public Information Office, Room 202, Legislative Office Building, 2nd Floor, Albany, NY 12248 (518) 455-4218 (800) 342-9860. New York State Senate Public Information Office, 214 Legislative Office Building, (518) 455-3216. These offices can provide information on the status of House and Senate bills and send you copies of bills. They may refer you to your local library if you want a search done to identify all bills which pertain to a specific subject, or refer you to the House Document Room, Room 305, Washington and State Streets, Albany, NY 12204 Fax: (518) 455-4741; or the Senate Document Room, Room 317, State Capitol Building, Albany, NY 12247 Fax: (518) 432-3389. For bill status, call (518) 342-9860.

NORTH CAROLINA

Clerk of the House, State Legislative Building, Room 2320, Jones Street, Raleigh, NC 27601-1096 (919) 733-7760. This office can provide information about House and Senate bills and will refer you to the appropriate offices within the State Capitol to obtain copies of bills, such as the Printed Bills Office at (919) 733-5648 Fax: (919) 733-2599.

NORTH DAKOTA

Legislative Counsel Library, State Capitol, 600 East Blvd., Bismarck, ND 58505-0360 (701) 224-2916. This office can provide information about House and Senate bills year-round and will refer you to appropriate offices in the State Capitol. Copies of bills can be obtained from the Secretary of State's Office at (701) 244-2900 Fax: (701) 244-2992. Charge is $1.00 per faxed copy. The legislature maintains an in-state toll-free number during the biannual session.

OHIO

Legislative Information, Statehouse, Columbus, OH 43266-0604 (614) 466-8842 (800) 282-0253. This office can provide information on the status of House and Senate legislation and do subject searches. This telephone bank of researchers will route your requests (i.e., copies of bills). With the bill number, you may call directly: House Bill Room, (614) 466-8207; or Senate Bill Room, (614) 466-7168.

OKLAHOMA

Chief Clerk's Office, House of Representatives, Room 405, State Capitol Bldg., Oklahoma City, OK 73105 (405) 521-2711. This

office can respond to questions about bills pending before the House and Senate. It can refer you to the appropriate offices within the State Capitol.

OREGON

Legislative Library, S-427, State Capitol, Salem, OR 97310 (503) 378-8871 Fax: (503) 378-3289. This office can provide information and copies on House and Senate bills year-round. During the biannual session the legislature offers an in-state toll-free number for bill information.

PENNSYLVANIA

Legislative Reference Bureau, History Room, Main Capitol Building, Room 648, Harrisburg, PA 17120-0033 (717) 787-2342. This office can provide information on the status of House and Senate bills by consulting its card index and computerized database. It will refer you to the appropriate offices where you can obtain copies of bills. Copies of House bills can be obtained from the House Document Room at (717) 787-5320; Senate bills can be obtained from the Senate Document Room at (717) 787-6732.

RHODE ISLAND

State Library, Statehouse Room 208, Providence, RI 02903 (401) 277-2473. This office can provide you with information on the status of House and Senate bills and send you copies of bills. It will refer you to the appropriate legislators or committees. Copies of bills are 50¢ per page.

SOUTH CAROLINA

Legislative Information Systems, Room 112, Blatt Building, 1105 Pendleton St., Columbia, SC 29201 (803) 734-2923. This office can respond to inquiries about House and Senate bills and will refer you to the appropriate offices where you can obtain copies of bills. It can do subject searches and mail printouts.

SOUTH DAKOTA

Public Information Clerk, Legislative Research Counsel, State Capitol Building, 500 East Capitol, Pierre, SD 57501 (605) 773-4498 Fax: (605) 773-4576. Ms. Clare Cholik can provide information on the status of House and Senate bills. She can access a computerized database and do a search to identify legislation which pertains to a specific subject. However, research collection is not online, thus no printouts are available.

TENNESSEE

Office of Legislative Services, State Capitol, Room G-20, War Memorial Bldg, Nashville, TN 37243-0058 (615) 741-3511. This office can provide information on House and Senate bills and will send you copies of bills for 25¢ per page, plus $1.00 for mailing costs. It can identify all legislation pending on specific subjects.

TEXAS

Legislative Reference Library, PO Box 12488, Capitol Station, Austin, TX 78711 (512) 463-1252 Fax: (512) 475-4626. This office can provide information on the status of all House and Senate bills. It can search its computerized database to identify all legislation which pertains to a specific subject. It will refer you to the appropriate offices such as the document room. Fees are: 15¢ per page for printouts; $10.00 for faxed bills; 15¢ per page for bills mailed over ten pages.

UTAH

Legislative Research and General Counsel, 436 State Capitol, Salt Lake City, UT 84114 (801) 538-1032 Fax: (801) 538-1712. This office can respond to questions about House and Senate bills. It will give you the bill number and refer you to the appropriate offices within the State Capitol for copies.

VERMONT

Clerk of the House, Attn: Cathleen Cameron, Statehouse, Montpelier, VT 05602 (802) 828-2247. Ms. Cameron can provide you with information on legislation pending before the House and do subject searches by accessing a computerized database. She will refer you to the appropriate offices in the Statehouse.

Secretary of the Senate, Statehouse, Montpelier, VT 05602 (802) 828-2241. This office can respond to questions about legislation pending before the Senate and will refer you to the appropriate legislators, committees, document rooms, etc., such as the Legislative Counsel Office for status and copies of bills (802) 828-2231 Fax: (802) 828-2424. No charge for bills. Transcripts are 10¢ per page.

VIRGINIA

Legislative Information, House of Delegates, PO Box 406, Richmond, VA 23203 (804) 786-6530 Fax: (804) 786-3215. This office can provide information on House and Senate bills and can send you copies of bills. It can consult a printed cumulative index which is updated daily to identify bills which pertain to a specific subject and a digest of acts that have already passed.

WASHINGTON

House Workroom, Legislative Building, Third Floor Capitol Campus, Olympia, WA 98504 (206) 786-7780 Fax: (206) 786-7021 (800) 562-6000. This office can provide information on the status of bills pending before the House. It can also provide copies of bills. Searches with printouts are not available. The toll-free number is in operation only during the session.

Senate Workroom, Legislative Building, Room 307, Mail Stop AS32, Third Floor Capitol Campus, Olympia, WA 98504 (206) 786-7592 (800) 562-6000 Fax: (206) 786-7520. This office can provide information on bills pending before the Senate and can

supply you with copies of bills. The in-state toll-free number provides both House and Senate bill information but only during the session. The out-of-state number is (206) 786-7274. Copies of Senate and House bills are available from the Bill Room, (206) 786-7573.

WEST VIRGINIA

Clerk of the House, House of Delegates, Room 212, State Capitol, Charleston, WV 25305 (304) 340-3200 Fax: (304) 348-2182. This office can respond to questions about legislation pending before the House of Delegates and House committees. It will refer you to appropriate offices in the State Capitol to obtain legislative documents. Manual searches go back two years. No printouts are available.

Clerk of the Senate, Room 211M, State Capitol, Charleston, WV 25305 (304) 357-7800 Fax: (304) 357-7829. No documents over five pages will be faxed. This office can provide information on the status of bills pending before the Senate. It will refer you to the appropriate offices in the State Capitol.

WISCONSIN

Legislative Reference Bureau, 100 North Capitol Street, PO Box 2037, Madison, WI 53701-2037 (608) 266-0341; (800) 362-9696; Fax: (608) 266-5648. The legislature operates a Legislative Hotline during the session; if calling from outside the state, dial (608) 266-9960. The Legislative Reference Bureau can respond to questions year-round and will refer you to the document room, etc.

WYOMING

Legislative Service Office, State Capitol Building, Room 213, Cheyenne, WY 82002 (307) 777-7881 Fax: (307) 777-5466. When the Wyoming legislature is not in session, it is necessary to contact this office. During the session, bill status questions are best directed to the two offices noted below.

Senate Information Clerk, State Capitol Building, Cheyenne, WY 82002 (307) 777-6185 Fax: (307) 777-7711. This office can respond to questions about the status of bills pending before the Senate. It will refer you to the Bill Room to obtain copies of bills.

House Information Clerk, State Capitol Building, Cheyenne, WY 82002 (307) 777-7765 Fax: (307) 777-7852. This office can provide current information on legislation pending before the House. It will refer you to the appropriate offices in the State Capitol, such as the Bill Room. Copies of House and Senate bills, if bill number is known, can be obtained for 10¢ per page plus postage. Call (307) 777-7648.

Bibliography

Here is an eclectic list of free and inexpensive pamphlets, manuals and books. Some focus on just one component of a campaign. *Note By Note*, for example, describes in detail how to choreograph a benefit concert. Other books cover different aspects of organizing a campaign, or explain out the quirks of the legislative process. The publications below which include a complete address are not available at bookstores or libraries.

Advocacy Institute. *The Elements of A Successful Public Interest Advocacy Campaign* (1730 Rhode Island Avenue NW, Washington, DC 20036)

Anzalone, Joan. *Good Works: A Guide to Careers in Social Change* (Barricade Books, New York, NY)

Benton Foundation. *Op-Eds: A Cost-Effective Strategy for Advocacy* (1710 Rhode Island Avenue NW, Washington, DC 20036)

Biagi, Bob. *Working Together: A Manual for Helping Groups Work More Effectively* (Center for Organizational and Community Development, 225 Furcolo Hall, University of Massachusetts, Amherst, MA 01003)

Bobo, Kim and Steve Max of the Midwest Academy. *A Manual for Activists in the 1990s* (Seven Locks Press, Washington, DC)

Boyte, Harry and Kathyrn Stoff Hogg. *dOing pOlitics* (Project Public Life, Humphrey Institute, 301 19th Avenue South, Minneapolis, MN 55455)

Center for Research and Development in Law-Related Education. *Righting Your Future: LRE Lesson Plans for Today and Tomorrow* (CRADLE, Wake Forest University School of Law, PO Box 7206, Reynolda Station, Winston-Salem, NC 27109)

Common Cause. *Common Cause Action Manual* (2030 M Street NW, Washington, DC 20036)

C-SPAN and the Benton Foundation. *Gavel To Gavel: A Guide to the Televised Proceedings of Congress* (1710 Rhode Island Avenue NW, Washington, DC 20036)

Gardner, John W. *Self-Renewal: The Individual and The Innovative Society* (W. W. Norton & Co., New York, NY)

Goldberg, Kim. *The Barefoot Channel: Community Television as a Tool for Social Change* (New Star Books, Vancouver, Canada)

Grifin, Kelley and Ralph Nader. *More Action for a Change: Students Serving the Public Interest* (Center for Study of Responsive Law, PO Box 19367, Washington, DC 20036)

Independent Sector. *Lobby? You?* (1828 L Street NW, Washington, DC 20036)

Kentucky Youth Advocates. *Fairness Is A Kid's Game* (2034 Frankfurt Avenue, Louisville, KY 40206)

Lappe, Frances Moore. *Rediscovering America's Values* (Ballantine Books, New York, NY)

League of Women Voters. *Know Your County; Know Your School; Tell It To Washington* (1730 M Street NW, Washington, DC 20036)

Lewis, Barbara A. *The Kid's Guide To Social Action* (Free Spirit Publishing, Minneapolis, MN)

National Institute for Citizen Education in the Law. *Excel In Civics* (711 G Street SW, Washington, DC 20003)

Northern Rockies Action Group. *Be It Enacted By The People: A Citizens Guide to Initiatives* (9 Placer Street, Helena, MT 59601)

Oshsiro, Carl and Harry Snyder. *Getting Action: How To Petition State Government* (Consumers Union, 256 Washington Street, Mt. Vernon, NY 10550)

Pertschuk, Michael. *Giantkillers* (W.W. Norton & Co., New York, NY)

Quigley, Charles N. and Charles F. Bahmueller. *CIVITAS: A Framework for Civic Education* (NCSS Publications, c/o Maxway Data Corporation, 225 West 45th Street, New York, NY)

Reid, T. R. *Congressional Odyssey: The Saga of a Senate Bill* (W. H. Freeman & Co, San Francisco, CA)

Shoemaker, Joanie. *Note By Note: A Guide to Concert Production* (Redwood Cultural Work, Community Music & Friends, PO Box 10408, Oakland, CA 94608)

Smith, Devon Cottrell. *Great Careers: The Fourth of July Guide to Careers, Internships, and Volunteer Opportunities in the Nonprofit Sector* (Garrett Park Press, Garrett Park, MD)

Woods Institute. *The Dynamics of Congress: A Guide to the People and Process in Lawmaking* (2231 California Street NW, Washington, DC 20008)

A Final Word or Two

I prefer the errors of enthusiasm
to the indifference of wisdom.
— Anatole France

Don't wait to get actively involved in our democracy. Now is the time to challenge the status quo. Set an example for your friends, peers, teachers, neighbors, even your parents and siblings. Imagine if every family, community or youth group adopted a cause and plugged into the political process in the coming decade. The Activism 2000 Project wants to help jump-start your campaign to effect change. If you are stumped about a particular strategy, have difficulty obtaining information, or are puzzled by a parliamentary procedure, we can provide leads and offer suggestions and plenty of encouragement. Call, send a letter, or fax us at: Activism 2000 Project, PO Box E, Kensington, MD 20895 Tel: (301) 929-8808 Fax: (301) 929-8907.

We want to hear from you. Your story might be included in the next edition of *No Kidding Around!*. Once you activate, expect a lot of people to jump on the bandwagon.

INDEX

Washington, Booker T., 115
Washington, D.C.
  homeless, 17
  see also District of Columbia
water, 100, 210
  conservation, 20
  erosion, 37
  Marine Conservation Center videos, 15
  purification process, 33, 95
  Senate committee, 218
  stream pollutants, 3
Water Pollution Control Federation, 215
watershed development, 221
weapons, 206, 207, 209
  teen center security, 108
  see also guns; war
welfare, 205
Weller Elementary School, 37
Wells, Diane, 188, 190
West Virginia
  House of Delegates, 227
  Clerk of the Senate, 227
  Shepherd College, 15
wetlands, 11, 77, 97, 103
  Environmental Law Institute, 103
  Hatch Act, 96
  master plan, 33
  National Wetlands Coalition, 103
  National Wetlands Newsletter, 103
  National Wildlife Federation, 104
  U.S. Army Corps of Engineers, 104
  U.S. Fish and Wildlife Service, 104
  zoning approval, 33
whales, 210
White House 41-42, 54, 131, 183, 202
Wilderness Society, 215
wildlife, 215
  National Wildlife Federation, 104
  regulation and protection, 221
  U.S. Fish and Wildlife Service, 161
Williams, John, 27
Wilson Phillips band, 181
Winfrey, Oprah, 168
Winkler, Henry, 177
Winkler, Representative Lenny, 46
Wisconsin
  Legislative Reference Bureau, 227
  smoke-free schools legislation, 171
women, 212
Women's Policy Research, 212
Woodland Park Zoo, 23
Woods Institute, 231

Worden, Scott, 34
World Food Day, 56
world population, 135
World Resources Institute, 204, 205
World Summit for Children, 41, 136
World Wildlife Fund, 215
Worldwatch Institute, 205
WWTC-AM, 69
WXPN-FM, 69
Wyoming
  Legislative Service Office, 227
  Senate Information Clerk, 227

Yanda, Katy, 40, 60-61, 88
yearbooks, 32, 201
Young and Teen Peacemakers, 118, 119, 211
Young Minds That Care, 48
youth, 22, 87, 121
  21st Century Youth Leadership, 149
  career projections, 209
  Center for Youth Development and Policy
    Research, 147
  community centers, 52
  House Select Committee on Children,
    Youth and Families, 205
  National Black Youth Leadership Council,
    148
  National Network of Runaway and Youth
    Services, 201
  unemployment, 209
  youth groups tree planting matching
    fund, 54, 127
Youth Action, 215
Youth Earth Action, 205
Youth Ending Hunger, 23, 41, 42, 58, 129, 131,
  136, 209
Youth For Environmental Sanity, 205
Youth News Service, 69
Youth Policy Institute, 112
Youth Service America, 202
Youth Suicide National Center, 212
Youth Suicide Prevention National
  Committee, 212
YouthVoice, 60

Zero Population Growth, 136, 209
Zillions, 88
Zoning, 26, 100
  master plan, 34, 98
Zoos, 49, 215

About the Author

Wendy Schaetzel Lesko is the founder of the Activism 2000 Project, a clearinghouse created primarily to encourage the political participation of young people. The idea behind the project and this book has been evolving for many years, growing out of her experience as both a grassroots organizer and a journalist. While a student at Rollins College in Florida, her involvement with Head Start tutoring migrant farmworker children spurred her to jump from volunteerism to advocacy. Immediately after graduation she worked for Cesar Chavez and the United Farmworkers Union, mobilizing public support for their struggle to break out of the cycle of poverty.

She coauthored *The People Rising: The Campaign against the Bork Nomination* (Thunder's Mouth Press, 1989) with Michael Pertschuk, co-director of the Advocacy Institute and former chairman of the Federal Trade Commission. This in-depth oral history is filled with critical lessons relevant to both the novice and the veteran activist, including building coalitions, mobilizing a national constituency, bridging "inside" Washington-based strategists and "outside" grassroots activists, gaining media attention, maintaining momentum, and winning.

From 1975 to 1980 she was managing editor of the *Congressional Monitor*, a daily newsletter reporting on future House and Senate committee activities, floor votes and conference negotiations. Wendy Schaetzel Lesko and her colleagues taught hundreds of lobbyists at biweekly seminars entitled "Understanding the Legislative Process." Between 1978 and 1980 she also broadcast "Today on the Hill" each weekday for WTOP radio, the CBS affiliate in the nation's capital. This live commentary highlighted upcoming legislative skirmishes.

Her first book, *The Maternity Sourcebook: 230 Basic Decisions for Pregnancy, Birth, and Baby Care* (Warner Books, 1984), was coauthored with her husband, Matthew Lesko. In 1983 she broadcast "Conversation for Consumers," a nationally syndicated weekly radio program sponsored by the Council of Better Business Bureaus.

ORDER FORM

★ ACTIVISM 2000 PROJECT ★
Information USA, Inc.
P.O. Box E
Kensington, MD 20895
Tel: (301) 942-6303

TOLL-FREE
Order Line
(800) 955-POWER

☐ Please put me on the Activism 2000 Project mailing list.

☐ Please send me a free catalog of all Information USA, Inc. publications and books.

☐ I want to order additional copies of *NO KIDDING AROUND!*
    (263 pages with illustrations)

    1 - 3 copies = $18.95 each plus $4.00 postage & handling (total $22.95)
    4 - 9 copies = 10% discount
  10 - 50 copies = 20% discount
  Over 50 copies = negotiable

Order
by **Fax**
(301) 929-8907

Quantity _____

TOTAL $ _____

☐ Check or Money Order - Amount Enclosed $ _____

☐ Purchase Order PO # _____

☐ Credit Card Charge ____ VISA ____ MasterCard ____ American Express

    Credit card # _____ Exp. date_____

NAME _____

ADDRESS _____

_____

CITY/STATE _____ ZIP _____

TELEPHONE _____

★ 100% MONEY BACK GUARANTEE ★

Mail to Activism 2000 Project, Information USA Inc.,
P.O. Box E, Kensington, MD 20895.

OTHER INFORMATION USA PUBLICATIONS

Lesko's Info-Power Newsletter

This monthly newsletter shows decision makers and researchers how to take advantage of unusual sources of information on markets, companies, investments, and personal finance. Each twelve-page issue also identifies little known data bases, free experts, hotlines and reports available from federal, state and local governments. Annual subscription is $128.00. Free sample copies available upon request.

The Federal Data Base Finder

This unique resource identifies thousands of government data sources. This book describes free data bases which your computer can access, for example, news about the latest economic indicators, weather, or crude oil availability. Instead of paying as much as $100 per hour to a commercial vendor, *The Federal Data Base Finder* will show how to tap into the same computerized files on international demographics, health markets, etc. Also, this directory describes hundreds of tapes that can be loaded into a large mainframe. The third edition costs $125.00.

The Federal Data Base Finder is also available on search and retrieval software for IBM or compatible computers. This powerful package allows you to instantly access thousands of data bases with as little as three key strokes. The software and book are available for $199.95.

Government Giveaways For Entrepreneurs

The third edition of this 640-page book reveals over 9,000 sources of money and free expertise that are available to entrepreneurs who want to start or expand their business. It identifies over 300 federal, state and private sources of loans, grants and venture capital, as well as literally thousands of free sources of expertise to help with problems on markets, competition, and technology. The cost is $33.95 plus $4.00 postage and handling (only prepaid or credit card orders are accepted on this product).

Government Giveaways For Entrepreneurs is also available on search and retrieval software for IBM or compatible computers. This powerful package allows you to instantly access thousands of money and information sources with as little as three key strokes. The software and book are available for $79.95.

The Great American Gripe Book

This engaging pocket guide identifies over 1,000 government offices you can contact to learn your rights, get back your money, tackle a corporate giant or win a neighbor dispute. When trouble strikes you don't have to hire a lawyer at $100 an hour. Instead you can call a government office which will investigate your problem, make sure you are treated fairly under the law and they will even take the guilty to court. Available for $13.95 (this includes postage and handling).

Government Giveaways
For Entrepreneurs Video

This fast-paced video serves as a companion to Matthew Lesko's book, *Government Giveaways For Entrepreneurs*. This program walks you through the process of starting or expanding a business. As a bestselling author, Matthew Lesko, a small business owner himself, has appeared on such well-known television shows as Late Night With David Letterman, the Larry King Show, Good Morning America, and Donahue. Now he has put his talents to work creating this energetic video which introduces the viewer to several federal, state, and local government bureaucrats whose job it is to help you launch your own business. VHS only. Cost is $33.94 (this includes postage and handling).

Lesko's Info-Power Sourcebook

For those who truly appreciate the power of information, this book with over 30,000 sources will show you where to get the most up-to-date information on virtually every subject imaginable, from business finance and modern art to extraterrestrials, surplus property and even iguana farming. So whether you are a consumer who needs to know the best woodburning stove to buy or a business executive who needs to know the market potential of a product in Brazil, this one-of-a-kind sourcebook will help you get the answers you need when you need them. The cost is only $38.95 (this includes postage a.nd handling).

Lesko's Info-Power is also available on search and retrieval software for IBM or compatible computers. This powerful package allows you to instantly access thousands of data bases with as little as three key strokes. The software and book are available for $79.95.

_____

_____

_____

Stamp

ACTIVISM 2000 PROJECT
Information USA, Inc.
P.O. Box E
Kensington, MD 20895